A HISTORY OF ENGLISH LANGUAGE

A HISTORY OF ENGLISH LANGUAGE

SAMUCA CARECA

ANMOL PUBLICATIONS PVT. LTD.
NEW DELHI - 110 002 (INDIA)

ANMOL PUBLICATIONS PVT. LTD.

H.O.: 4374/4B, Ansari Road, Darya Ganj,
New Delhi-110 002 (India)
Ph.: 23278000, 23261597

B.O.: No. 1015, Ist Main Road, BSK IIIrd Stage
IIIrd Phase, IIIrd Block
Bangalore - 560 085 (India)
Visit us at: www.anmolpublications.com

PRINTED IN INDIA

Printed at Mehra Offset Press, Delhi.

Contents

Preface

The English language has undergone many changes with the changes of time. The history and development of English, from the earliest known writings to its status today as a dominant world language, is a subject of major importance to linguists and historians. Today the tenets of this nineteenth-century philosophy of liberalism are almost forgotten. In continental Europe it is remembered only by a few.

In England the term "liberal" is mostly used to signify a programme that only in details differs from the totalitarianism of the socialists. In the United States "liberal" means today a set of ideas and political postulates that in every regard are the opposite of all that liberalism meant to the preceding generations.

Every measure aiming at confiscating some of the assets of those who own more than the average or at restricting the rights of the owners of property is considered as liberal and progressive. Practically unlimited discretionary power is vested in government agencies the decisions of which are exempt from judicial review.

The few upright citizens who dare to criticize this trend toward administrative despotism are branded as extremists, reactionaries, economic royalists, and Fascists. It is suggested that a free country ought not to tolerate political activities on the part of such "public enemies." With such changes, the English language has a long history of its own.

Author

Chapter 1

Introduction

LANGUAGE AND ITS HISTORY

Nothing is perfectly static. Every word, every grammatical element, every locution, every sound and accent is a slowly changing configuration, molded by the invisible and impersonal drift that is the life of language. The evidence is overwhelming that this drift has a certain consistent direction. Its speed varies enormously according to circumstances that it is not always easy to define. We have already seen that Lithuanian is to-day nearer its Indo-European prototype than was the hypothetical Germanic mother-tongue five hundred or a thousand years before Christ. German has moved more slowly than English; in some respects it stands roughly midway between English and Anglo-Saxon, in others it has of course diverged from the Anglo-Saxon line.

When I pointed out that dialects formed because a language broken up into local segments could not move along the same drift in all of these segments, I meant of course that it could not move along identically the same drift. The general drift of a language has its depths. At the surface the current is relatively fast. In certain features dialects drift apart rapidly. By that very fact these features betray themselves as less fundamental to the genius of the language than the more slowly modifiable features in which the dialects keep together long after they have grown to be mutually alien forms of speech.

But this is not all. The momentum of the more fundamental, the pre-dialectic, drift is often such that languages long disconnected will pass through the same or strikingly similar phases. In many such cases it is perfectly clear that there could have been no dialectic interinfluencing. Every one knows that language is variable. Two individuals of the same generation and locality, speaking precisely the same dialect and moving in the same social circles, are never absolutely at one in their speech habits.

A minute investigation of the speech of each individual would reveal countless differences of detail-in choice of words, in sentence structure, in the relative frequency with which particular forms or combinations of words are used, in the pronunciation of particular vowels and consonants and of combinations of vowels and consonants, in all those features, such as speed, stress, and tone, that give life to spoken language. In a sense they speak slightly divergent dialects of the same language rather than identically the same language. There is an important difference, however, between individual and dialectic variations.

If we take two closely related dialects, say English as spoken by the "middle classes" of London and English as spoken by the average New Yorker, we observe that, however much the individual speakers in each city differ from each other, the body of Londoners forms a compact, relatively unified group in contrast to the body of New Yorkers. The individual variations are swamped in or absorbed by certain major agreements — say of pronunciation and vocabulary — which stand out very strongly when the language of the group as a whole is contrasted with that of the other group.

This means that there is something like an ideal linguistic entity dominating the speech habits of the members of each group, that the sense of almost unlimited freedom which each individual feels in the use of his language is held in leash by a tacitly directing norm. One individual plays on the norm in a way peculiar to himself, the next individual is nearer the dead average in that particular respect in which the first speaker most characteristically departs from it but in turn diverges from the average in a way peculiar to himself, and so on. What keeps the individual's variations from rising to dialectic importance is not merely the fact that they are in any event of small moment — there are well-marked dialectic variations that are of no greater magnitude than individual variations within a dialect — it is chiefly that they are silently "corrected" or canceled by the consensus of usage.

If all the speakers of a given dialect were arranged in order in accordance with the degree of their conformity to average usage, there is little doubt that they would constitute a very finely intergrading series clustered about a well-defined centre or norm. The differences between any two neighboring speakers of the series would be negligible for any but the most microscopic linguistic research. The differences between the outermost members of the series are sure to be considerable, in all likelihood considerable enough to measure up to a true dialectic variation. What prevents us from saying that these untypical individuals speak distinct dialects is that their peculiarities, as a unified whole, are not referable to another norm than the norm of their own series.

If the speech of any member of the series could actually be made to fit into another dialect series, we should have no true barriers between dialects (and languages) at all. We should merely have a continuous series of individual variations extending over the whole range of a historically unified linguistic area, and the cutting up of this large area (in some cases embracing parts of several continents) into distinct dialects and languages would be an essentially arbitrary proceeding with no warrant save that of practical convenience.

But such a conception of the nature of dialectic variation does not correspond to the facts as we know them. Isolated individuals may be found who speak a compromise between two dialects of a language, and if their number and importance increases they may even end by creating a new dialectic norm of their own, a dialect in which the extreme peculiarities of the parent dialects are ironed out.

In course of time the compromise dialect may absorb the parents, though more frequently these will tend to linger indefinitely as marginal forms of the enlarged dialect area. But such phenomena—and they are common enough in the history of language – are evidently quite secondary. They are closely linked with such social developments as the rise of nationality, the formation of literatures that aim to have more than a local appeal, the movement of rural populations into the cities, and all those other tendencies that break up the intense localism that unsophisticated man has always found natural. The explanation of primary dialectic differences is still to seek.

It is evidently not enough to say that if a dialect or language is spoken in two distinct localities or by two distinct social strata it naturally takes on distinctive forms, which in time come to be divergent enough to deserve the name of dialects. This is certainly true as far as it goes. Dialects do belong, in the first instance, to very definitely circumscribed social groups, homogeneous enough to secure the common feeling and purpose needed to create a norm.

But the embarrassing question immediately arises, if all the individual variations within a dialect are being constantly leveled out to the dialectic norm, if there is no appreciable tendency for the individual's peculiarities to initiate a dialectic schism, why should we have dialectic variations at all? Ought not the norm, wherever and whenever threatened, automatically to reassert itself? Ought not the individual variations of each locality, even in the absence of intercourse between them, to cancel out to the same accepted speech average?

If individual variations "on a flat" were the only kind of variability in language, I believe we should be at a loss to explain why and how dialects arise, why it is that a linguistic prototype gradually breaks up into a number of mutually unintelligible languages. But language is not merely something that is spread out in space, as it were — a series of reflections in individual minds of one and the same timeless picture. Language moves down time in a current of its own making. It has a drift. If there were no breaking up of a language into dialects, if each language continued as a firm, self-contained unity, it would still be constantly moving away from any assignable norm, developing new features unceasingly and gradually transforming itself into a language so different from its starting point as to be in effect a new language. Now dialects arise not because of the mere fact of individual variation but because two or more groups of individuals have become sufficiently disconnected to drift apart, or independently, instead of together.

So long as they keep strictly together, no amount of individual variation would lead to the formation of dialects. In practice, of course, no language can be spread over a vast territory or even over a considerable area without showing dialectic variations, for it is impossible to keep a large population from segregating itself into local groups, the language of each of which tends to drift independently.

Under cultural conditions such as apparently prevail today, conditions that fight localism at every turn, the tendency to dialectic cleavage is being constantly counteracted and in part "corrected" by the uniformizing factors already referred to. Yet even in so young a country as America the dialectic differences are not inconsiderable. Under primitive conditions the political groups are small, the tendency to localism exceedingly strong. It is natural, therefore, that the languages of primitive folk or of non-urban populations in general are differentiated into a great number of dialects.

There are parts of the globe where almost every village has its own dialect. The life of the geographically limited community is narrow and intense; its speech is correspondingly peculiar to itself. It is exceedingly doubtful if a language will ever be spoken over a wide area without multiplying itself dialectically.

No sooner are the old dialects ironed out by compromises or ousted by the spread and influence of the one dialect which is culturally predominant when a new crop of dialects arises to undo the leveling work of the past. This is precisely what happened in Greece, for instance. In classical antiquity there were spoken a large number of local dialects, several of which are represented in the literature. As the cultural supremacy of Athens grew, its dialect, the Attic, spread at the expense of the rest, until, in the so-called Hellenistic period following the Macedonian conquest, the Attic dialect, in the vulgarized form known as the "Koine," became the standard speech of all Greece. But this linguistic uniformity did not long continue.

During the two millennia that separate the Greek of to-day from its classical prototype the Koine gradually split up into a number of dialects. Now Greece is as richly diversified in speech as in the time of Homer, though the present local dialects, aside from those of Attica itself, are not the lineal descendants of the old dialects of pre Alexandrian days.

The experience of Greece is not exceptional. Old dialects are being continually wiped out only to make room for new ones. Languages can change at so many points of phonetics, morphology, and vocabulary that it is not surprising that once the linguistic community is broken it should slip off in different directions. It would be too much to expect a locally diversified language to develop along strictly parallel lines. If once the speech of a locality has begun to drift on its own account, it is practically certain to move further and further away from its linguistic fellows. Failing the retarding effect of dialectic inter influences, which I have already touched upon, a group of dialects is bound to diverge on the whole, each from all of the others.

In course of time each dialect itself splits up into sub dialects, which gradually take on the dignity of dialects proper while the primary dialects develop into mutually unintelligible languages. And so the budding process continues, until the divergences become so great that none but a linguistic student, armed with his documentary evidence and with his comparative or reconstructive method, would infer that the languages in question were genealogically related, represented independent lines of development, in other words, from a remote and common starting point.

Yet it is as certain as any historical fact can be that languages so little resembling each other as Modern Irish, English, Italian, Greek, Russian, Armenian, Persian, and Bengali are but end-points in the present of drifts that converge to a meeting-point in the dim past. There is naturally no reason to believe that this earliest "IndoEuropean" (or "Aryan") prototype which we can in part reconstruct, in part but dimly guess at, is itself other than a single "dialect" of a group that has either become largely extinct or is now further represented by languages too divergent for us, with our limited means, to recognize as clear kin. All languages that are known to be genetically related, i.e., to be divergent forms of a single prototype, may be considered as constituting a "linguistic stock."

There is nothing final about a linguistic stock. When we set it up, we merely say, in effect, that thus far we can go and no farther. At any point in the progress of our researches an unexpected ray of light may reveal the "stock" as but a "dialect" of a larger group. The terms dialect, language, branch, stock – it goes without saying – are purely relative terms. They are convertible as our perspective widens or contracts. It would be vain to speculate as to whether or not we shall ever be able to demonstrate that all languages stem from a common source.

Of late years linguists have been able to make larger historical syntheses than were at one time deemed feasible, just as students of culture have been able to show historical connections between culture areas or institutions that were at one time believed to be totally isolated from each other.

The human world is contracting not only prospectively but to the backward probing eye of culture-history.

Nevertheless we are as yet far from able to reduce the riot of spoken languages to a small number of "stocks." We must still operate with a quite considerable number of these stocks. Some of them, like Indo-European or Indo-Chinese, are spoken over tremendous reaches; others, like Basque, have a curiously restricted range and are in all likelihood but dwindling remnants of groups that were at one time more widely distributed.

As for the single or multiple origin of speech, it is likely enough that language as a human institution (or, if one prefers, as a human "faculty") developed but once in the history of the race, that all the complex history of language is a unique cultural event. Such a theory constructed "on general principles" is of no real interest, however, to linguistic science. What lies beyond the demonstrable must be left to the philosopher or the romancer.

We must return to the conception of "drift" in language. If the historical changes that take place in a language, if the vast accumulation of minute modifications which in time results in the complete remodeling of the language, are not in essence identical with the individual variations that we note on every hand about us, if these variations are born only to die without a trace, while the equally minute, or even minuter, changes that make up the drift are forever imprinted on the history of the language, are we not imputing to this history a certain mystical quality? Are we not giving language a power to change of its own accord over and above the involuntary tendency of individuals to vary the norm?

And if this drift of language is not merely the familiar set of individual variations seen in vertical perspective, that is historically, instead of horizontally, that is in daily experience, what is it? Language exists only in so far as it is actually used — spoken and heard, written and read. What significant changes take place in it must exist, to begin with, as individual variations.

This is perfectly true, and yet it by no means follows that the general drift of language can be understood from an exhaustive descriptive study of these variations alone. They themselves are random phenomena, like the waves of the sea, moving backward and forward in purposeless flux. The linguistic drift has direction. In other words, only those individual variations embody it or carry it which moves in a certain direction, just as only certain wave movements in the bay outline the tide.

The drift of a language is constituted by the unconscious selection on the part of its speakers of those individual variations that are cumulative in some special direction. This direction may be inferred, in the main, from the past history of the language. In the long run any new feature of the drift becomes part and parcel of the common, accepted speech, but for a long time it may exist as a mere tendency in the speech of a few, perhaps of a despised few.

As we look about us and observe current usage, it is not likely to occur to us that our language has a "slope," that the changes of the next few centuries are in a sense prefigured in certain obscure tendencies of the present and that these changes, when consummated, will be seen to be but continuations of changes that have been already effected. We feel rather that our language is practically a fixed system and that what slight changes are destined to take place in it are as likely to move in one direction as another.

The feeling is fallacious. Our very uncertainty as to the impending details of change makes the eventual consistency of their direction all the more impressive. Sometimes we can feel where the drift is taking us even while we struggle against it. Probably the majority of those who read these words feel that it is quite "incorrect" to say "Who did you see?" We readers of many books are still very careful to say "Whom did you see?" but we feel a little uncomfortable (uncomfortably proud, it may be) in the process. We are likely to avoid the locution altogether and to say "Who was it you saw?" conserving literary tradition (the "whom") with the dignity of silence. The folk makes no apology.

"Whom did you see?" might do for an epitaph, but "Who did you see?" is the natural form for an eager inquiry. It is of course the uncontrolled speech of the folk to which we must look for advance information as to the general linguistic movement. It is safe to prophesy that within a couple of hundred years from to-day not even the most learned jurist will be saying "Whom did you see?" By that time the "whom" will be as delightfully archaic as the Elizabethan "his" for "its." No logical or historical argument will avail to save this hapless "whom."

The demonstration "I: me = he: him = who: whom" will be convincing in theory and will go unheeded in practice. Even now we may go so far as to say that the majority of us are secretly wishing they could say "Who did you see?" It would be a weight off their unconscious minds if some divine authority, overruling the lifted finger of the pedagogue, gave them carte blanche. But we cannot too frankly anticipate the drift and maintain caste. We must affect ignorance of whither we are going and rest content with our mental conflict — uncomfortable conscious acceptance of the "whom," unconscious desire for the "who."

Meanwhile we indulge our sneaking desire for the forbidden locution by the use of the "who" in certain twilight cases in which we can cover up our fault by a bit of unconscious special pleading. Imagine that some one drops the remark when you are not listening attentively, "John Smith is coming to-night." You have not caught the name and ask, not "Whom did you say?" but "Who did you say?" There is likely to be a little hesitation in the choice of the form, but the precedent of usages like "Whom did you see?" will probably not seem quite strong enough to induce a "Whom did you say?"

Not quite relevant enough, the grammarian may remark, for a sentence like "Who did you say?" is not strictly analogous to "Whom did you see?" or "Whom did you mean?" It is rather an abbreviated form of some such sentence as "Who, did you say, is coming to-night?" This is the special pleading that I have referred to, and it has a certain logic on its side.

Yet the case is more hollow than the grammarian thinks it to be, for in reply to such a query as "You're a good hand at bridge, John, aren't you?" John, a little taken aback, might mutter "Did you say me?" hardly "Did you say I?" Yet the logic for the latter ("Did you say I was a good hand at bridge?") is evident. The real point is that there is not enough vitality in the "whom" to carry it over such little difficulties as a "me" can compass without a thought.

The proportion "I: me = he: him = who: whom" is logically and historically sound, but psychologically shaky. "Whom did you see?" is correct, but there is something false about its correctness. It is worth looking into the reason for our curious reluctance to use locutions involving the word "whom," particularly in its interrogative sense. The only distinctively objective forms which we still possess in English are me, him, her (a little blurred because of its identity with the possessive her), us, them, and whom. In all other cases the objective has come to be identical with the subjective — that is, in outer form, for we are not now taking account of position in the sentence.

We observe immediately in looking through the list of objective forms that whom is psychologically isolated. Me, him, her, us, and them form a solid, well-integrated group of objective personal pronouns parallel to the subjective series I, he, she, we, they. The forms who and whom are technically "pronouns" but they are not felt to be in the same box as the personal pronouns. Whom has clearly a weak position, an exposed flank, for words of a feather tend to flock together, and if one strays behind, it is likely to incur danger of life.

Now the other interrogative and relative pronouns (which, what, that), with which whom should properly flock, do not distinguish the subjective and objective forms. It is psychologically unsound to draw the line of form cleavage between whom and the personal pronouns on the one side, the remaining interrogative and relative pronouns on the other. The form groups should be symmetrically related to, if not identical with, the function groups. Had which, what, and that objective forms parallel to whom, the position of this last would be more secure. As it is, there is something unesthetic about the word. It suggests a form pattern which is not filled out by its fellows. The only way to remedy the irregularity of form distribution is to abandon the whom altogether, for we have lost the power to create new objective forms and cannot remodel our which-what-that group so as to make it parallel with the smaller group who whom.

Once this is done, who joins its flock and our unconscious desire for form symmetry is satisfied. We do not secretly chafe at "Whom did you see?" without reason. But the drift away from whom has still other determinants. The words who and whom in their interrogative sense are psychologically related not merely to the pronouns which and what, but to a group of interrogative adverbs — where, when, how — all, of which are invariable and generally emphatic. I believe it is safe to infer that there is a rather strong feeling in English that the interrogative pronoun or adverb, typically an emphatic element in the sentence, should be invariable. The inflective -m of whom is felt as a drag upon the rhetorical effectiveness of the word.

It needs to be eliminated if the interrogative pronoun is to receive all its latent power. There is still a third, and a very powerful, reason for the avoidance of whom. The contrast between the subjective and objective series of personal pronouns (I, he, she, we, they: me, him, her, us, them) is in English associated with a difference of position. We say I see the man but the man sees me; he told him, never him he told or him told he.

Such usages as the last two are distinctly poetic and archaic; they are opposed to the present drift of the language. Even in the interrogative one does not say Him did you see? It is only in sentences of the type whom did you see? That an inflected objective before the verb is now used at all. On the other hand, the order in whom did you see? is imperative because of its interrogative form; the interrogative pronoun or adverb normally comes first in the sentence (What are you doing? When did he go? Where are you from?).

In the "whom" of whom did you see? There is concealed, therefore, a conflict between the order proper to a sentence containingan inflected objective and the order natural to a sentence with an interrogative pronoun or adverb. The solution did you see whom? or You saw whom? is too contrary to the idiomatic drift of our language to receive acceptance.

The more radical solution Who did you see? is the one the language is gradually making for. These three conflicts — on the score of form grouping, of rhetorical emphasis, and of order — are supplemented by a fourth difficulty. The emphatic whom, with its heavy build (half-long vowel followed by labial consonant), should contrast with a lightly tripping syllable immediately following. In whom did, however, we have an involuntary retardation that makes the locution sound "clumsy." This clumsiness is a phonetic verdict, quite apart from the dissatisfaction due to the grammatical factors which we have analyzed. The same prosodic objection does not apply to such parallel locutions as what did and when did.

The vowels of what and when are shorter and their final consonants melt easily into the following d, which is pronounced in the same tongue position as *t* and *n*. Our instinct for appropriate rhythms makes it as difficult for us to feel content with whom did as for a poet to use words like dreamed and hummed in a rapid line. Neither common feeling nor the poet's choice need be at all conscious. It may be that not all arc equally sensitive to the rhythmic flow of speech, but it is probable that rhythm is an unconscious linguistic determinant even with those who set little store by its artistic use.

In any event the poet's rhythms can only be a more sensitive and stylicized application of rhythmic tendencies that are characteristic of the daily speech of his people. We have discovered no less than four factors which enter into our subtle disinclination to say "Whom did you see?" The uneducated folk that says "Who did you see?" with no twinge of conscience has a more acute flair for the genuine drift of the language than its students. Naturally the four restraining factors do not operate independently.

Their separate energies, if we may make bold to use a mechanical concept, are "canalized" into a single force. This force or minute embodiment of the general drift of the language is psychologically registered as a slight hesitation in using the word whom. The hesitation is likely to be quite unconscious, though it may be readily acknowledged when attention is called to it. The analysis is certain to be unconscious, or rather unknown, to the normal speaker.

How, then, can we be certain in such an analysis as we have undertaken that all of the assigned determinants are really operative and not merely some one of them? Certainly they are not equally powerful in all cases. Their values are variable, rising and failing according to the individual and the locution But that they really exist, each in its own right, may sometimes be tested by the method of elimination. If one or other of the factors is missing and we observe a slight diminution in the corresponding psychological reaction (" hesitation" in our case), we may conclude that the factor is in other uses genuinely positive.

The second of our four factors applies only to the interrogative use of whom, the fourth factor applies with more force to the interrogative than to the relative. We can therefore understand why a sentence like Is he the man whom you referred to? though not as idiomatic as Is he the man (that) you referred to? (Remember that it sins against counts one and three), is still not as difficult to reconcile with our innate feeling for English expression as Whom did you see?

If we eliminate the fourth factor from the interrogative usage, say in Whom are you looking at? where the vowel following whom relieves this word of its phonetic weight, we can observe, if I am not mistaken, a lesser reluctance to use the whom. Who are you looking at? might even sound slightly offensive to ears that welcome Who did you see? We may set up a scale of "hesitation values" some- what after this fashion:

Value 1: factors 1, 3. "The man whom I referred to."

Value 2: factors 1, 3, 4. "The man whom they referred to."

Value 3: factors 1, 2, 3. "Whom are you looking at?

Value 4: factors 1, 2, 3, 4. "Whom did you see?"

We may venture to surmise that while whom will ultimately disappear from English speech, locutions of the type Whom did you see? will be obsolete when phrases like The man whom I referred to are still in lingering use. It is impossible to be certain, however, for we can never tell if we have isolated all the determinants of a drift. In our particular ease we have ignored what may well prove to be a controlling factor in the history of who and whom in the relative sense.

This is the unconscious desire to leave these words to their interrogative function and to concentrate on that or mere word order as expressions of the relative (e.g., The man that I referred to or The man I referred to). This drift, which does not directly concern the use of whom as such (merely of whom as a form of who), may have made the relative who obsolete before the other factors affecting relative whom have run their course.

A consideration like this is instructive because it indicates that knowledge of the general drift of a language is insufficient to enable us to see clearly what the drift is heading for. We need to know something of the relative potencies and speeds of the components of the drift. It is hardly necessary to say that the particular drifts involved in the use of whom are of interest to us not for their own sake but as symptoms of larger tendencies at work in the language.

At least three drifts of major importance are discernible. Each of these has operated for centuries, each is at work in other parts of our linguistic mechanism, each is almost certain to continue for centuries, possibly millennia. The first is the familiar tendency to level the distinction between the subjective and the objective, itself but a late chapter in the steady reduction of the old Indo-European system of syntactic cases.

This system, which is at present best preserved in Lithuanian, was already considerably reduced in the old Germanic language of which English, Dutch, German, Danish, and Swedish are modern dialectic forms. The seven Indo-European cases (nominative, genitive, dative, accusative, ablative, and locative, instrumental) had been already reduced to four (nominative, genitive, dative, and accusative). We know this from a careful comparison of and reconstruction based on the oldest Germanic dialects of which we still have records.

In the group of West Germanic dialects, for the study of which Old High German, Anglo-Saxon, Old Frisian, and Old Saxon are our oldest and most valuable sources, we still have these four cases, but the phonetic form of the case syllables is already greatly reduced and in certain paradigms particular eases have coalesced. The case system is practically intact but it is evidently moving towards further disintegration.

Within the Anglo-Saxon and early Middle English period there took place further changes in the same direction. The phonetic form of the case syllables became still further reduced and the distinction between the accusative and the dative finally disappeared. The new "objective" is really an amalgam of old accusative and dative forms; thus, him, the old dative (we still say I give him the book, not "abbreviated" from I give to him; compare Gothic imma, modern German ihm), took over the functions of the old accusative and dative.

The distinction between the nominative and accusative was nibbled away by phonetic processes and morphological levelings until only certain pronouns retained distinctive subjective and objective forms. In later medieval and in modern times there have been comparatively few apparent changes in our case system apart from the gradual replacement of thou — thee (singular) and subjective ye — objective you (plural) by a single undifferentiated form you. All the while, however, the case system, such as it is (subjective-objective, really absolutive, and possessive in nouns; subjective, objective, and possessive in certain pronouns) has been steadily weakening in psychological respects.

At present it is more seriously undermined than most of us realize. The possessive has little vitality except in the pronoun and in animate nouns. Theoretically we can still say the moon's phases or a newspaper's vogue; practically we limit ourselves pretty much to analytic locutions like the phases of the moon and the vogue of a newspaper. The drift is clearly toward the limitation, of possessive forms to animate nouns.

All the possessive pronominal forms except its and, in part, their and theirs, are also animate. It is significant that theirs is hardly ever used in reference to inanimate nouns, that there is some reluctance to so use their, and that its also is beginning to give way to of it. The appearance of it or the looks of it is more in the current of the language than its appearance. It is curiously significant that its young (referring to an animal's cubs) is idiomatically preferable to the young of it. The form is only ostensibly neuter, in feeling it is animate; psychologically it belongs with his children, not with the pieces of it. Can it be that so common a word as it's is actually beginning to be difficult?

Is it too doomed to disappear? It would be rash to say that it shows signs of approaching obsolescence, but that it is steadily weakening are fairly clear. In any event, it is not too much to say that there is a strong drift towards the restriction of the inflected possessive forms to animate nouns and pronouns. How is it with the alternation of subjective and objective in the pronoun? Granted that whom is a weak sister, that the two cases have been leveled in you (in it, that, and what they were never distinct, so far as we can tell), and that her as an objective is a trifle weak because of its formal identity with the possessive her, is there any reason to doubt the vitality of such alternations as I see the man and the man sees me?

Surely the distinction between subjective I and objective me, between subjective he and objective him, and correspondingly for other personal pronouns, belongs to the very core of the language. We can throw whom to the dogs, somehow make shift to do without an its, but to level I and me to a single case – would that not be to un English our language beyond recognition? There is no drift toward such horrors as Me see him or I see he.

True, the phonetic disparity between I and me, he and him, we and us, has been too great for any serious possibility of form leveling. It does not follow that the case distinction as such is still vital. One of the most insidious peculiarities of a linguistic drift is that where it cannot destroy what lies in its way it renders it innocuous by washing the old significance out of it. It turns its very enemies to its own uses. This brings us to the second of the major drifts, the tendency to fixed position in the sentence, determined by the syntactic relation of the word. We need not go into the history of this all-important drift. It is enough to know that as the inflected forms of English became scantier, as the syntactic relations were more and more inadequately expressed by the forms of the words themselves, position in the sentence gradually took over functions originally foreign to it.

The man in the man sees the dog is subjective; in the dog sees the man, objective. Strictly parallel to these sentences are he sees the dog and the dog sees him. Are the subjective value of he and the objective value of him entirely, or even mainly, dependent on the difference of form? I doubt it. We could hold to such a view if it were possible to say the dog sees he or him sees the dog. It was once possible to say such things, but we have lost the power.

In other words, at least part of the case feeling in he and him is to be credited to their position before or after the verb. May it not be, then, that he and him, we and us, are not so much subjective and objective forms as pre-verbal and post-verbal forms, very much as my and mine are now pre-nominal and post-nominal forms of the possessive (my father but father mine; it is my book but the book is mine)?

That this interpretation corresponds to the actual drift of the English language is again indicated by the language of the folk. The folk says it is me, not it is I, which is "correct" but just as falsely so as the whom did you see? that we have analyzed. I'm the one, it's me; we're the ones, it's us that will win out – such are the live parallelisms in English today. There is little doubt that it is I will one day be as impossible in English as c'est je, for c'est moi, is now in French. How differently our I: me feels than in Chaucer's day is shown by the Chaucerian it am I. Here the distinctively subjective aspect of the I was enough to influence the form of the preceding verb in spite of the introductory it; Chaucer's locution clearly felt more like a Latin sum ego than a modern it is I or colloquial it is me.

We have a curious bit of further evidence to prove that the English personal pronouns have lost some share of their original syntactic force. Were he and she subjective forms pure and simple, were they not striving, so to speak, to become caseless absolutives, like man or any other noun, we should not have been able to coin such compounds as he-goat and she-goat, words that are psychologically analogous to bull-moose and mother-bear.

Again, in inquiring about a new-born baby, we ask Is it a he or a she? quite as though he and she were the equivalents of male and female or boy and girl. All in all, we may conclude that our English case system is weaker than it looks and that, in one way or another, it is destined to get itself reduced to an absolutive (caseless) form for all nouns and pronouns but those that are animate. Animate nouns and pronouns are sure to have distinctive possessive forms for an indefinitely long period.

Meanwhile observe that the old alignment of case forms is being invaded by two new categories — a positional category (pre-verbal, post-verbal) and a classificatory category (animate, inanimate). The facts that in the possessive animate nouns and pronouns are destined to be more and more sharply distinguished from inanimate nouns and pronouns (the man's, but of the house; his, but of it) and that, on the whole, it is only animate pronouns that distinguish pre-verbal and post-verbal forms are of the greatest theoretical interest.

They show that, however the language strive for a more and more analytic form, it is by no means manifesting a drift toward the expression of "pure" relational concepts in the Indo-Chinese manner. The insistence on the concreteness of the relational concepts is clearly stronger than the destructive power of the most sweeping and persistent drifts that we know of in the history and prehistory of our language.

The drift toward the abolition of most case distinctions and the correlative drift toward position as an all-important grammatical method are accompanied, in a sense dominated, by the last of the three major drifts that I have referred to. This is the drift toward the invariable word. In analyzing the "whom" sentence I pointed out that the rhetorical emphasis natural to an interrogative pronoun lost something by its form variability (who, whose, whom).

This striving for a simple, unnuanced correspondence between idea and word, as invariable as may be, is very strong in English. It accounts for a number of tendencies which at first sight seem unconnected. Certain well-established forms, like the present third person singular -s of works or the plural -s of books, have resisted the drift to invariable words, possibly because they symbolize certain stronger form cravings that we do not yet fully understand. It is interesting to note that derivations that get away sufficiently from the concrete notion of the radical word to exist as independent conceptual centres are not affected by this elusive drift.

As soon as the derivation runs danger of being felt as a mere nuancing of, a finicky play on, the primary concept, it tends to be absorbed by the radical word, to disappear as such. English words crave spaces between them, they do not like to huddle in clusters of slightly divergent centres of meaning, each edging a little away from the rest.

Goodness, a noun of quality, almost a noun of relation, that takes its cue from the concrete idea of "good" without necessarily predicating that quality (e.g., I do not think much of his goodness) is sufficiently spaced from good itself not to need fear absorption. Similarly, unable can hold its own against able because it destroys the latter's sphere of influence; unable is psychologically as distinct from able as is blundering or stupid. It is different with adverbs in -ly. These lean too heavily on their adjectives to have the kind of vitality that English demands of its words. Do it quickly! drags psychologically.

The nuance expressed by quickly is too close to that of quick, their circles of concreteness are too nearly the same, for the two words to feel comfortable together. The adverbs in -ly are likely to go to the wall in the not too distant future for this very reason and in face of their obvious usefulness. Another instance of the sacrifice of highly useful forms to this impatience of nuancing is the group whence, whither, hence, hither, thence, thither.

They could not persist in live usage because they impinged too solidly upon the circles of meaning represented by the words where, here and there. In saying whither we feel too keenly that we repeat all of where. That we add to where an important nuance of direction irritates rather than satisfies. We prefer to merge the static and the directive (Where do you live? like Where are you going?) or, if need be, to overdo a little the concept of direction (*Where are you running to?*). Now it is highly symptomatic of the nature of the drift away from word clusters that we do not object to nuances as such, we object to having the nuances formally earmarked for us.

As a matter of fact our vocabulary is rich in near-synonyms and in groups of words that are psychologically near relatives, but these near-synonyms and these groups do not hang together by reason of etymology. We are satisfied with believe and credible just because they keep aloof from each other. Good and well go better together than quick and quickly. The English vocabulary is a rich medley because each English word wants its own castle.

Has English long been peculiarly receptive to foreign words because it craves the staking out of as many word areas as possible, or, conversely, has the mechanical imposition of a flood of French and Latin loan-words, unrooted in our earlier tradition, so dulled our feeling for the possibilities of our native resources that we are allowing these to shrink by default? I suspect that both propositions are true.

Each feeds on the other. I do not think it likely, however, that the borrowings in English have been as mechanical and external a process as they are generally represented to have been. There was something about the English drift as early as the period following the Norman Conquest that welcomed the new words. They were a compensation for something that was weakening within.

One would be inclined to surmise that these dialectic forms go back to old Germanic or West-Germanic alternations of the same type. But the documentary evidence shows conclusively that there could have been no plurals of this type in primitive Germanic. There is no trace of such vocalic mutation ("umlaut") in Gothic, our most archaic Germanic language. More significant still is the fact that it does not appear in our oldest Old High German texts and begins to develop only at the very end of the Old High German period (circa 1000 A.D.).

In the Middle High German period the mutation was carried through in all dialects. The typical Old High German forms are singular *fuoss,* plural *fuossi;* singular *mus,* plural *musi.* The corresponding Middle High German forms are *fuoss, füesse; mus, müse.* Modern German *Fuss: Füsse, Maus: Mäuse* are the regular developments of these medieval forms. Turning to Anglo-Saxon, we find that our modern English forms correspond to *fot, fet; mus, mys.*

These forms are already in use in the earliest English monuments that we possess, dating from the eighth century, and thus antedate the Middle High German forms by three hundred years or more. In other words, on this particular point it took German at least three hundred years to catch up with a phonetic-morphological drift that had long been under way in English.

The mere fact that the affected vowels of related words (Old High German *uo,* Anglo-Saxon *o*) are not always the same shows that the affection took place at different periods in German and English. There was evidently some general tendency or group of tendencies at work in early Germanic, long before English and German had developed as such, that eventually drove both of these dialects along closely parallel paths.

Chapter 2

History of Grammar and Composition

HISTORICAL OVERVIEW

The first attempts to study grammar began in about the 4th cent. B.C., in India with Panini's grammar of Sanskrit and in Greece with Plato's dialogue *Cratylus*. The Greeks, and later the Romans, approached the study of grammar through philosophy. Concerned only with the study of their own language and not with foreign languages, early Greek and Latin grammars were devoted primarily to defining the parts of speech. The biblical commentator Rashi attempted to decipher the rules of ancient Hebrew grammar.

It was not until the Middle Ages that grammarians became interested in languages other than their own. The scientific grammatical analysis of language began in the 19th cent. with the realization that languages have a history; this led to attempts at the genealogical classification of languages through comparative linguistics. Grammatical analysis was further developed in the 20th cent. and was greatly advanced by the theories of structural linguistics and transformational-generative grammar.

The relationship between the teaching of writing and the various bodies of knowledge and prejudice called "grammar" has always been problematical. In a volume such as this, which investigates, among other issues, the relation of writing to the most modern linguistic phenomena, it might at first seem unwarranted to cover the "bad old days," when pinch-faced champions of "literacy" forced gobs of questionable prescription down adolescent throats.

A look, however, into the handbooks and the workbooks that still pour from the presses for use in both remedial and freshman English will show that the old days may be gone theoretically but remain with us on the level of practical pedagogy. We ought, I think, to learn more about them.

During the Middle Ages, *grammar* was often used to describe learning in general, including the magical, occult practices popularly associated with the scholars of the day. People in Scotland pronounced *grammar* as "glam-our," and extended the association to mean magical beauty or enchantment. In the 19th century, the two versions of the word went their separate ways, so that our study of English grammar today may not be *quite* as glamorous as it used to be.

English Grammar

In order to understand how grammar has affected the teaching of writing, it will first be necessary to look briefly at the ways in which traditional grammar was taught in America prior to the rise of modern linguistics. The study of formal English grammar became a popular subject in the common schools of America around the time of the American Revolution. Rollo L. Lyman has set 1775 as the date for the beginning of a fifty-year rise of vernacular grammar in elementary and secondary schools.

English grammar replaced the study of Latin grammar among the earlier school grades as Latin and Greek ceased to be the absolute core of every curriculum. Soon grammar was so much at the centre of elementary study that elementary schools became known as "grammar schools," an appellation that exists even today. Study of English grammar reached its peak influence around 1850, at a time when grammar was the main subject of a pupil's first six grades.

Early grammar instruction – before 1850 or so – had nothing to do with composing essays or even with constructing sentences. It was an absolutely formal discipline that demanded a great deal of rote memorization of terms, complex analyses of given sentences, and suspicious patrols through other sentences searching for "errors." As Charles C. Fries says, the basis of this early formal grammar study was very different from modern linguistic science and had as its end not "*description* for the sake of *prediction*" but "*analysis* for the sake of *classification*."

Grammar was not, in any sense, a creative field of study; rather, it was meant as a "mental discipline," training the mind for rigorous thought. Before 1850, traditional grammar methods were threefold, and none of the three traditional pedagogies was concerned with the development of writing skill. First, pupils were made to memorize the parts of speech, all the "rules" of declension, conjugation, gender, number, case, degree, tense, mood, person, and countless others. Second, they were forced to apply and demonstrate these rules in oral exercises called "parsing," which asked pupils to give definitions and applicable rules for every word in a sentence provided by the teacher. Here is an example of a sentence partially parsed, from what was the paradigmatic grammar text for nineteenth-century America, Lindley Murray best-selling English Grammar of 1795:

"We should be kind to them, who are unkind to us."

We is a personal pronoun, of the first person, the plural number, and in the nominative case. (*Decline it.*) *Should be* is an irregular verb neuter, in the potential mood, the imperfect tense, and the first person plural. (*Repeat the present tense, etc.*) *Kind* is an adjective, in the positive state. (*Repeat the degrees of comparison.*) *To* is a preposition. *Them* is a personal pronoun, of the third person, the plural number, and in the objective case. (*Decline it.*) *Who* is a relative pronoun, and in the nominative case.

The example goes on, but the point is made. The third sort of grammar exercise was introduced by Robert Lowth in his *Short Introduction* of 1758, and was used by every major grammar textbook through 1850. It consisted of the teacher's providing examples of ungrammatical sentences, either orally or in written form, and asking pupils to correct the ungrammaticality and then state the rules and definitions by which the repair was made. These "false syntax" exercises fostered a spirit of anxiety and suspicion about grammar that was not long in pervading the entire linguistic culture of the new nation. Around 1850 the methods of teaching grammar began to change as inductive forms of pedagogy were imported from Europe.

Creative and compositional elements were gradually added to the memorization and dissection exercises already used. Most important to this movement toward incorporating writing and grammar were the many editions of Samuel S. Greene *Analysis* of 1847. Greene was the first important grammarian to include the writing of original sentences as part of each of his grammar lessons, usually ending a series of models and parsing exercises with instructions. For instance, "Write fifteen sentences of your own, limiting the subjects of the first five by a compound adjective element, the predicates of the next five by a compound objective element, and the predicates of the last five by a compound adverbial element."

In spite of Greene's popularity, however, the field of grammar continued to be overwhelmingly formalistic and abstract, having little to do with communications skills as they really existed. Grammarians contrived to accept Lindley Murray's definition of grammar as "the art of speaking and writing the English language with propriety," and school grammar was still an attempt to instill, through rigid taxonomic practice, this knowledge of correctness. Teaching of formal grammar in American elementary and high schools reached its high point around 1850 and then began to lose popularity. More and more teachers and school board officials began to see the "mental discipline" claims of grammar instructions as will-o'-the-wisps and the claims that knowledge of grammatical categories fostered literate skills as demonstrably false.

William H. Wells, one of the earliest professors of the system of inductive grammar, had lost faith in grammatical study by 1865, when he wrote that a student "may have the whole grammar book by heart, and yet not be able to make a respectable speech. . . . The great object to be attained is not the mastery of a text-book in grammar, but the acquisition of language."

Indeed, some began to question whether English had a grammar, so poorly did the language seem to fit into the accepted inflected structure of Latin grammar. In Words and Their Uses in 1870 Richard Grant White claimed that English was a "grammarless" language, and many believed the claim. The traditional teaching of formal grammar was in deep trouble by the 1880s.

The state of Connecticut dropped all grammar teaching during this period, claiming it was "hateful" to students and did not help them to speak or write better. On the level of theory, more and more philologists were coming to agree with pioneer linguist George P. Marsh:

> So far as respects English or any other uninflected speech, a knowledge of grammar is rather a matter of convenience as a nomenclature, a medium of thought and discussion about language than a guide to the actual use of it, and it is as impossible to acquire the complete command of our own tongue by the study of grammatical precept, as to learn to walk or swim by attending a course of lectures on anatomy.

Marsh believed that in English "grammar has little use except to systematize," and more and more people were questioning why such an abstract system should be at the core of American school education.

Yet grammar, though its early methods were being seriously questioned, was far from defunct. Educators, a conservative group in the nineteenth century, were shoring up fragments against the ruin of their central subject, and between 1850 and 1880 a new pedagogy for grammar was born, one based not on abstract learning of formal grammar but rather on using grammar in sentences.

This method, based on Greene Analysis, came to be called "sentence building" or "language lessons," after William Swinton extremely popular textbook Language Lessons, which appeared in 1873. This pedagogy focused on writing and then examining the student's own sentences rather than on rote memorization and parsing. It was given a great boost in 1877, when Alonzo Reed and Brainerd Kellogg first published their Higher Lessons in English.

Reed and Kellogg admitted that grammar "is very insecure. Children are not enthusiastic in praise of grammar, most parents recall without pleasure their own trials with it, and many men of culture and of wisdom openly advise its banishment from the school-room." Reed and Kellogg believed that grammar is necessary, but warned that "it must bear on its branches more obvious and more *serviceable* fruit, or the tree will be hewn down and cast out of the way". The answer in Higher Lessons was to "make the Science of the Language, of which all the essentials are thoroughly presented, tributary to the Art of Expression". The book was filled with practices, exercises, and drills, but these were not so different from Swinton's drills. What really set Reed and Kellogg apart was their invention of the sentence diagram, the familiar straightline diagram that was still used in the 1970s to demonstrate sentence structure.

Grammar and Rhetoric

When assessing grammar's affect on the teaching of writing, we need to remember that the conflation of grammar and rhetoric is an exclusively modern phenomenon, unknown before 1870 or so. The Greek or Roman rhetorician would have been scandalized by the suggestion that he profess the structure of the language on any level. That job, dirty but necessary, was the responsibility of the grammaticus, the lower-grade teacher who made certain that pupils could speak with correctness.

Only when this knowledge of pure and correct language was assured would the rhetorician take over and teach the pupil to discourse with eloquence. This essential split between grammar and rhetoric existed unchanged through the eighteenth century. As the brilliant George Campbell, hardly a purveyor of unexamined tradition, put it in 1776,

Now, the grammatical art hath its completion in syntax; the oratorical, as far as the body of expression is concerned, in style. Syntax regards only the composition of many words into one sentence; style, at the same time that it attends to this, regards further the composition of many sentences into one discourse. Nor is this the only difference; the grammarian . . . requires only purity. . . . The orator requires also beauty and strength. The highest aim of the former is the lowest aim of the latter; where grammar ends eloquence begins. Thus the grammarian's department bears much the same relation to the orator's which the art of the mason bears to that of the architect.

Campbell is not sneering here at grammar — he discusses grammatical purity at some length when covering good usage — but he does wish to differentiate it clearly from the rhetorical theory that absorbed his interest.

Campbell's attitude toward grammar was not, however, shared by Hugh Blair, whose 1783 *Lectures on* Rhetoric and Belles-Lettres became the most influential of the eighteenth-century rhetorics. Instruction in formal English grammar had begun in both England and America around 1750, and Blair saw, as Campbell did not, that an English rhetoric would have to come to terms with English grammar. Grammar, wrote Blair in one of his two chapters covering it, is apt to be slighted by superficial thinkers as belonging to those rudiments of knowledge, which were inculcated upon us in our earliest youth. But what was then inculcated before we could comprehend its principles, would abundantly repay our study in maturer years; and to the ignorance of it, must be attributed many of those fundamental defects which appear in writing.

Blair gave grammar a place in two of his forty-six lectures, covering all the parts of speech and something of the origins of English. This discussion, thought Blair, was necessary, for without a knowledge of grammar as a formal system good writing was impossible. Good style demanded grammatical purity and propriety, and "If any imagine they can catch it merely by the ear, or acquire it by a slight perusal of some of our good authors, they will find themselves much disappointed." This statement became an article of faith for several generations of teachers of vernacular composition, who came to see a complete knowledge of English grammar as a panacea for all ills in writing.

The gradual absorption of grammar by rhetoric began slowly, however. There were early textbooks with titles like *A Grammar of Composition*, but most of the texts of the pre-1850 period are either based upon Blair Lectures and contain much rhetorical theory and a passing mention of grammar, or upon Lindley Murray English Grammar and are overwhelmingly grammatical with perhaps a few pages on "purity, propriety, precision, and perspicuity" in writing. Rhetoricians were generally able to assume preexisting understanding of the "rules" and terms of grammar on the parts of their readers. At the very least, students of rhetoric were supposed to have mastered the necessities of "Correctness," which, as Samuel Newman put it in his *Practical System* of 1827, "is to be learned from the rules and principles of syntax."

Rhetoric, however, was still mostly thought a higher mystery, one concerned with more than the grammarian's correctness. The rhetoric of the period before 1850 was overwhelmingly abstract and theoretical, concerned with systems of rules and principles rather than with creative methods. There was very little actual practice in composition in rhetoric courses before 1875 or so; such courses consisted of lectures on or textbook study of a system. For such a rhetorical tradition, chock full of its own theoretical content, there was little need for the "rules" and definitions of grammar, a separate system.

Beginnings of Composition

But rhetoric in America was changing. The period 1850-1900 was a time when systematic theoretical rhetoric was replaced by an intensely practical course in correct writing, and a large part of this change came about as a result of the mixture of the "practical" sentence based grammar of Greene and Reed and Kellogg with the newly practical subject of English composition.

Different prepositions in certain contexts

- In the United States, the word *through* can mean "up to and including" as in *Monday through Friday*. In the UK *Monday to Friday*, or *Monday to Friday inclusive* is used instead; *Monday through to Friday* is also sometimes used. (In some parts of Northern England the term *while* can be used in the same way, as in *Monday while Friday*, whereas in Northern Ireland *Monday till Friday* would be more natural.)
- British athletes play *in a team*; American athletes play *on a team*. (Both may play *for* a particular team.)
- The word *heat* meaning "mating season" is used with *on* in the UK and with *in* in the U.S.
- The intransitive verb *affiliate* can take either *with* or *to* in BrE, but only *with* in AmE.
- The verb *enrol(l)* usually takes *on* in BrE and *in* in AmE (as in "to enrol(l) on/in a course") and the on/in difference is also used when *enrolled* is dropped (as in "I am (enrolled) on the course that studies....").

- In AmE, one always speaks of the street *on* which an address is located, whereas in BrE *in* can also be used in some contexts. *In* suggests an address in a city street, so a service station (or a tourist attraction or indeed a village) would always be *on* a major road, but a department store. Moreover, if a particular place on the street is specified then the preposition used is whichever is idiomatic to the place, thus "*at* the end of Churchill Road", and thus also the lyric "our house, in the middle of our street" from "Our House" by the British band Madness, whose intended meaning is "halfway along our street" but is confusing to many Americans—in AmE, the lyric suggests that the house is literally in the middle of the *roadway*.

- The preposition used with the word *weekend* is *on* in the U.S. and *at* (sometimes *on*; the ratio in the British National Corpus is about 9:1) in Britain - for example, in "at the weekend/at weekends" vs. "on the weekend/on weekends". Such usages as "this weekend", "over the weekend", etc. are found in both dialects, but the use of "weekends" adverbally (and also "Mondays", etc.), with no preposition, is AmE rather than BrE.

- After *talk* American can use the preposition *with* but British always uses *to* (that is, "I'll talk with Dave / I'll talk to Dave". The American form is sometimes seen as more politically correct in British organisations, inducing the ideal of discussing (with), as opposed to lecturing (to). This is, of course, unless talk is being used as a noun, for example: "I'll have a talk with him" in which case this is acceptable in both BrE and AmE.

- In both dialects *from* is the preposition prescribed for use after the word *different*: "American English is different from British English in several respects." However, *different than* is also commonly heard in the U.S., and is often considered standard when followed by a clause ("American English is different than it used to be"), whereas *different to* is the alternative common in BrE.

- It is common in BrE to say *opposite to* as an alternative to *opposite of*, the only form normally found in AmE. The use of *opposite* as a preposition ("opposite the post office") has long been established in both dialects, but appears to be more common in British usage.
- The noun *opportunity* can be followed by a verb in two different ways: *opportunity* plus *to*-infinitive ("the opportunity to do something") or *opportunity* plus *of* plus gerund ("the opportunity of doing something"). The first construction is the most common in both dialects, but the second has almost disappeared in AmE and is often regarded as a Briticism.
- Both British and Americans may say (for example) that a river is named *after* a state, but "named *for* a state" would rightly be regarded as an Americanism.
- BrE sometimes uses *to* with *near* ("we live near to the university"), while AmE avoids the preposition in most usages dealing with literal, physical proximity ("we live near the university"), although the "to" reappears in AmE when "near" takes the superlative form, as in, "Of all of us, she lives nearest to the deranged axe murderer's house."
- In BrE, you *call* (or *ring*) someone *on* their telephone number; in AmE, you *call* someone *at* their telephone number.

During the 1850s and 1860s, instruction in actual writing was in its infancy in American colleges, but it became quickly apparent to teachers who demanded writing from students that the older theoretical rhetoric of Blair, like the formal grammar of Murray and his imitators, had no effect on students' abilities to write. Only one early text, G. P. Quackenbos ' *Advanced Course of Composition and Rhetoric,* tried mixing the new "sentence-building" grammar with rhetorical lessons.

During the 1860s, however, several phenomena converged to create a new situation for grammar. First, formal grammar, as we have seen, came under attack as sterile and impractical. Second, the teaching of rhetoric came to be more and more concerned with writing, and thus with *correctness* as well as eloquence. Third, the United States culture as a whole began to become more aware of correct speaking and writing as indices of status and professional worth.

In 1865 Henry Alford, dean of Westminster, published his *Plea for the* Queen's English, an attack on the poor grammar and bad usage he saw all around him – and noted especially in America. Several American writers answered and debated him, and the prescriptive-usage debate that raged throughout the 1860s and '70s drew the attention of the American intellectual community to linguistic issues as never before. After the Civil War, with the Union saved and the beginnings of the drastic social stratification of the Gilded Age, proper language came to have new importance.

A few theorists saw that rhetoric and grammar would be melded in the developing discipline of composition and strove to create an intellectually defensible systhesis of the two. Some, like grammarian William Wells, saw a new discipline in which practice in writing would be the central pedagogical technique, "where analysis and parsing will find their appropriate place as collateral aids in connection with the daily living exercises in the use of the English tongue."

Rhetorician Henry Day, always a theoretical pioneer, published his Grammatical Synthesis: The Art of English Composition in 1867. This book, which meant to unite grammar, rhetoric, and logic in one study because all were "grounded in the basis of Thought," never attained great popularity; like most of Day's work it was too original for its own good. *Grammatical Synthesis* showed, however, that by the late 1860s at least some colleges were beginning to mix grammar with composition.

In the 1870s grammatical elements advanced even more rapidly into the teaching of writing, largely because of the influence of Harvard College. Harvard teachers of English had been noticing for some years that their students had trouble with the written language, and as the older academic system of lectures and exams gave way to the newer classroom discussion and essay writing methods, this problem became even more obvious.

In addition, the growing importance of linguistically influenced class structures and Harvard's desire to demonstrate that it had the highest standards and deserved its leadership position led to the introduction in 1874 of a written examination that determined admission to the college. When the Harvard faculty read these first exams they were shocked by the poor writing and the number of egregious grammatical errors produced by the graduates of America's best academies. More than half of the students taking these early tests failed.

This began an "illiteracy" uproar in academia that lasted for more than two decades and resulted in the interment of most of the old traditions of rhetoric and the creation of a new course and subject that soon became de rigueur in American colleges: freshman composition courses patterned after "English A," the course Harvard instituted to grapple with its literacy problems.

Much anxiety was apparent in the public prints after the mid-seventies bemoaning the "illiteracy of American boys" and suggesting various solutions to the problem. The most popular remedy prescribed for the cure of "illiteracy" was the collection of form-based mechanical lessons that came to be known as "grammar." College students could not write, the reasoning went, because their early grammar lessons had not "taken."

Thus the lessons needed to be repeated until the knowledge of parts of speech and rules would transform into the ability to write. We now see this as an *essentially* incorrect idea, and identify students' poor writing in 1874 as a result of their lack of composition practice in the academies and schools. Yet the power of grammar as a panacea for writing ills was still strong in the 1870s and '80s.

Several books appeared in the mid-seventies which reflect the rather sudden introduction of grammar to the composition course. Joseph H. Gilmore's textbook *Outlines of the Art of Expression* set out, quite clearly, to make grammar a college-level subject. Gilmore, a professor at the University of Rochester, stated in his preface:

This little book has grown, in the author's class-room, out of an attempt to supplement the defective early training of his pupils.

Those pupils had, when they entered college, some practical acquaintance with English composition. . . . English Grammar, many of them had never studied at all – few if any, of them, as the author conceives it should be studied.

For Gilmore, grammar was "the art of correctly expressing our thoughts," and his 112-page book mixed formal grammar and prescriptive advice with some low-level stylistic rhetoric. *Outlines* was neither a grammar book nor a true rhetoric, but its combination of sentence-level advice and grammatical rules made it popular until nearly the turn of the century. Much more popular and important was a book that originated in England, Edwin A.

Abbott How to Write Clearly. Abbott had originally written his book to help his students translate Greek and Latin into acceptable English, since "the flat, vague, long-winded Greek-English and Latin-English imposture that is often tolerated in our examinations . . . diminishes instead of increasing the power that our pupils should possess over their native language." Abbott's answer, unlike Gilmore's, was to try to discern the main grammatical principles most commonly violated and to create a new sort of prescriptive rule that would warn against that specific violation. This was often a grammar-based rule but was by no means always a grammatical rule.

For instance, where Gilmore covers adverbs according to their traditional definitions and classes, Abbott assumes this knowledge and proffers three specific prescriptions: "Adverbs should be placed next to the words they are intended to affect"; "'Only' requires careful use"; and "When 'not only' precedes 'but also,' see that each is followed by the same part of speech." In short, *How to Write Clearly* is the first identifiable handbook of composition. Amazingly popular in the U.S., it remained in print from 1875 until 1914 and was required by colleges in all parts of the country.

Gilmore and Abbott together illustrate how pervasively grammar had infiltrated composition by 1880. Curiously, however, we find little evidence of the advance of grammar in most rhetoric texts of the day. Alexander Bain, A. S. Hill, Barrett Wendell, and Fred Newton Scott all wrote extremely popular rhetoric texts that had no important grammatical components at all. Of all the major rhetoricians of the last two decades of the century, only John Genung in his *Practical Elements of Rhetoric* and *Outlines of Rhetoric* touched on grammar in any important way.

Genung's willingness to deal with grammatical elements (he called them "Fundamental Processes") in his books was part of the reason for his tremendous success: between 1887 and 1894 or so, *Practical Elements* was the most popular composition textbook. Genung realized that rhetoric was going to have to make peace with grammar one way or another and figured that it might as well be done with dignity. "But even in employing grammatical processes as working-tools," Genung wrote, "rhetoric imparts to them a new quality distinctively rhetorical, the quality by which they become methods in an art, means to an end."

His Outlines of Rhetoric of 1893 was even more open in its acceptance of grammatical theory and syntactic exercises. *Outlines* is a collection of 125 illustrated rules not unlike an expanded version of Abbott's How to Write Clearly. Of these, thirty-one were overtly grammatical rules. Outlines was the first major text to be so practice-oriented and prescriptively organized. Genung may have been the only rhetorician of the "Big Four" to include grammatical elements in his rhetoric, but beginning in the late eighties other text authors made the jump from "rhetoric" to "composition."

The words "composition" and "by practice" in a book title were often the code terms for books that included lower-level formal sections and sections on grammar. William Williams' *Composition and Rhetoric by Practice* devoted its first sixty pages to grammar and to sentence practice and remained extremely popular into the 1920s. Williams was immediately copied by Edward Shaw, whose 1892 English Composition by Practice was even less concerned with traditional nongrammatical rhetoric than was Williams' book.

The period of the nineties was a time of warfare between the old fashioned rhetoricians and teachers who believed that grammar and rhetoric should remain separate and the newer teachers and authors who had no such qualms. The old guard, many of whom had been educated in Blair's systematic tradition, looked down on the new field of composition as it burgeoned.

They decried the illiteracy of students but insisted that secondary schools take the responsibility for education in grammar and formal correctness. E. L. Godkin, one of the authors of the famous *Harvard Report* of 1892, pleaded that college teachers be "delivered, in large part at least, from the necessity of teaching the rudiments of the language." It was increasingly clear, however, that they would not soon be so delivered, and younger numbers of the authorial community increasingly produced textbooks that took advantage of the trend toward grammar.

Though more and more traditional grammar was included in college rhetorics after 1895, those who wrote about English pedagogy seemed at that time curiously reticent about admitting that the "practicalization" of the course in rhetoric, so much lauded, really meant the supplanting of abstract lectures by low-level formal exercises.

The very word "grammar" seldom appeared in many books except as part of a short discussion about its relation to rhetoric. Hardly mentioned was the fact that basic grammatical correctness was coming to be regarded as the prime desideratum for composition. One must look at some of the student papers of the period and the comments teachers made upon them to realize how essentially formal the criteria for good writing were.

At the same time that article-writers in *Educational Review* were discussing "philological training" and "the science of language," however, teachers were making their students buy Abbott How to Write Clearly, A. S. Hill's pamphlet on grammatical correctness, or one of the newer texts that carefully straddled the line between high school and college composition.

Teaching grammatical correctness in college accelerated after 1900, and it soon became obvious that new tools would be needed to make college grammar more effective. In 1907, Edwin Woolley Handbook of Composition reduced the system of English grammar to a series of prescriptive error-based rules. Woolley was much more complete than Abbott, covering 350 rules to Abbott's 56. Woolley Handbook was not a grammar treatise of the old soil; as he said in his preface, "The aim of the book is not scientific, but practical.

The purpose is to make clear the rules in regard to which many people make mistakes. No material has been put into the book for the sake of formal completeness." A far cry from the aims of traditional grammarians from Lowth onward, but Woolley defined here the sort of "grammar" that would henceforward be most people's definition: a set of rules about words and sentences that define mistakes as perceived by an English teacher. The development and use of handbooks after Woolley is another story, one told elsewhere.

For the purposes of this essay, it is enough to say that insofar as grammar was part of composition after 1910, it was found in the increasingly popular — eventually almost ubiquitous — handbooks. As the handbook moved closer and closer to centrality in the teaching practices and especially in the paper-grading and marking practices of teachers, the field of grammar became more and more important.

For secondary-school students, grammar meant the "sentence-building" book or the "language" book; for college students, grammar meant the handbook. Rhetoric waned during the period 1910-1930. Frank Scott wrote in 1918 that "for ten years or so there has been a steady diminution of the amount of rhetorical theory offered in [college textbooks]; that which has been retained has been made more and more elementary."

Meanwhile, the son of grammar being taught in college courses reflected the most old-fashioned, rigid, and puristic prejudices of the nineteenth century.

Where ever you may be (UK, Canada, Ireland, Malta, USA, New Zealand, India, anywhere really) if you want to learn English, then the obvious thing to do is attend classroom instructor-led training - depending on the time available to you, that will be day-time or evening classes.

But what are your options other than classroom? You time is limited and classroom training isn't always possible. English books? CBT (Computer Based Training) English CDs? Cassettes? Or videos? What about learning English online? Book is probably the most convenient form allowing you brush-up while on a bus, during your lunch break or during those regular traffic jams.

Phrasal Verbs

- In the U.S., forms are usually but not invariably *filled out*, but in Britain they can also be *filled in*. However, in reference to individual parts of a form, Americans may also use *in* ("fill in the blanks"). In AmE the direction "fill it all in" (referring to the form as a collection of blanks, perhaps) is as common as "fill it all out."

- Britons facing extortionate prices may have no option but to *fork out*, whereas Americans are more likely to *fork (it) over* or sometimes *up*; both usages are however found in both dialects.
- British thugs will *beat* someone *up*, while their American counterparts will also *beat on* (as both would for an inanimate object, such as a drum) or *beat up on* their victim, though "beat up on" is only used in some locations, and would generally be avoided by Americans who consider themselves well-educated. Both *beat on* and *beat up on* are often considered slang in AmE.
- When an outdoor event is postponed or interrupted by rain, it is *rained off* in the UK and *rained out* in the U.S.
- In AmE, some prescriptionists feel that *which* should not be used as an antecedent in restrictive relative clauses. According to *The Elements of Style*, "*that* is the defining, or restrictive pronoun, *which* the nondefining, or nonrestrictive." This distinction was endorsed by Fowler's Modern English Usage, but the use of *which* as a restrictive pronoun is common in great literature produced on both sides of the Atlantic.
- In names of American rivers, the word *river* usually comes after the name (for example, *Colorado River*), whereas for British rivers it comes before (as in *River Thames*). One exception present in BrE is the *Fleet River*, which is rarely called the *River Fleet* by Londoners outside of official documentation. Exceptions in the U.S. are the *River Rouge* and the *River Raisin*, both in Michigan and named by the French. This convention is mixed, however, in some Commonwealth nations, where both arrangements are often seen.
- In BrE the word *sat* is often colloquially used to cover *sat, sitting* and *seated*: "I've been sat here waiting for

half an hour." "The bride's family will be sat on the right-hand side of the church." This construction is not often heard outside the UK. In the 1960s, its use would mark a speaker as coming from the north of England but by the turn of the 21st century this form had spread to the south. Its use often conveys lighthearted informality, as many speakers intentionally use an ungrammatical construction they would probably not use in formal written English. This colloquial usage is widely understood by British speakers. Similarly *stood* can be used instead of *standing*. To an American these usages are passive, and may imply that the subject had been involuntarily forced to sit or stand, or directed to hold that location.

- In most areas of the United States, the word *with* is also used as an adverb: "I'll come with" instead of "I'll come along". However, in some British Dialects, 'come with' is used as an abbreviation of 'come with me', as in "I'm going to the office - come with" instead of "I'm going to the office - come with me". This particular usage is also used by speakers in Minnesota and parts of the adjoining states: "Want to come with?" Possibly, this is another expression arising from German (*kommst du mit?*) in parts of the United States with high concentrations of German American populations. It is similar to South African English, where the expression comes from Afrikaans, and is also used by Dutch speakers when speaking in English.

- The word *also* is used at the end of a sentence in AmE (just as *as well* and *too* are in both dialects), but not so commonly in BrE, although it is encountered in Northern Ireland. Additionally, sentence-ending *as well* is more formal in AmE than in BrE.

Word Derivation and Compounds

- Directional suffix *-ward(s)*: British *forwards, towards, rightwards,* etc.; American *forward, toward, rightward.*

In both dialects, distribution varies somewhat: *afterwards, towards,* and *backwards* are not unusual in America; while in Britain *forward* is common, and standard in phrasal verbs like *look forward to.* The forms with *-s* may be used as adverbs (or preposition *towards*), but rarely as adjectives: in Britain as in America one says "an upward motion". The Oxford English Dictionary in 1897 suggested a semantic distinction for adverbs, with *-wards* having a more definite directional sense than *-ward*; subsequent authorities such as Fowler have disputed this contention.

- AmE freely adds the suffix *-s* to *day, night, evening, weekend, Monday,* etc. to form adverbs denoting repeated or customary action: "I used to stay out evenings"; "the library is closed Saturdays". This usage has its roots in Old English, but many of these constructions are now regarded as American (for example, the OED labels *nights* "now chiefly N.Amer. colloq."; but *to work nights* is standard in BrE).
- In BrE, the agentive *-er* suffix is commonly attached to *football* (also *cricket*; often *netball*; occasionally *basketball*). AmE usually uses *football player.* Where the sport's name is usable as a verb, the suffixation is standard in both dialects: for example, *golfer, bowler* (in Ten-pin bowling and in Lawn Bowls), and *shooter.* AmE does, however, sometimes use *baller* as slang for a basketball player, as in the video game "NBA Ballers."
- English writers everywhere occasionally (and from time immemorial) make new compound words from common phrases; for example, *health care* is now being replaced by *healthcare* on both sides of the Atlantic. However, AmE has made certain words in this fashion which are still treated as phrases in most Commonwealth countries. For example, Americans write *trademark,* but some other countries write *trade-mark* or *trade mark.*

- In compound nouns of the form <verb><noun>, sometimes AmE favours the bare infinitive where BrE favours the gerund. Examples include (AmE first): *jump rope/skipping rope; racecar/racing car; rowboat/rowing boat; sailboat/sailing boat; file cabinet/filing cabinet; dial tone /dialling tone.*

- More generally, AmE has a tendency to drop inflectional suffixes, thus favouring clipped forms: compare *cookbook /cookery book; Smith, age 40/Smith, aged 40; skim milk/skimmed milk.* The first form is rarely encountered in British usage.

- Singular attributives in one country may be plural in the other, and *vice versa.* For example, the UK has a *drugs problem* while the United States has a *drug problem* (although the singular usage is also commonly heard in the UK); Americans read the "sports" section of a newspaper, while the British are more likely to read the "sport" section. However, BrE *maths* is singular, just as AmE *math* is: both are abbreviations of *mathematics.*

Chapter 3

Early Linguistic Theory

BASIC LINGUISTIC THEORY

The science, that is, the general and universal properties, of language. The middle of the twentieth century saw a shift in the principal direction of linguistic inquiry from one of data collection and classification to the formulation of a theory of generative grammar, which focuses on the biological basis for the acquisition and use of human language and the universal principles that constrain the class of all languages. Generative grammar distinguishes between the knowledge of language (linguistic competence), which is represented by mental grammar, and the production and comprehension of speech (linguistic performance). If grammar is defined as the mental representation of linguistic knowledge, then a general theory of language is a theory of grammar.

A grammar includes everything one knows about a language; its phonetics and phonology (the sounds and the sound system), its morphology (the structure of words), its lexicon (the words or vocabulary), its syntax (the structure of sentences and the constraints on well-formed sentences), and its semantics (the meaning of words and sentences). Linguistics is not limited to grammatical theory.

Descriptive linguistics analyzes the grammars of individual languages; anthropological linguistics, or ethnolinguistics, and sociolinguistics focus on languages in relation to culture, social class, race, and gender;

dialectologists investigate how these factors fragment one language into many. In addition, sociolinguists and applied linguists examine language planning, literacy, bilingualism, and second-language acquisition. Computational linguistics encompasses automatic parsing, machine processing, and computer simulation of grammatical models for the generation and parsing of sentences.

If viewed as a branch of artificial intelligence, computational linguistics has as its goal the modeling of human language as a cognitive system. A branch of linguistics concerned with the biological basis of language development is neurolinguistics. The form of language representation in the mind, that is, linguistic competence and the structure and components of the mental grammar, is the concern of theoretical linguistics.

The branch of linguistics concerned with linguistic performance, that is, the production and comprehension of speech (or of sign language by the deaf), is called psycholinguistics. Psycholinguists also investigate how children acquire the complex grammar that underlies language use. If a gap had developed between rhetoric as it perceived itself and the grammar-oriented composition course as it was taught, a gap just as large began to open between the grammar that English teachers taught and the growing insights of the scientific philologists and linguists active in English studies during the late nineteenth and early twentieth centuries.

Such important early linguistic scholars began, in the years after 1900, to suggest that a new way of viewing grammar, one based on a descriptive and flexible objectivity rather than on the prescriptive purism of the older grammar, might be the linguistics of the future. The expression "basic linguistic theory" refers to the theoretical framework that is most widely employed in language description, particularly grammatical descriptions of entire languages.

It is also the framework assumed by most work in linguistic typology. The status of basic linguistic theory as a theoretical framework is not often recognized. People using basic linguistic theory often characterize their work as atheoretical or theory-neutral or theoretically eclectic.

However, there is really no such thing as atheoretical or theory-neutral description, since one cannot describe anything without making some theoretical assumptions. The extent to which most descriptive work shares the same theoretical assumptions is actually rather striking, especially when one considers how much such work has in common in its assumptions compared to other theoretical frameworks. It is probably the most widely used and best known theoretical framework in the field, especially outside the United States.

It is particularly popular among linguists who are more interested in languages than in language. Many linguists who are adherents of other theoretical frameworks assume it as a point of departure, as a framework they wish to improve on. Unlike many theoretical frameworks in linguistics, which are often ephemeral and pass quickly into obsolescence, basic linguistic theory is a cumulative framework that has slowly developed over the past century as linguists have learned how to describe languages better.

It is grounded in traditional grammar and can be seen as having evolved out of traditional grammar. It has also been heavily influenced by pre-generative structuralist traditions, particularly in emphasizing the need to describe each language in its own terms, rather than imposing on individual languages concepts whose primary motivation comes from other languages, in contrast to traditional grammar and many recent theoretical frameworks.

It has taken analytic techniques from structuralist traditions, particularly in the areas of phonology and morphology. But it also contrasts with work that is more purely structuralist in attempting to describe languages in a more user-friendly fashion, in including semantic considerations in its analyses, and in employing terminology that has been used for similar phenomena in other languages.

Basic linguistic theory has also been influenced to a certain extent by generative grammar, though the influence has primarily been from early generative grammar (before 1970) and is often indirect. The influence largely reflects the fact that early generative grammar examined many aspects of the syntax of English in great detail, and the insights of that research have influenced how basic linguistic theory looks at the syntax of other languages, especially in terms of how one can argue for particular analyses.

The influence of generative grammar can be seen in the way that certain constructions in other languages are identified and characterized in ways reminiscent of constructions in English, from cleft constructions to "topicalizations" to reflexive constructions. More recent work in generative grammar, especially Government-Binding Theory, has had essentially no impact on basic linguistic theory. In the past 30 years, the primary influence on basic linguistic theory has come from work in linguistic typology.

This influence has come primarily from the recognition of recurrent sorts of phenomena cross linguistically and basic linguistic theory has incorporated many substantive concepts discussed in the typological literature. This includes such notions as split intransitivity, antipassive constructions, internally-headed relative clauses, switch reference, and head-marking.

Work in typology has also influenced the way linguists describing languages think about such things as negativity and relative clauses. Basic linguistic theory differs from many other theoretical frameworks in that it is not a formal theory but an Informal theory. That is, many grammatical phenomena can generally be characterized with sufficient precision in English (or some other natural language), without the use of formalism. The above discussion focuses on the morphosyntactic side of basic linguistic theory (or what one might call "basic syntactic theory"), but one can also trace the historical influences on phonology in basic linguistic theory.

The concept of the phoneme is probably the most central phonological concept in basic linguistic theory: identifying the phonemes in a language remains the most fundamental task in describing the phonology of a language. But generative phonology has also influenced basic linguistic theory: language descriptions often find the generative notion of phonological rule useful, and the descriptive tools of more recent phonological theories, especially autosegmental phonology, have proven useful for descriptive linguists.

Support for a universal grammar and a rigid purism in usage declined rapidly among genuine philosophers of language after 1900, but, sadly, little was carried over from the descriptive language studies. As early as the 1880s a few philologists had criticized teachers' total acceptance of traditional rigid grammar, but before 1900 there was no organized critique of this purblind dependence on an increasingly discredited system. With the work of Lounsbury, Matthews, and Krapp a new scientific and descriptive spirit appeared in philology.

Arguing against a fixed standard of grammatical propriety in The Standard of Usage in English, Lounsbury grittily proclaimed that "in order to have a language become fixed, it is first necessary that those who speak it should become dead. . . ." George Krapp, in his Modern English of 1909, made an important differentiation between standard English as taught by the rigid prescriptive grammarians of the schools and good English, language that treads the boundary between convention and invention.

"Language is valuable only as it effects the purposes one wishes to attain," wrote Krapp, unconsciously echoing George Campbell's definition of rhetoric in 1776 as "that art or talent by which the discourse is adapted to its end." By World War I a whole generation of philologically trained teachers had made themselves conversant with both the history of the English language and with its similarities to and differences from other language systems.

This generation of scholars — no more than a few hundred in number, in comparison to the thousands of literary specialists and composition teachers — founded the Linguistic Society of America in 1924. Linguistics thus officially declared itself independent of English, classics, anthropology, and psychology, complaining that "the standing of our science in the academic community leaves much to be desired."

In an almost anguished apologia for the LSA, published in the first volume of Language, Leonard Bloomfield charged that our schools are conducted by persons who, from professors of education down to teachers in the classroom, know nothing of the results of linguistic science; not even the relation of writing to speech or of standard language to dialect. In short, they do not know what language is, and yet must teach it. . . .

The National Council of Teachers of English had been formed in 1911, but only slowly did it come to be a prime mover behind attacks on purism and prescriptivism in grammar. Most early NCTE members, it appears, were satisfied with Woolley's prescriptive-handbook approach, but a few of the most active and influential members were aware of the trends in linguistics and began in the late teens to fire off salvoes against prescriptive grammar and usage. Fred N. Scott, as reliably ahead of his time on this issue as on others, attacked inflexible prescriptive standards in the 1917 English Journal.

In the following year, he was seconded by G. P. Krapp, who was still exploring the question of acceptability of usages, and the youthful Sterling A. Leonard, whose "Old Purist Junk" still remains a classic of witty denigration. It begins, "The purist is surely one of the strangest of God's creatures," and includes the plaint, modern sounding even in the eighties, that in our weary preoccupation with a hundred mere insignificant conventions of wording and idiom we have left almost untouched more fruitful topics. . .

Our nice conscientiousness has been sadly misled by dictatorial and wise-sounding but often densely ignorant pronouncements, into a teaching, not only of fiddle faddle niceties, but of positive untruth about present usage. I suggest that for a very considerable part of the actual difficulties and regrettable ill successes of our English teaching – I know at least that it is true of my own – the blind leading of purists is responsible.

Leonard was one of the most important figures in establishing the empirical reality of the doctrine of usage with his posthumously published Current English Usage of 1932. But as early as 1917 he had already spoken out strongly in favour of the liberal and reformist ideas he had learned as Scott's student at Michigan.

The decade of the teens also brought forth the first series of attempts to measure empirically the worth of grammar to literacy skills. Most of these early experiments involved elementary and secondary schools and affected college grammar only indirectly. Yet the fact that they were done at all indicates a new professionalism in education, an unwillingness to accept the received wisdom that gramnmar was indispensable.

Studies in 1917 cast increasing doubt on the idea that grammar instruction carried over into composition. William Asker in 1923 correlated the grammatical knowledge of high school seniors with their freshman composition grades in college and found that "knowledge of formal grammar influences ability to judge the grammatical correctness of a sentence and ability in English composition only to a negligible degree."

By the 1920s, the antiprescriptivists had begun to assemble an impressive array of theorists and studies unbified by the belief that traditional grammar was not useful. Krapp, Leonard, and Scott insisted that the insights of Bloomfield, Sapir, Jespersen, and other scientific linguists could be ignored only at peril. Around the mid-twenties Charles C. Fries added his voice to this chorus of criticism.

Throughout his long and active career in the LSA, the MLA, and NCTE, Fries constantly strove to make English teachers aware of linguistic insights. In Fries's first important book, The Teaching of the English Language, he wrote:

> Even after more than a hundred years of linguistic study based upon the historical method, the fundamental principles upon which the modern scientific view of language rests and the results of scholarly investigations in the English language have not reached the schools. On the whole the schools still perpetuate with very little change the eighteenth century point of view. This book is an effort to interpret the modern scientific view of language in a practical way for teachers.

Fries discusses at length the folly of rule-worship, the doctrine of the standard of usage, where the concept of acceptable grammar originated, and other elements of informed language teaching. For the next forty years, which included presidencies of the LSA and NCTE, Fries would continue to press the fight against destructive prescription in grammar.

By the mid-twenties the defenders of formal grammar, while ascendant in the classroom, were on the defensive in scholarly journals. Leon Mones was one of the few who made any attempt to defend the teaching of formal grammar against the flood of attacks. Grammar was under such an attack, complained Mones that "an argument in its favour must ring like either grumpy reaction or hysteric reform. Well, grumpy some of us are, and hysteric too.

We have seen the 'No Formal Grammar' army march on to victory and leave chaos behind it." Mones' nostalgia for an ordered past was not the usual position found in journals after 1920, however. The greater number of post-1920 journal articles on grammar either report the findings of ill-designed studies about whether grammar helps students read and write, or attack the idea of prescriptive usage, or report on minor teaching techniques involving grammar without taking sides, or make technical descriptive points within traditional grammar.

Meanwhile, in the classrooms, handbooks and their sinister new siblings, "drillbooks" and "workbooks," held almost unchallenged sway. During this period, the public attitude toward grammar instruction was mixed; most people had hated their school grammar, but large numbers felt it had done them good and many thought traditional grammar needed to be continued.

The public had little idea of the formidable forces building a case against grammar instruction within academe until Sterling Leonard Current English Usage in 1932 and Marckwardt and Walcott Facts about Current English Usage in 1938. These books were widely perceived as surrender on the part of English teachers to an "anything goes" ethic in usage, and various funerals were held in popular magazines for "grammar."

When the NCTE in 1935 published its Experience Curriculum in English, a document which more or less summed up the pedagogical opinions of the Deweyite wing that composed the group's vocal minority, few were surprised to see a general comdemnation of grammar teaching:

Because scientific investigators haved failed to show the effectiveness of grammar in the elimination of usage errors, it is not here organized for that purpose. There is no scientific evidence of the value of grammar which warrants its appearance as a prominent or even distinct feature of the course of study.

Linguistics and English

After 1935 a number of factors came together to make the relations between linguistics and composition complex and polemical. Edward Sapir and Leonard Bloomfield had published their magniopi, both entitled Language, in 1921 and 1933, and in the thirties their students moved more and more rapidly toward a genuinely scientific linguistics.

In practice, this meant that after 1930 linguistics and composition moved further and further apart in terms of their ultimate goals. Linguistics was becoming exclusively interested in comparative and structural description that had nothing at all to do with teaching or specifying good or bad usage. Such labels, dear to English teachers, were becoming genuinely embarrassing to linguists.

Except for a few teachers like Fries, who had deep roots in both English and linguistics, there were not many who could carry the message of this essential disjunction over to English. Since Bloomfield Language in 1933, linguistics had hardly concerned its investigations with writing at all, assuming that writing was secondary to oral speech, but few teachers were even aware of that.

Most had never had specific training in linguistics, although the NCTE had been calling for such training for English teachers since 1928. English teachers knew something was happening in linguistics, and they had heard it was scientific and impressive; when, they tended to ask, would this new grammar give them something they could use in classrooms to replace the oft-critiqued old grammar?

Such applications were not forthcoming. Linguists after 1940 hardly bothered to criticize the soil of grammar taught in English. They merely rolled their eyes and sighed. The linguistic frontiers were far away from the handbook and the classroom. As many large universities formed departments of linguistics, linguists literally moved away from English and away from the turmoil that continued in English over the use of "grammar" to teach writing.

For the period after 1940 we must carefully distinguish the controversies within the field of linguistics from those in English whose ostensible subject was linguistics. Linguists increasingly disputed analytical techniques, categories, philosophical and psychological perspectives, and purposive paradigms.

English teachers disputed two questions: what should "grammar" be and how can it help students read and write better? While this is not the place for a history of linguistics in America (those interested can turn to a number of books on that subject), it must be noted that the knowledge and attitudes of most English teachers were increasingly outdated. Fries' American English Grammar of 1940, financed by the NCTE, was meant to inform teachers about contemporary grammatical knowledge and thus reduce the "futile and even harmful practices which have resulted from ignorance."

The book seems not to have had much impact, however, despite its practical intentions and readability. During the forties and early fifties grammar teaching in college was damped down by the growth of two trendy movements: General Semantics and the Communications movement. The General Semantics movement concerned itself with words and their representational functions. The "communications" movement in general education wished to concentrate on all four communications skills – reading, writing, speaking, and listening – and thus had a great deal of non grammatical material to cover.

Meanwhile, handbooks of grammar grew from small home-reference manuals into fairly large books that attempted to rule-govern the entire process of composition. It is unfortunate but true that of the dozens of handbooks published between 1930 and 1960 only a handful even attempted to utilize the insights of linguistics, and only one of these had any influence – Porter Perrin An Index to English, which, like all of Perrin's .work, was rigorous in its scholarship and not satisfied to mouth the contemporary pieties. In 1952, the indefatigable Charles Fries published. "The Structure of American English", a textbook which attempted to apply the insights of linguists since Bloomfield to constructing English sentences.

Fries's basically descriptive, non normative approach would gradually come to be called "structural grammar" and would be one of the key issues in grammatical arguments that would rage a few years later. In 1952, however, The Structure of English caused barely a ripple. Many teachers examined it, but few taught it. Most English teachers continued to slumber through a long summer of lethargic acceptance of linguistic ignorance, leading W. Melson Francis to cry in 1953 that in no reputable academic discipline is the gap between the pioneers of research and the pedagogical rank and file more shockingly great. . . . Our situation is as anomalous as if our scientific colleagues were to teach geocentric astronomy, pre-Darwinian biology, and chemistry based on the four elements.

The combination of ignorance and willful refusal to abandon traditional grammar and the "standards" that many people thought it represented continued throughout most of the 1950s. Many teachers shared the common public attitude that "standards" had been sliding in English for many years, and especially since Sterling Leonard and Charles Fries and their band of radical hotheads had begun cutting the ground out from under traditional grammar.

By the mid-fifties, however, this position was little defended except in sotto voce staffroom complaints. Most of the publishing members of the profession were increasingly coming to see a pro-traditional grammar attitude as a hallmark of ignorance and solipsism. With the mid-fifties we enter a fascinating era, one that really deserves an essay all its own. I cannot do full justice to the complexity of the positions held or the arguments advanced; such huge theoretical shifts rocked both linguistics and composition between 1956 and 1965 that the picture is often less than clear.

Before 1956 or so there was relatively little interest in or activity concerning grammar as a intellectual concept or a pedagogical challenge, and after 1965 we emerge into the recognizable modern landscape well described. Between those two dates, however, a veritable ferment of interest in linguistics came to English, leaving the discipline shaken and changed forever. This new era probably began with Fries' 1952 *Structure* as much as with anything else.

Though not a popular textbook, it motivated several other authors to write textbooks using "structural grammar" as their essential model. Paul Roberts 'Patterns of English, Donald Lloyd and Harry Warfel American English in Its Cultural Setting and Harold Whitehall Structural Essentials of English all appeared in 1956.

Suddenly, like it or not, English teachers were faced with having to choose between books that tacitly supported the old dispensation and those that trumpeted the new. As happens so often in composition, the knowledge that journal authors had been trying to promote for years was actually delivered by textbooks.

Not, I hasten to add, that the "structural" textbooks took over the field; in fact, they did rather poorly, considering how much had been said about the "new grammar." Some teachers tried the structural approach, hopeful, perhaps that this "new" grammar could rekindle the flame of belief that seemed to be guttering for the old grammar. But Roberts, Fries, and Lloyd-Warfel never became the touchstones they sought to be.

If we are to attempt teaching English in the near future by extensive use of structural linguistics, we are presented with at least the following staggering facts:

1. Structural linguistics is a difficult concept and an exacting practice, when compared, for instance, with an engaging amusement like general semantics;
2. The linguists themselves do not as yet agree entirely, either in the analysis of English or in a method of teaching it;
3. No large-scale test of the approach using unselected teachers has yet been attempted, and
4. There is no immediate prospect of producing a considerable body of teachers versed in structural linguistics.

Laird went on to question the entire structuralist enterprise, but he was aware even as he critiqued descriptivism that the old grammar was no more defensible. His essay provoked several responses.

By 1959, the question of structural linguistics and its relation to English was getting ready to explode. In late 1958 the venerable Wilbur Hatfield had come out in favour of teaching structural grammar in English, and the fuse was lit in 1959 by Harry Warfel's argument in the February College English. In his typically winsome and delicate fashion, Warfel began:

The science of structural linguistics has put new tools into our hands. Just as nucleonics has penetrated into the minute operations of the atom, so structural linguistics has unlocked the secrets of language. The established conclusions and the emerging theories seem likely to force other disciplines to reshape current procedures wherever they are dependent upon or impinge upon language. . . . The teaching of composition must undergo a revolutionary change.

From this humble beginning, Warfel went on to lecture his audience on the "vast array of facts" amassed by structural linguists from which come "principles, rules, and laws that have relevance to general composition." Warfel argued that the function-based grammar then accepted by most linguists was a better basis for composition learning than anything else.

He inveighed against the "outmoded gadgetry" of traditional handbooks, workbooks, and grammars, but he also condemned the (sometimes extreme) "thought" and "general education" methods of the period. "The study of semantics has been a will-o-thewisp. . . . Most books of reading selections have been productive of little good. The preoccupation with ideas as opposed to the student's mastery of the language system has been self-defeating". This hectoring tone continued throughout the article.

Warfel's structuralist boosterism seems vaguely sad and ironic to us today – "Look upon my works, ye mighty, and despair" – but in 1959 it was little less than a call to arms.

He was replied to quickly, and soon the journals were filled with essays for and against structural linguistics in English. The denigration of linguistics in the popular prints was continuing, with Jacques Barzun leading the charge against the "new grammarians," and from 1960 through 1963, linguistics and its impact on composition were fighting issues.

College English devoted the better parts of four issues to the linguistic controversy between 1960 and 1965, and the battles raged. Structuralists explained patiently again and again why their discipline better explained the facts of language than did the traditional grammar, while at the same time numerous English teachers wrote essays complaining about the nonjudgmental aspects of descriptive linguistics. The entire discipline seemed to feel that a great question impended; as Allain Renoir put it, "The necessity to make a considered choice between traditional grammar and structural linguistics is one which teachers of freshman composition can no longer avoid. . . ."

In the midst of this controversy a number of rational points of view also appeared. Among those who took this rational middle ground were Renoir, who admitted that the structuralists' "extreme accuracy in linguistic description is certainly desirable but by no means necessary to the teaching of composition. The main job of the teacher of composition is not to describe language, but rather to teach his students how to compose."

And Charles Fries himself, in several magisterial statements in 1960 and 1961, defended linguistics but tried to disassociate himself from its thoughtless popularizers. "Linguistic science, like all science, is concerned with knowing and understanding, not with doing," wrote Fries. If applications were to be made, he was certain that they could not be the result of forcing English teachers to take one or two linguistics courses to master techniques.

Nor did Fries believe in the simple-minded adaptations that some of the "linguistic science-fiction" writers like Warfel had proposed. Fries was utterly certain that such adaptations were futile, and his statement is worth noting today:

> In my view, it is not the tools and the techniques of linguistic science that should be brought into the classroom; but in some way, the substance of the knowledge and understanding won by linguistic science must be thoroughly assimilated and then used to shed new light upon the problems that arise wherever language is concerned.

The structuralist controversy seemed to many teachers and English based linguists to be a battle for the very soul of composition teaching itself. Some asked: would the discipline stagnate, a purveyor of outworn and discredited conventions, or would it take the high road of science and accept the future? Others asked: would English surrender to the "anything goes" radical wing or proudly continue its traditional role as safeguarder of standard?

Only a few early saw the futility of the battle, the foredoomed fate of both structuralists and traditionalists. While the usual suspects — Warfel, Fries, Francis, Barzun, Allen, Roberts, and many others — worried the question of structuralism from 1959 through 1963, a young student of Zellig Harris's named Noam Chomsky readied the linguistic revolution that would, at least in America, relegate the entire structuralist enterprise to the history books. As early as 1961 James Sledd saw it coming in a thoughtful article called "A Plea for Pluralism." As usual, Sledd minced no words":

> For American teachers of English, the year's principal developments in language-study have been two. First, Chomsky, Halle, Lees, and their disciples have sustained their attacks on structural linguistics with increasing vigor and success. Second, with increasing success and vigor the evangels of the Anglists have sustained their effort to convert the high schools and colleges to structural linguistics.

Yesterday's Left has thus become today's Right, a new Left has emerged which is in some ways closer to yesterday's Right than to today's, and today's Right, internally divided and calling itself the Centre, works at ignoring the new Left as it evangelizes the old Right. The result may well be that men who have argued creditably against traditional dogmas will now saddle the country's schools with the opposite dogmas of American structuralism at the precise moment when many of those dogmas are being discredited.

That is what happened for a little while, but not for long. After 1965, linguistics in America was clearly in the hands of the MIT axis, and the structuralist debate was effectively over. The old Right, handbook traditionalists, remained in English, but even the tenuous bridges between linguistics and handbook grammar that the structuralists had built were impossible to maintain after the ascent of transformational-generative grammar. If Friesian function categories and juncture theory were hard for English teachers to follow, phrase-structure rules and obligatory transformations were completely impossible for most of them.

After 1965, linguistics as an ongoing exploration had less and less to do with teaching English. As genuine linguistics became less accessible, "grammar" in English became the strange amalgam of buzzwords, legends, handbook nostrums, half-understood transformational concepts, and decayed eighteenth-century prescription that most of us know today.

Traditional grammar did not flourish openly, especially after the famous and seemingly final verdict of *Research in Written Composition* in 1963 that "the teaching of formal grammar has a negligible or, because it usually displaces some instruction and practice in actual composition, even a harmful effect on the improvement of writing," but it continued its malevolent half-life in its accustomed lair: handbooks and workbooks.

In 1963, the concerted leap forward in rhetorical theory that we now think of as the "rhetorical revolution" was just beginning, and some nonmainstream linguistic theories such as tagmemics were instrumental parts of it. A few enthusiasts believed that transformational-generative theory could be made the keystone of the new rhetoric, but results were inconclusive, and the full story of TG applications takes me beyond 1965, where I arbitrarily mean to end this history.

The tale of grammar is by no means over; even today sentence diagramming has voluble champions, and traditional grammar, against all odds, is attempting a comeback. A great deal of the history of composition in America seems to be a clumsy shuffle-dance of grammar with rhetoric, with first one and then another leading.

It will not end soon, for the wish for certainty and algorithmic closure represented by the one struggles always with the desire for originality and creativity represented by the other. So long as language is part science, part art, and part magic, the grammarians and the rhetoricians will be struggling with each other to lead the dance. If your educational experience in any way resembled mine, you have been uncertain about what style is.

Style was a familiar enough word for you, but your concept of style was probably vague. You sensed that certain authors had a distinctive style, but you were not quite sure what it meant to say that an author "has style" and even less sure about what made a style distinctive. In reading a piece of prose, you experienced an undeniable effect, but you could not designate just what it was in that collection of sentences that caused that effect.

Consequently, you still may not know how to analyze style or how to talk about it in any meaningful way. Style may be a vague concept to us because our own teachers spent little or no time talking about style. They may have used such general terms as "lucid," "elegant," "laboured," "Latinate," "turgid," or "flowing" in commenting on an author's syle, but they never bothered to analyze the features or the constituents of the styles that bore those epithets.

Those were largely impressionistic labels, and if we too regarded a certain author's style as, say, "turgid" — whatever *that* was — then we agreed with our teacher's classification of the style. But if we felt that this same author had a "lilting style," we knew no way of describing a "lilting style" or no way of refuting our teacher's judgment. So we dutifully copied down in our notebooks the appropriate epithets for each author we read and discussed in class, and we delighted in moving on to talk about more determinable matters, like the content or the structure of the piece of literature.

If we listed ourselves as members of that post-World War II generation of students who regularly practiced the Brooks-and-Warren method of close analysis, we could talk about the linguistic features of a poem with great specificity. Yet we may well have been stymied when we wanted to talk about the linguistic features of a prose text.

If you could put these questions concerning style (what is it? what effects does it produce in a reader? what does one look for in studying it?) to a Renaissance schoolboy, he could give you satisfactory answers. His education was predominatly language-oriented. From the beginning to the end of the school day, he was steeped in words – English words, Latin words, sometimes even Greek words.

He had to recite the grammatical rules that he had memorized the night before; he had to parse sentences; he had to translate Latin sentences into English sentences or English sentences into Latin sentences; he had to be able to write original sentences according to a prescribed pattern; he had to paraphrase sentences in a variety of ways; he had to be able to recognize, classify, and define the schemes and tropes in a passage being studied (and there were more than a hundred of those listed in the Renaissance rhetoric texts).

T. W. Baldwin's William Shakspere's Small Latine & Lesse Greeke, or Sister Miriam Joseph Shakespeare's Use of the Arts of Language, or Donald L. Clark's John Milton at St. Paul's School will give you a generous sense of the language-arts regimen that the Tudor school boy was subjected to in the grammar schools. If we required of our students what Renaissance schoolmasters demanded of theirs, we would no doubt face a general revolt.

This rigorous regimen, however, produced students who really learned grammar and rhetoric and who knew not only the meaning of style but also the procedures for analyzing someone else's style and improving their own. They could tell you that style represented the choices that an author made from the lexical and syntactical resources of the language. Style represented a curious blend of the idiosyncratic and the conventional.

The more idiosyncratic a style, the more distinctive it became; the more conventional, the more bland it likely became — although not necessarily less serviceable for being bland. In one sense, then, "Style was the man," because it represented the characteristic way in which a person expressed his or her thoughts and feelings. For that reason, everyone can be said to "have a style."

But some styles are more pleasing, more distinctive, more effective than others. Some writers can command several styles — a range of styles into which they can readily shift as the subject-matter, the occasion, or the audience necessitates. There are high styles and low styles and middle styles. In his book *The Five Clocks,* Martin Joos compares these various styles to what he calls the five registers — the frozen, the formal, the consultative, the casual, and the intimate.

Joos also notes that sophisticated language-users can shift into and out of these registers as the occasion demands. Some people do not command the full range of styles or registers, simply because they have not yet acquired the full repertory of diction and syntax needed for stylistic versatility. As the philosophers would say, they have the command *potentially* but not *actually*. Our task as teachers is to turn the *potency* into *act*.

If we as teachers want to engage our students in the study of style, the first point that needs to be made is that the circumstances in which we teach may not allow us to deal with style at all. Many of us teach in a curriculum so crowded that there simply is not enough time to deal adequately with style. And the study of style does take time.

The Renaissance schoolmaster had the same group of pupils for the full academic year, often had them six days a week for six to eight hours a day.

That generous allotment of time allowed for relentless recitation, rigorous drill, and reinforcing repetition. And the curriculum then was not as cluttered as it is now. If you cannot devote at least two weeks to the study of style, either in a concentrated period or in scattered sessions throughout the semester, you had better not deal with style at all.

The relative sophistication of your students in language matters may also determine whether you can deal with style in the classroom. I can imagine some teachers saying, "Good heavens, I have all I can do just to get my students to the point where they can consistently write sentences that parse. My students have to learn how to walk before I can teach them how to run." There is no question that a minimal grammatical competence is a *sine qua non* for stylistic studies.

If style represents the choices one makes from the available grammatical options, then students must have at least a basic awareness of what the grammatical options are if they are to profit from stylistic studies. But a deficiency in conscious knowledge of grammar is not an insuperable disqualification for studying style.

Many students can learn their grammar while studying style. I have found that students are invariably fascinated by style – not only because it offers something new and different but also because it provides an element of fun in changing words and shifting parts. And in such a positive and creative atmosphere, students may well be more inclined to develop an interest in grammar or at least to absorb grammar subconsciously. Studying style in English courses can have two focuses or objectives: to learn either how to analyze someone else's style or how to improve our own.

These two objectives are ancillary rather than countervailing. As teachers, we can pursue either or both, but we should determine our main objective for the course at the outset. Learning how to analyze someone else's style belongs primarily to the literature class; learning how to improve one's own style belongs primarily to the composition class. But there is no reason why both kinds of learning cannot take place in both classes.

In fact, learning how to analyze someone else's style in the composition class is almost a necessary prelude for learning how to improve one's own style. By analyzing an accomplished writer's style, we can recognize the marks of effective style, and then we can begin, either consciously or unconsciously, to incorporate some of those features into our own style. The process works in reverse too.

By deliberately working on our own style to refine it, we learn what to look for in analyzing someone else's style. Studying style begins with some awareness of what we should look at or look for. In the chapter on style in my *Classical Rhetoric for the Modern Student* and in my "A Method of Analyzing Prose Style, with a Demonstration Analysis of Swift's 'A Modest Proposal,'" I outline the features that can be observed and analyzed. I divide these features into four main categories: diction, sentence patterns, figures of speech, and paragraphing. But my designating those main cagetories may not be very helpful to you. What about diction? What about sentence patterns? Just what aspects of diction and sentence patterns are significant?

Let me be a little more specific here. A writer's choice of words contributes to the effects that style has on readers. If we think about it for a moment, we must acknowledge that choosing a big word or a little word, a general word or a specific word, an abstract word or a concrete word does make a difference in what the text conveys to us either explicitly or implicitly. And when we observe that certain kinds of words are recurrent, when we observe that sets of words exemplify certain motifs, these words become even more significant because of what they tell us about an author's characteristic way of saying things.

A writer's working vocabulary — the stock of words that a writer actually uses in a piece of writing rather than the words that he or she can recognize in someone else's writing — reflects the range of a writer's knowledge and interests. The larger one's working vocabulary, the more likely it is that one can choose precise diction. Shakespeare's working vocabulary of over 21,000 words was an extraordinary lexicon — and not only for his time.

The study of the lexical element of style involves fewer objectively observable items than the study of any other stylistic element. By the term "objectively observable item," I mean an item which can be definitely classified by observation rather than by judgment. For instance, one can decide whether a particular word is monosyllabic or polysyllabic by simply looking at the word. The decision, however, about whether a word is abstract or concrete, general or specific, often involves a judgment, because those dichotomies are more relative than absolute. Consider, for example, a sentence like "The wealthy Texan owned huge herds of cattle." Is the word *cattle* general or specific? It is more specific than *livestock* but less specific than *steers*.

Because of the relativity of the general-specific dichotomy, the classifier has to make an arbitrary judgment about the word *cattle* in this particular context. In this respect, it is worth remembering that any tabulating of percentages of words in a text according to whether the words are abstract or concrete, general or specific, formal or informal, denotative or connotative is likely to be somewhat less than precise, simply because in many instances the yes-no decision represents someone's arbitrary judgement. When we move on to study collocations of words in sentences, we find not only more objectively observable items but more significant features of writing habits.

Most of the stylistic features of sentences are objectively observable items: length of sentences (in number of words); grammatical types of sentences (simple, compound, complex, compound-complex); rhetorical types of sentences (loose, periodic, balanced, antithetical); functional types of sentences (statement, question, command, exclamation); types and frequency of sentence-openers; methods and location of expansions in sentences; amount of embedding. Analysis and classification of features like those tell us a great deal about the level of a writer's "syntactic fluency."

Syntactic patterns also tell us something about the way a writer structures his or her thoughts, about a writer's "epistemic orientation," to use Richard Ohmann's term. The frequent occurrence, for instance, of balanced or antithetical patterns in Dr. Johnson's sentences suggests that he tended to structure his thinking in terms of parrallel or opposing dichotomies. The many levels of subordination in John Henry Newman's prose suggests that he tended to see things in terms of hierarchies.

The stringing together of independent clauses in Hemingway's prose, often with redundant use of coordinating conjunctions, indicates that Hemingway tended to view the phenomenal world as a flux of discrete, coordinate elements. Henry James's heavy use of parenthetical elements reflects a mind disposed to meticulous qualifications. And so on.

The gathering of data about syntactic patterns involves a lot of tedious counting and tabulating. Data of that sort were not previously available because the counting and measuring had to be done by hand and took hours and weeks. When Edwin Lewis and L. A. Sherwin did their studies in the 1890s of sentence and paragraph length in the works of several British writers, they did all their counting by hand. Today, the computer facilitates such tedious data-gathering, and as a result, stylistic studies of large corpuses of prose and poetry have proliferated.

Collecting data — once tedious and time-consuming — still must be done. We are much more impressed when someone pronounces that a certain writer strings together unusually long sentences and supports that claim with the empirically derived evidence that the writer's average sentence length is 37.8 words. And we are further impressed by the disclosure that 18 percent of that writer's sentences are ten or more words longer than that average.

How much of a corpus has to be studied before valid generalizations can be made about someone's style? I have told undergraduate students studying style – either their own or some professional writer's – that they must analyze somewhere between 1000 and 1500 words of a piece of prose. That is not very much really – at most four double-spaced typescript pages, maybe two pages of printed text.

But it is substantial enough to allow for some valid inferences to be drawn. Students writing a dissertation or a scholarly article on someone's prose style should be reminded not only that they would have to study a much larger corpus but also that they would have to study several specimens of a writer's prose, pieces written at different periods and on different subject matters for different audiences. As in any inductive study, the larger and the more representative the sampling, the safer the conclusions will be.

The gathering of data is a necessary stage but should not be the stopping point. Necessary as the gathering of the data is, what one does with the data matters more. Data – even raw statistical data – can convey some illuminating information. But often the full or the most salient significance of the data depends upon interpretation. The act of interpretation calls upon all of one's intellectual and imaginative powers; it requires that one shift from the role of a mere counter to the role of a critic.

Critical interpretation demands that one be able to detect the relevance or the relationship of the data to the exigencies of the rhetorical situation – to the occasion, purpose, subject matter, audience, or author of the discourse. We may find, for instance, that in a particular discourse, the author used an unusually high percentage of interrogative sentences – let us say 18 percent, almost one out of every five sentences. Why? A question like that poses a real challenge for the critic.

The critic may find the answer by relating the statistical fact to the nature of the subject matter that the author addressed. The writer may have been writing on a subject about which he was uncertain. He was exploring the subject, probing for answers. So he frequently resorted to questions, knowing that sometimes asking the right questions can be as illuminating as proposing hesitant answers.

Or the critic might relate the statistical fact to the disposition of the audience for this piece of discourse. The author, let us say, knew that his audience harbored certain hostility to the position he was espousing. He knew that he could exacerbate that hostility if he were dogmatic in his pronouncements. So he decided that it would be a prudent strategy to soften his assertiveness by frequently resorting to the tentativeness of questions. But looking closely at his questions might reveal, for example, that many of them are framed as rhetorical questions in which the writer has subtly implied the answers he wants to elicit from his audience.

That kind of interpretation, that kind of relating of fact to function, may be beyond the capacity of some students in basic writing courses. After all, that kind of interpretation requires a great deal of linguistic and rhetorical sophistication. Some students may not be mature enough to make such connections and to come forth with anything more than the most superficial interpretation.

But the present incapacity of some students for such critical insights is not the issue. They have learned something valuable about the text simply from gathering the data. They have learned something too from the mere *attempt* to interpret the data. Inadequate as their interpretation may be, they have grown a few inches in the attempt. In addition to diction and syntax, there are other aspects of style that we might have our students look at: the incidence of figures of speech, the rhythms of sentences, the manner of paragraphing.

A figure of speech may be defined as any artful deviation from the ordinary way of speaking or writing. The classical rhetoricians commonly divided the *figura* into two main groups: schemes and tropes. A scheme involves a deliberate deviation from the ordinary pattern or arrangement of words. In addition to common patterns like parallelism and antithesis, schemes include such artistic patterns as the inversion of the natural or normal word order (*anastrophe*), deliberate omission of the normally expected conjunctions in a series of related words, phrases, or clauses (*asyndeton*), repetition of the same word or group of words at the beginning of successive clauses (*anaphora*), repetition of initial consonants in two or more adjacent words (*alliteration*), and reversal of the grammatical structures in successive clauses (*chiasmus or crisscross*).

Tropes, the second main kind of figurative language, are deliberate deviations from the ordinary *meaning* of words and include such familiar figures as metaphor, simile, hyperbole, synecdoche, metonymy, oxymoron, and irony. In the schools of rhetoric, pupils were expected to be able to identify, define, and illustrate the figures they encountered in the texts they read and to be able to invent similar figures. Their task was complicated by the fact that the number of schemes and tropes had proliferated enormously.

Rhetorica ad Herennium, an influential Roman rhetoric text, listed 65 figures; the 1577 edition of Henry Peacham *The Garden of Eloquence* identified 184. Undoubtedly, the proliferation of the figures resulted from overly subtle anatomizing, but amazingly, once students were made aware of the many kinds of artful deviations from the normal meanings or arrangements or words, they readily found the figures in the prose and poetry they read.

In the second edition of my *Classical Rhetoric for the Modern Student*, more than half of the schemes and tropes illustrated there were supplied to me by two classes of freshman students who, over a six-week period, searched for examples in their reading. They found a surprising number of examples in magazine advertisements and television commercials. Once students become familiar with a wide range of schemes and tropes, they find them everywhere, even where authors were not conscious that they were creating figures.

What should teachers encourage students to look for when studying the figures, and what does the occurrence of figures tell them about an author's style? First of all, we ought to ask them simply to look for the schemes and tropes. When they find them, they ought to identify and tabulate them and perhaps draw up some statistical information about them. If there are many schemes and tropes, they can begin to classify them into groups or clusters.

A particular author, let us say, uses mainly schemes of repetition. Most of this author's metaphors are based on agricultural analogies. Certain patterns or motifs begin to emerge that tell students something about a particular author's mind-set. The presence – or the absence – of figures tells students something about the texture and flavor of an author's prose. In the modern classroom, teachers rarely, if ever, consider prose rhythms, but our forebears in Greek and Latin schools regularly engaged their pupils in analyzing and composing various prose rhythms.

The Greeks and the Romans, of course, had developed elaborate prosodies for their synthetic languages, and since a good deal of their formal communication took place in the oral medium, they were much more conscious than we of the sounds and rhythms of words when they composed their orations. We have only to read sections of Cicero's rhetoric texts or his orations to find out the careful attention this rhetorician gave to the composition of euphonious prose.

English-speaking people probably lost their ear for verbal rhythms when written or printed documents superseded oral discourse as the primary mode of communication. In the late eighteenth century, the elocutionary movement in England, fostered by former actors like Thomas Sheridan, tried to revive interest in the sounds of prose.

Although English teachers continued to teach students how to scan lines of poetry, they began to lose all interest in the aural dimensions of prose early in the twentieth century, along about 1915, when teachers of speech formally divorced themselves from the National Council of Teachers of English and formed their own speech association.

But at a time when the aural element has become dominant again and music is the favourite medium of young people, perhaps we should revive the study of prose rhythms in the classroom. Litterateurs like George Saintsbury have shown us that there is an elaborate prosody for scanning prose rhythms, but I would not recommend that we spend valuable time in the classroom exploring the technicalities of that system. If we would revive the practice of reading prose aloud, we might be able to cultivate our students' ears for the harmonies of prose.

In the February 1977 issue of *College Composition and Communication*, Thomas Kane published an engaging article about what teachers might do in the classroom to cultivate a sense for the ring and rhythm of well-constructed sentences. Prose, of course, is most often read silently, but curiously enough, euphonious sentences somehow disclose their meanings more easily than awkwardly constructed sentences do, even when read silently.

Rhythm is a neglected area of stylistic study, but the classical rhetoricians were right when they preached that the harmonies of prose did make a positive contribution to the conveyance of a message. For the classical rhetoricians, stylistic study rarely extended beyond the limits of the sentence. Maybe the reason for that neglect was that the concept of paragraphing had not yet developed, even in their writing system.

The typographical device of paragraphing was largely the invention of printers, and it was not until the late nineteenth century that a systematic rhetoric of the paragraph was developed by Alexander Bain. Recently, however, such rhetoricians as Francis Christensen, Alton Becker, Paul C. Rodgers, and Frank D'Angelo have convinced us that there is such a thing as a "style" of paragraphing.

What should teachers and students look for in studying the "style" of paragraphing? They can, for example, examine the length of paragraphs, measured in number of words or sentences per paragraph. Information about the average length of paragraphs reveals whether an author tends to break up the discourse into small units or into large units and whether an author tends to develop topics elaborately or minimally.

Teachers and students can also note whether an author uses explicit topic sentences and where those topic sentences are placed in the paragraph. Moreover, they can observe the coherence devices that an author uses to articulate sequences of sentences within and between paragraphs. Using Francis Christensen's system, they can diagram the levels of coordination and subordination in paragraphs.

They can also catalogue the methods of development that an author uses. Indeed, the kinds of choices that an author makes in composing a paragraph are comparable to, if not identical with, the kinds of choices an author makes in composing a sentence. There is, then, a style of paragraphing. Each aspect that teachers and students can look at when studying someone else's style can be applied to studying specimens of their own prose. And I would strongly urge teachers to analyze their own style.

They can take a paper of 1000 to 15000 words that they wrote for one of their college classes or a paper that they have published and subject it to some of the kinds of counting and measuring that I outlined. They will find the investigation fascinating, and they will discover some surprising features about their style — some felicitous characteristics and some regrettable mannerisms.

Improving our students' analytical skills is a proper concern of English teachers, but improving our students' synthetical skills should be our main concern as teachers of composition. And let me suggest, although in the broadest terms, the kinds of exercises that can help our students refine their style and enhance their stylistic virtuosity.

In my own rhetoric texts, I have suggested a number of imitative exercises that have proven fruitful for me and for my students. Let me just mention those exercises, without elaborating on them. (1) Simply copying verbatim admired passages of prose. (2) Copying a passage but changing one element in it – for instance, changing all the past-tense verbs to present-tense verbs. (3) Composing a sentence on the pattern of a sentence written by some admired author. (4) Taking a sentence that someone else has written and seeing in how many different way one can say essentially what the model sentence says. (5) Taking a group of isolated kernel sentences and combining them into a single sentence.

You can get more details about these exercises by consulting the chapters on style in my two rhetoric texts, in Francis Christensen article "A Generative Rhetoric of the Sentence," in the two NCTE monographs on sentence-combining by John Mellon and Frank O'Hare, in Walker Gibson *Tough, Sweet, and Stuffy,* in Winston Weathers and Otis Winchester *Copy and Compose,* in Joseph Williams' *Style: Ten Lessons in Clarity and Grace,* or in Thomas Whissen *A Way with Words.* Perhaps the classroom practices I have suggested here are wholly impracticable for your situation. With all the requirements – and time constraints – of a composition course, the study of style may be more than you can handle.

Or some of your students may be so minimally literate that engaging them in any of the analyses or exercises I have proposed would prove futile. But even if your students are not ready to engage in stylistic studies, you can do so yourself. Such a regimen promises to help you grow immeasurably in your awareness of the remarkable richness and variety of our language and in your resourcefulness as a teacher of language, literature, and composition.

Rhetoric, and Style

It may be well to start our speculations with the obvious before we begin to probe the not-so-obvious and even the esoteric. Obviously, then, the skilled writer of exposition must be able to generalize (state or adumbrate a thesis) and then to organize the exposition of that thesis in some meaningful way. This idea can be stated in a variety of terms: the writer of exposition must be able to think deductively, must be coherent in the development of ideas, must be "logical." And just as obviously, the skilled writer must be able to supply appropriate local detail, to texture the exposition so that it is something more than an elegant structure in which all of the major segments fit.

In this essay, I will argue that the writer needs those skills which are characteristic of both the left and the right hemispheres of the brain; I will further suggest that some unsuccessful writers are extremely left-hemispheric while some are extremely right-hemispheric; finally, I will suggest that the skills of both hemispheres can be taught (though a great deal of empirical work must be done before we will be on solid ground in this regard).

So this essay will concern composition, but our interest does (and must) spill over from that homely subject into the headier realms of poetry. In fact, I believe that there can be no sharp division between composition theory and literary theory without the impoverishment of each. I intend *not* to keep a sharp focus in these pages, but to maintain a lambency of interest.

As composition is the construction of texts, so reading is their reconstruction, and composition theory must take account of reading theory. In fact, it is virtually impossible to consider the construction of texts without also dealing with their reconstruction.

All of which is to say, really, that the following essay will deal with reading and writing in the light of brain theory — the reading of *anything* and the writing of *anything*.

This discussion calls upon the most reliable theories of brain function and uses the consensus of brain researchers for its conclusions and speculations. The reader must determine for him- or herself where conclusiveness ends and speculation begins, for I do not hesitate to use brain theory and research metaphorically, heuristically. The facts about the brain are accurate; in this paper, I often use them as speculative instruments.

And yet I think that alert readers will know perfectly well when the paper becomes highly speculative, for I have made every attempt to keep not only my audience but myself oriented. No small task, when one considers the drama and glamour of brain theory, the seductive possibilities of using one finding about cognition or brain mechanism for much more than it is worth.

All in all, however, I have approached my materials with caution. I hope that my readers agree on two points: where I am relatively assured in my conclusions, I have good warrant for my certainty; when I am less assured, I have nonetheless pointed the way for future inquiry and research.

By "rhetoric" in the following discussion, I mean the generation, reception, and pragmatics of natural language and even more narrowly, reading and writing.

The story of brain and language began in the mid-nineteenth century when, performing an autopsy on an aphasic, the French neurologist Paul Broca found massive damage to an area of the left cerebral cortex and concluded that this area — now identified with his name — was the speech centre. It is indeed known to be *one* of the areas controlling speech.

Since Broca's discovery — and especially since the end of World War II — brain research has been pursued with increasingly dramatic results. An ecumenical endeavor involving neurologists, neurosurgeons, biochemists, linguists, and psychologists (among others), brain science has, will demonstrate, much to contribute to rhetoric and stylistics, and, conversely, both of these fields have much to contribute to brain science.

For example, in discussing the brain as mechanism of language, A. R. Luria tells us that expression begins with a *motive* or general idea, while perception (decoding, understanding) ends with the interpretation of the motive lying behind the utterance. That is to say, rhetoric is the alpha and omega of the brain's handling of speech, for rhetoric is, in large part, the study of motives.

However, I do not want to give the impression that brain research is meaningful to rhetoric and stylistics only in the large philosophical sense; its details help clarify many of the premises of these fields and suggest pedagogical strategies.

Left-Brain, Right-Brain

Our interest in the brain centres on hemisphericity, the different ways in which the left hemisphere (LH) and the right hemisphere (RH) function.

The LH controls the right hand, and the RH controls the left hand. By and large, in right-handed people language is a function of the LH, often called the "dominant hemisphere." Localization studies by such researchers as Wilder Penfield have resulted in "maps" detailing the areas of speech mechanisms.

The two hemispheres of the brain are joined by the corpus callosum, a white sheet of axons or nerve fibers that provides the communicative link between the two halves of the brain. If the corpus callosum is severed (through a surgical procedure known as *commissurotomy*), the left hand quite literally does not know what the right hand is doing if there are no visual or verbal clues. Obviously, commissurotomized patients are a major source of knowledge about the functioning of the hemispheres.

Information from the left side of the visual field is transmitted to the RH, and information from the right side of the visual field is transmitted to the LH. Since language is, by and large, a function of the LH, if the right portion of the visual field is covered in a split-brain (commissurotomized) patient, only the RH receives information, and as a result, the patient cannot name items shown to him or her even though there is evidence that this patient knows what the items are. For instance, in the situation just described, a patient will be able to use a spoon properly, but will not be able to name it.

While it is generally agreed that the LH is the side of the brain with language, the role of the RH in regard to language is disputed. One study suggests that the RH does have language, which is released when the control of the LH is weakened or removed as in the case of massive injury to or removal of the LH.

An even more dramatic view of the RH and language is provided by the study of three subjects, nine and ten years old, who had either the RH or the LH removed before five months of age. The study concludes the following: (1) both the LH and the RH are efficient in phonemic discrimination; (2) both the LH and the RH provide "an adequate substrate for semantic skills"; (3) the LH is far better at syntax than is the RH. "What is the characteristic of the left hemispheric defect? It appears to be an organizational, analytical, syntactic, and hierarchic problem rather than a difficulty with the conceptual or semantic aspects of language." In regard to the LH, those adjectives have resonance: organizational, analytical, syntactic, hierarchic.

Perhaps the best-known terms for characterizing the hemispheres are J. E. Bogen's *propositional* (LH) and *appositional* (RH), in regard to which he hazards the generalization that "simultaneous patterns rather than sequential order distinguish appositionality from propositionality." As we shall see, the terms "propositional" and "appositional" have great meaning for the present discussion, implying as they do that the LH is sequential, logical and that the RH, on the other hand, works with an all-at-onceness, a temporally and non sequentially.

In this discussion, I will suggest that language use can be rated on a scale according to its degree of propositionality or appositionality. On the one hand, some language use approaches the pure propositionally of mathematics or symbolic logic; that is, it is structure almost without specific content. Other language use is almost purely appositional in the sense that idea after idea or image after image occurs in a string of appositions, with no apparent propositional connection.

At these extremes, language is, I think, pathological, and indeed the best illustrations of what I mean come from the language of schizophrenics. In a later section of this paper, we will return to my notions of propositional and appositional language, particularly in relation to the teaching of written composition.

To characterize the RH, then. It is often called the "dark," "intuitive" side of the brain. In the normal right-handed person, either it has very little language or its language function is suppressed by the "dominant" LH. The RH is superior at establishing pail-whole relationships, that is, at gestalt formation or closure. (As will be seen, this idea is extremely important.)

For instance, with the left hand (controlled by the RH), the split-brain patient is proficient at determining what a whole object will be on the basis of feeling one part of that object; from the part, the patient can infer or construct a gestalt. With the right hand, this is impossible.

As Bogen points out, perhaps the RH's lack of the linear concept of time in ordering thought is the most important distinction between the two modes. (This will be important to us when we consider reading.)

The RH emotes, learns, remembers, and initiates responses. It is superior in "managing spatial tasks."

Robert D. Nebes provides a succinct description of the activity of the RH:

It is evident that the right cerebral hemisphere makes an important contribution to human performance having functions complementary to those of the left hemisphere. The right side of the brain probably processes information differently from the left, relying more on imagery than on language, and being more synthetic and holistic than analytic and sequential in handling data.

It is certainly important in perceiving spatial relationships. It is also probably the neural basis for our ability to take the fragmentary sensory information we receive, and construct from it a coherent concept of the spatial organization of the outside world — a sort of cognitive spatial map within which we plan our actions.

If we think about the process of speech — which characterizes the LH-we begin to get a notion of how the LH must operate: "what is essentially involved in language production is the programming of an idea, itself containing no intrinsic temporal order, into a sequence of linguistic units, which are also intrinsically unordered."

As Luria characterizes the process, first "the motive or general idea of the expression . . . is coded into a speech scheme and put into operation with the aid of internal speech; finally, these schemes are converted into narrative speech, based on a 'generative' grammar." The temporal nature of these operations is illustrated by the fact that, in some cases at least, the speaker must choose or project a structure before selecting a lexical item, as in the following: "That she didn't recognize Jim surprised Mary."

The left (dominant) hemisphere (in right-handers) begins to play an essential role not only in the cerebral organization of speech, but also in the cerebral organization of all higher forms of cognitive activity connected with speech-perception organized into logical schemes, active verbal memory, logical thought — whereas the right (non-dominant) hemisphere either begins to play a subordinate role in cerebral organization of these processes or plays no part whatsoever in their course.

I cannot resist ending this characterization of the hemispheres with a paradox — which will seem a good deal less paradoxical as our discussion progresses. I have implied that the LH is the logical half of the brain and that the RH works in images, a logically. Now ponder Einstein's description of his own cognition:

The words of the language, as they are written or spoken, do not seem to play any role in my mechanism of thought. The psychical entities which seem to serve as elements in thought are certain signs and more or less clear images which can be "voluntarily" reproduced and combined. As Nebes hints, perhaps the apparent inverse relationship between creativity and verbal skills could be due to the overtraining of verbal skills at the expense of nonverbal abilities.

Brain, Creativity, and the Comp Class

It is a common experience in composition classes to find two diametrically opposed styles, the one which is highly general, the student writer never seeming able to get down to cases, and the other which is extremely specific and concrete, but chaotic, as if the writer is unable to order ideas and impressions, unable to establish the logical connections and hierarchies among them. In the one style, we have the skeleton of coherence without the substance of tangible content; in the other, there is substance without form.

We can characterize the highly abstract but "coherent" style as propositional and the concrete style as appositional. We will further discuss the characteristics of propositionality and appositionality, but for the moment, we must relate these styles to brain function.

As we have seen, the LH is the propositional side of the brain; it works well with deductive structures, handling the ghostliness of symbolic logic and the bare-bonedness of the syllogism and the sorites with a proficiency of which the RH is incapable. The RH is the appositional side of the brain, "seeing" with an all-at-onceness, taking a gestaltist view of sensory input, perceiving patterns in the gouache which the LH would process as merely a jumble of disconnected fragments. (It is the RH that enables us to recognize faces.)

That much said, we can look at some specific examples of propositional and appositional styles.

Some years ago, quite by chance, I found an article on schizophrenic language. When I read the piece it occurred to me that the author, Brendan Maher, could well have been speaking of the more extreme cases of propositionality and appositionality that I had discovered in my composition classes. Here are two examples of schizophrenic language:

Propositional

The subterfuge and the mistaken planned substitutions for that demanded American action can produce nothing but the general results of negative contention and the impractical results of misplacement, of mistaken purpose and unrighteous position, the impractical serviceabilities of unnecessary contradictions. For answers to this dilemma, consult Webster.

Appositional

I hope to be home soon, very soon. I fancy chocolate eclairs, Doenuts. I want some doenuts, I do want some golden syrup, a tin of golden syrup or treacle, jam. . . . See the Committee about me coming home for Easter my twentyfourth birthday. I hope all is well at home, how is Father getting on. Never mind there is hope, heaven will come, time heals all wounds, Rise again Glorious Greece and come to Hindoo Heavens, the Indian Heavens. The Dear old times will come back. We shall see Heaven and Glory yet, come everlasting life. I want a new writing pad of note paper.

"Normal" students write themes that are only a shade less schizoid than the passages quoted above. The following two themes are reproduced exactly as I received them, with all errors intact.

Propositional

Before a person can say whether the best things in life are free, he must first deturmine what in his opinion the best things are. Naturally every person has his own ideas concerning the objects or things that are important.

I believe that friendship, health, and beauty are three of the most important things a person can enjoy. When I say "beauty" I mean having things around you that you like or being places that make you feel good.

When I say that friendship is not fun, I don't mean that you can go out and buy five dollars worth of it when you need a friend. Instead of using money you use yourself. Your ideals and attitudes to buy friends. To fit into a group you must drop some and maybe most of your attitudes before you will be considered normal in the group. If you don't, you will be considered rebellious or off-beat and become an outcast from that group. Therefore, to have friends is to pay by changing yourself for their benefit.

Good health is very important to me because without it I can not enjoy myself. To maintain a healthy physical condition one must get the proper amounts of exercise, food, and sleep. Exercise and sleep are free but food is by no means free. Every time one turns around he is paying for food by working at some type of job to get money for food.

Beauty is the only thing that comes close to being free. Aside from having to buy most of the articles that a person likes to have — such as a car, skiis or any other material object — beauty is mostly free. I love to go into the forest and enjoy nature's beauty. The trees, forest creatures, brooks and streams all mean a lot to me. I enjoy hunting and camping in the forest and just walking there alone, thinking to myself. But to keep these forests we must pay to see that some careless hunter or camper doesn't burn them down. We have to set aside parks and wilderness areas so they aren't cut into lumber by the mills. These parks all cost money. Everywhere you go, you have to pay some way or another.

Appositional

Are Motion Pictures Too Real?

"Film" Scene Is 'Too Real'"

Sao Paulo, Brazil (Reuters) — An assistant movie director shooting a Brazilian style western, fell dying with a rifle bullet in his back during a gunfight scene, Meridional News Agency reported here Wednesday.

Police halted film-making while they tried to find out who fired the fatal shot at Martino Martini as film extras blazed off blank ammunition. So far there has been no explanation of how there came to be a live bullet among the blanks.

Martini was a talented young member of the "new wave" of Brazil's film industry. The film, "Obliged to Kill," was to be completed in 10 days' time."

Senta of Vienna

"Brunette Senta Berger of Vienna has long been a glowing face in nondescript German movies. Last year fame took a leap across Europe and the world after she played the lusciously blonde German girl friend of a Russian soldier in the American-produced "The Victors.""I (Senta) was the aggressive girl in the film scenes. I stood out because when you're aggressive, audiences watch you." Senta also stood out, as mail from men everywhere proclaimed, because she is full-faced, full-bosomed, full-hipped — a frankly full female." "The 'Love Goddess' who never found love." — Marilyn Monroe

"Here (Miss Monroe) fans saw her pictures as reflections of her beauty, fame, fortune, and sex. They show the evolution of the Love Goddess in all her sexuality — the role that Marilyn knew and enjoyed and most feared to lose. First — and most famous — was the 1949 nude calendar pose, which brought her a worldwide flood of welcome publicity while she was just a long-haired model who had a few walk-on parts in the movies."

Elizabeth Taylor and Sophia Loren among the few, are too explicit in their acting on and off the scene. Producers seem to put realism in front of morals and dignity.

The public wants more sex from female actresses, more realistic looking and sounding killings, etc.

The Walt Disney type programme is fast becoming obsolete. Programmes on the educational line seem to have died. I want to go to a movie to be entertained by good acting, but moral conduct. Now days, I walk away from a movie with a sick feeling in my stomach. My feelings are caused by simpley vulgar entertainment. Of course, there are a few good movies, such as Lorance of Arabia and others, but to the handful that is acceptable in my terms, there are hundredes that are poor. The producers' ought to put this realistic thought into good and moral acting.

Not this garbage that is turned out in mass production.

"Of Human Bondage"

"Some women can't help what they are . . ."

"There would always be men in her life . . . all kinds of men . . . and always

Phillip to come back to . . . to degrade and despise."

As the billboard, a half naked woman!

The propositional and the appositional styles can be contrasted on the basis of these factors, among others:

Propositional	**Appositional**
Stated topic (enthymeme)	Implied topic
Organizational rigidity	Organizational flexibility
General examples, if any	Specific examples
Backgrounded style	Foregrounded style
Little presence	Great presence

In the propositional essay, the topic is clearly stated; at the end of the second paragraph, we know that the writer considers health, friendship, and beauty to be three of the best things in life, and we can predict with virtual certainty that the essay will explore these three values to determine whether or not they are free. The progression will be, in Kenneth Burke's term, syllogistic.

It follows then, that organization is predictable. The first two paragraphs enunciate the topic (which might, indeed, have been stated in one complex sentence), and the following three paragraphs each explore one aspect of the topic. Our expectations concerning organization are thwarted only by the writer's failure to supply cloture in the form of a summative paragraph.

There are no real examples in the piece, no narrative concerning a friendly relation, no anecdote concerning ebullient good health, no specific image of a beautiful place. The prose floats at least thirteen feet above the rich earth of specificty.

This lack of examples creates the backgrounded style and deprives the writing of presence, which is the sort of palpability that evokes attention from the reader.

Comments on the appositional essay would be the obverse of those on the propositional: the topic is unstated, there is no real organization, and the examples (which are the substance of the essay) create foregrounding and presence.

Although the ability to carry on propositional thinking is undoubtedly a sign of maturity, maturity in writing involves the ability to unite the appositional with the propositional in appropriate contexts. Such is the implication of Aristotle's mention of inductive thinking and of the whole concept of presence. (Such also, of course, is the implication of the poetic theory that this discussion will elaborate.)

Of course, writing teachers have intuitively understood this point all along. The master comment on the propositional theme above would be, I suppose, "Get down to cases. Give me some concrete examples. Help me to see what you're talking about, to experience." The "master" comment on the appositional theme would be, "Get a thesis, state it or imply it clearly, and then organize and explore your ideas."

When we give such advice, we are quite literally asking students to change the ratios between their cerebral hemispheres. In this regard, Luria tells us that it must be remembered that the absolute dominance of one (the left) hemisphere is not by any means always found, and the law of lateralization is only relative in character.

According to recent investigations, one-quarter of all persons are completely right-handed, and slightly more than one-third show marked dominance of the left hemisphere, whereas the rest are distinguished by relatively slight dominance of the left hemisphere, and in onetenth of all cases the dominance of the left hemisphere is totally absent.

Clearly, in the classroom we must take account of the fact that we will encounter instances of extreme LH or RH dominance, and I would postulate that in the example themes above, we have seen probable instances of such dominance. The situation becomes even more complicated when we realize that literacy may create or facilitate lateralization. Learning to read and write may well increase the dominance of the LH.

Can we conclude, then, that the appositional writer may increase proportional skills through intensive practice in reading and writing? Such would seem to be the case. Are appositional writers in general less literate than propositional writers are? At present, there is no answer to that question. In the absence of such evidence, I would suggest that carefully structured reading and writing exercises may well increase the versatility of the appositionalist. Drawing on work that I have done in the past and on my experience with secondary students in the Huntington Beach Union High School District, I am at present constructing materials intended to give the appositionalist propositional skills.

The materials are yet to be tested, but, in general, they are based on a progression from algorithmic to heuristic to aleatory exercises. In the materials, this progression will be applied to instruction in all of the "stadia" of discourse: sentence, paragraph, essay. The paragraph is the handiest example of what I am getting at. Drawing on both tagmemic theories and the theories of Francis Christensen, I ask students to construct paragraphs according to algorithms – for instance:

- Make a general statement about your English class.
  My English class is boring.

- Qualify, restrict, or explain that statement. We never do interesting things in the class.
- Illustrate the restrictedstatement three times. We spend a lot of timediagramming sentences. The teacher makes us read a lotof old-fashioned poetry. Every day we do grammardrills in our workbooks.

The result is a recognizable paragraph, with levels of generality and local details. The next step is heuristic: to recombine the "tagmemes" in the algorithmic paragraph in as many ways as possible:

1. In my English class, we spend a lot of time diagramming sentences. The teacher makes us read a lot of old-fashioned poetry, and every day we do grammar drills in our workbooks. My English class is boring. We never do interesting things in the class.
2. Because we never do interesting things in my English class, it is boring. We spend a lot of time diagramming sentences, and the teacher makes us read a lot of old-fashioned poetry. Not only that, we do grammar drills in our workbooks every day.
3. We spend our time doing uninteresting things in my English class: diagramming sentences, reading old-fashioned poetry, and doing grammar drills in our workbooks. My English class is boring.

The aleatory phase of instruction relies on creative devices such as metaphor and analogy to suggest relationships that can be expressed in paragraphs, the forms for which students have presumably "internalized" through their algorithmic and heuristic work. For example,

Compare a recent journey — to another country, another city, another part of your own city — with each of the following:

threading a needle
a nightmare
attending a play or a film

eating a tart apple
smelling a freshly painted room
touching suede
solving a math problem

Use the ideas that your comparisons generated to write a paragraph — or several paragraphs — about the journey.

One other possibility concerning the appositionalist is intriguing and deserves careful investigation. If the general skills of propositional thought are both learnable and transferable, then it might well be possible to increase the appositionalist's versatility by providing him or her with extensive exercises in propositional reasoning, e.g., syllogisms, enthymemes, sorites, and problems in symbolic logic.

As to the propositionalist, I can only suggest that intensive exposure to the most appositional of all written discourse may well bring about greater versatility. I am speaking, of course, of the reading the writing of lyric poetry. However, the common method of "explaining" the lyric poem by propositionalizing all of its images (a subject which is explored fully in a later section of this paper) should, according to my logic, tend to increase the propositional nature of the writing. It would seem, then, that "reader response" criticism and free writing would be in order.

Finally, of course, the ultimate goal is to increase the creativity of all writers — the ability to generate writings (whether poetic or non poetic, temporal or a temporal) that satisfy the writer's need for expression, the reader's need for understanding and empathy, and the world's need for meaningful communication. This creativity consists of the ability to use both propositional and appositional modes appropriately, and it comes about only in the proper environment.

Insofar as the composition classroom is an environment, it must be characterized by an atmosphere of freedom and writing tasks that are liberating. (Drills and exercises can be liberating at certain times for certain purposes with certain students.)

Carl Rogers defines creativity as "the emergence in action of a novel relational product, growing out of the uniqueness of the individual on the one hand, and the materials, events, people, or circumstances of his life on the other." The conditions that foster creativity are psychological safety ("Accepting the individual as of unconditional worth. . . . Providing a climate in which external evaluation is absent. . . . Understanding empathically") and psychological freedom.

In his magnificent book *The Act of Creation* Arthur Koestler has developed a model of the creative act. The creative person has been able to bisociate by leaping from one matrix to another. An excellent example of both matrix and leap is provided by James L. Adams in *Conceptual Blockbusting.*

At sunrise on the first morning, a monk laboriously climbs to the summit of a mountain, where he spends the rest of the day and all of the night meditating. At sunrise on the second day, he comes down the mountain on the same trail by which he ascended. Is there any time in his journey downward at which he would be in exactly the same spot as he was on the journey upward?

If one stays in the verbal matrix, this is a difficult problem to solve, but if one leaps to the visual matrix, the solution becomes obvious. Picture the monk going upward and downward simultaneously. Obviously he would meet himself at some point on the trail.

Koestler sets up three categories of creativity: comedy, in which there is a collision of matrices; science, in which there is an integration of matrices; and art, in which matrices are juxtaposed. The comic effect comes about, for example, through the juxtaposition of the ridiculous with the sublime; Kepler analogized the role of the Father in the Trinity with that of the sun in the solar system, thus integrating two matrices; in tragedy the matrix of the play is juxtaposed with the audience's knowledge that the play is just a play.

As there is matrix-hopping, so there is hemisphere-hopping: in fact, the two are apparently the same at times. Fluency in thought, like fluency in writing, is the ability to use both the appositional and the propositional, an ability that is very much like John Crowe Ransom's description of metaphysical poetry (as opposed to physical and Platonic poetry):

> Platonic poetry is too idealistic, but physical poetry is too realistic, and realism is tedious and does not maintain interest. The poets therefore introduce the psychological device of the miracle. The predication which it permits is clean and quick but it is not a scientific predication. For scientific predication concludes an act of attention but miraculism [in the form of the metaphysical conceit] initiates one. It leaves us looking, marveling, and reveling in the thick *dinglich* substance that has just received its strange representation.

The RH is the master of the appositional, *dinglich*, all-at-onceness of images; the LH is the master of metaphor, analogy, and proposition.

Chapter 4

Languages in Contact

GENERAL TRENDS

Most of the differences are in connection with concepts originating from the nineteenth century to the mid twentieth century, where new words were coined independently; almost the entire vocabularies of the car/automobile and railway/railroad industries are different between the UK and America, for example. Other sources of difference are slang or vulgar terms, where frequent new coinage occurs, and idiomatic phrases, including phrasal verbs. The differences most likely to create confusion are those where the same word or phrase is used for two different concepts.

Regional variations even within the U.S. or the UK can create the same problems. While the use of American expressions in the UK is often noted, movement in the opposite direction is less common. But such words as *book* (meaning "to reserve") and *roundabout* (otherwise called a *traffic circle* or *rotary*) are clearly current in AmE, although often regarded as British. Some other "Briticisms", such as *go missing* (as an alternative to *disappear*), *bespoke* (for *custom-made* or *made-to-order*), or *run-up* (for "period preceding an event") are increasingly used in AmE, and a few (for instance, *early on*) are now completely standard.

Though the influence of cross-culture media has done much to familiarize BrE and AmE speakers with each others regional words and terms, many words are still recognized as part of a single form of English. Though the use of a British word would be acceptable in AmE (and vice versa), most listeners would recognize the word as coming from the other form of English, and treat it much the same as a word borrowed from any other language. For instance: an American using the word "chap" or "mate" to refer to a friend, would be heard in much the same way as an American using the Spanish word "amigo".

Speakers of AmE are likely to be aware of some BrE terms, such as *lorry, biscuit, queue, chap, bloke, loo,* and *shag* although they would not generally use them, or may be confused as to whether one means the American or British meaning of some (such as *biscuit*). They will be able to guess approximately what is meant by some others, such as *driving licence*. However, use of many other British words, such as *naff* (unstylish - though commonly used to mean "not very good"), risks rendering a sentence incomprehensible to most Americans.

Speakers of BrE are likely to be aware of some AmE terms, such as *sidewalk, gas* (gasoline/petrol), *cookie* or *elevator*, although they would not generally use them. They will be able to guess approximately what is meant by some others, such as *cotton candy*. However, use of some other American words such as *semi* (articulated lorry), *stroller* (pram/ pushchair) or *kitty-corner* (diagonally opposite) risks rendering a sentence incomprehensible to most British people.

Words like "bill" (AmE "paper money", BrE "police") and "biscuit" (AmE: BrE's "scone", BrE: AmE's "cookie") are used regularly in both AmE and BrE, but mean different things in each form.

- In Southern Britain the word *whilst* is used almost interchangeably with *while* and *whilst* is the more common term. *Whilst* is more often used in instruction manuals, legal documents, etc. To Americans the word *whilst*, in any context, seems very archaic or pretentious or both. The words *amidst* (as opposed to *amid*), and to a lesser extent *amongst* (as opposed to *among*) are also rarer in AmE. ("In the midst of" is a standard idiom in both.)

- In Yorkshire, *while* means what *until* might mean elsewhere. So "we are open 9 while 5" means that a business opens at 9am and closes at 5pm.
- In the UK generally the term *fall* meaning "autumn" is obsolete. Although found often in Elizabethan and Dickensian literature, understanding of the word is usually ascribed to its continued use in America.
- In the UK, the term *period* for a *full stop* is now obsolete, even when used as a phrase, such as "Don't do that. Period." This in itself, though, is likely to be an American import; the use of *full stop* in its place is often preferred, as shown by the NSPCC Full Stop campaign.
- *Fitted* is used in both conventions as an adjective ("fitted sheets" are the same size as the mattress) and as the past tense of *fit* ("to suffer epilepsy", for example, "Leavitt fitted" in *The Andromeda Strain*); however *fit* and *fitting* do not denote epileptic seizure in ordinary British use (though that usage is common within medical circles), as the same effect is achieved by *to have a fit* or *to throw a fit*.

When saying or writing out numbers, the British will insert an "and" before the tens and units, as in "one hundred and sixty-two" and "two thousand and three", whereas Americans will typically drop the "and" as in "two thousand three"; however, "two thousand and three" is also common. The same rule applies when saying numbers in their thousands or millions: "four hundred and thirteen thousand" would be said by a British speaker, "four hundred thirteen thousand" by an American speaker.

American schools teach students to pronounce decimally written fractions (".5") as though they were longhand fractions ("^{1}D $_{2}$"), though this formality is often dropped in common speach. For example, "five hundred thirteen and seven tenths" for 513.7 – in the UK, this would be read "five hundred and thirteen point seven", although if it was written 513 $^7D_{10}$, it would still be pronounced "five hundred and thirteen and seven tenths").

Up to 1,900 it is common in both varieties of English to count in hundreds - so 1,200 may be "twelve hundred". But Americans use this pattern more consistently and for much higher numbers than is the norm in British English, referring to "twenty-four hundred" where British English would always use "two thousand four hundred". Even below 2,000, Americans are more likely than the British to read numbers like 1,234 as "twelve thirty-four", instead of "one thousand, two hundred and thirty-four".

In the case of years, however, "twelve thirty-four" would be the norm on both sides of the Atlantic for the year 1234. The year 2000 and years beyond it are read as "two thousand", "two thousand (and) one" and the like by both British and American speakers, although the BBC has recently taken the step of reading dates as "twenty-oh-six" for 2006.

For the house number (or bus number, etc) "272" British people would tend to say "two seven two" while Americans would tend to say "two seventy-two".

There was also a historical difference between billions, trillions, and so forth. Americans use "billion" to mean one thousand million (1,000,000,000), whereas in the UK, until the latter part of the 20th century, it was used to mean one million million (1,000,000,000,000) (although historically such numbers were not often required outside of mathematical and scientific contexts). One thousand million was sometimes described as a "milliard", the definition adopted by most other European languages. However, the "American" version has since been adopted for all published writing, and the word "milliard" is obsolete in English, as are billiard (but not billiards, the game), trilliard and so on. All major British publications and broadcasters, including the BBC, which long used "thousand million" to avoid ambiguity, now use "billion" to mean thousand million.

Many people have no direct experience with manipulating numbers this large, and many non-American readers may interpret "billion" as 10^{12} (even if they are young enough to have been taught otherwise at school); also usage of the "long" billion is standard in some non-English speaking countries. For these reasons, defining the word may be advisable when writing for the general public. See long and short scales for a more detailed discussion of the evolution of these terms in English and other languages.

When referring to the numeral 0, British people would normally use "zero", "nought", "oh", or "nil" in instances such as sports scores and voting results. Americans use the term "zero" most frequently; "oh" is also often used (though never when the quantity in question is nothing), and occasionally slang terms such as "zilch" or "zip". Phrases such as "the team won two-zip" or "the team leads the series, two-nothing" are heard when reporting sports scores. The digit 0, for example, when reading a phone or account number aloud, is nearly always pronounced "oh" in both language varieties for the sake of convenience.

When reading numbers in a sequence, such as a telephone or serial number, British people will usually use the terms *double* or *treble/triple*. Hence 007 is "double oh seven". Exceptions are the emergency telephone number 999, which is always "nine nine nine" and the apocalyptic "Number of the Beast" which is always "six six six". The directory enquiries prefix 118 is also "one one eight" in Britain due to its extensive advertising campaign with the slogan read out as "One one eight, what's your number?"; however, in Ireland it is "eleven-eight". In the U.S., 911 (the U.S. emergency telephone number) is almost always read "nine-one-one", while 9/11 (in reference to the September 11, 2001 attacks) is usually read "nine-eleven".

There are also variations in floor numbering between the U.S. and UK. In most countries, including the UK, the "first floor" is one above the entrance level while the entrance level is the "ground floor"; whereas normal American usage labels the entrance level as the "first floor" and does not use "ground floor." Some American buildings have a "ground floor" or another name for the entrance level, usually as part of a plan to cater to cosmopolitan persons. (This may also be the case in buildings built on hillsides or uneven ground, where the basement on one side of the structure may be at street level on the other.)

Nonetheless, the rest of the floors are numbered in the usual American manner. In Montreal, Canada, building floors are numbered in the American or British manner according to the whim of the original owner. Both BrE and AmE use the expression "I couldn't care less" to mean the speaker does not care at all. In AmE, the phrase "I could care less" (without the "n't") is synonymous with this in casual usage. Intonation no longer reflects the originally sarcastic nature of this variant, which is not idiomatic in BrE and might be interpreted as anything from nonsense (or sloppiness) to an indication that the speaker *does* care.

In both areas, saying "I don't mind" often means "I'm not annoyed" (for example, by someone's smoking), while "I don't care" often means "the matter is trivial or boring". However, in answering a question like "Tea or coffee?", if either alternative is equally acceptable, an American may answer "I don't care", while a British person may answer "I don't mind". Either sounds odd to the other.

In BrE, the phrase "I can't be arsed [to do something]" is a vulgar equivalent to the British or American "I can't be bothered [to do something]". This can be extremely confusing to Americans, as the Southern British pronunciation of the former sounds the same as "I can't be asked...", which sounds either defiantly rude or nonsensical.

In Appalachia, some speakers use "I don't care to" (as in "I don't care to talk to him") as the equivalent of "I don't mind (talking to him)." This usage is confusing (and sometimes offputting) to both non-Appalachian users of AmE and users of BrE.

In the Introduction we saw some of the ways in which we need to modify our conception of English as we observe its use in different kinds of communities throughout the world. The same type of adjustment must be made when we look at English across its fifteen centuries of history. In this chapter we shall outline the issues involved in the historical description of a language like English as it has been adapted to changing social functions in different periods, and as it has co-existed with other languages. The period covered is from the earliest records to the end of the Middle Ages. We shall trace the origins of English as the vernacular of certain Germanic tribes on the continent of Europe, at a time when much of that area was dominated by the institutions and language of the Roman Empire.

We can use the Latin of that period, with its patterns of contact with other languages, as a model for discussing a major kind of bilingual situation, and also that particular form of standardisation known as diglossia. In describing the Anglo-Saxon settlement of what is now England, we shall see how English came into contact with the Celtic language of the Britons, and how it developed a literature under the influence of Latin.

As the various kingdoms of the Anglo-Saxons created institutions and extended literacy, they came to be threatened by the Vikings, who spoke a different though closely related language. There followed two other cases of language-contact, involving different varieties of the same language: Norman French after the Norman Conquest, followed by the Central French of the Paris area after 1204. Finally, we shall see how an early form of what we can call language-loyalty surfaced in the fourteenth century, linking the English language with a patriotism based on antipathy towards France.

At no point during the period under discussion was there a standard variety of English accepted as such wherever the language was spoken. Rather we see a growing trend towards dialectal variation, as different centres of power exert their influence over local speech. We are not therefore describing English as a taught language; nor is it the case that the bilingual situations we shall discuss were primarily products of the schoolroom. We are dealing with language-learning, and language contact, in contexts that are more informal, more haphazard, and unplanned: as peoples migrate, as armies occupy new territory, as settlers intermarry. What may strike the modern monoglot speaker of English is the relative ease with which new languages seem to have been acquired or old ones discarded.

Just as there was no norm of language during the first thousand years of England's history, so there was no enduring political centre. Until the late Middle Ages the concept of England itself was a fragile one. The Anglo-Saxon kingdoms were often at war with each other, and for over two centuries they suffered militarily and politically at the hands of the Vikings. The periods of centralisation under Alfred and Athelstan were short-lived; one kingdom, Northumbria, was for centuries virtually isolated.

Although unity of a kind came with the Normans, it was a unity imposed by a foreign power, through a foreign language. Long after the early period of Norman settlement was over, many of the institutions of England remained saturated with French manners, ideals, and language. Some of the changes which took place during this period in the structure of English-its sounds, its words, its grammar-will be mentioned, and later in the book. But we shall predominantly be concerned here with changes of a different kind.

The English of the Germanic tribes people who first encountered the Celts of Britain was not the English of the Anglo-Saxon kingdoms at the time of the Viking invasions. By that time English had a written form, and was beginning to serve the functions of the developing institution of monarchy. The language had changed, that is to say, because it had been made to function in a different kind of society.

LANGUAGE AND SOCIAL FUNCTION

These considerations at once suggest the approach proposed in the Introduction: seeing language in terms of its functions, and relating language changes to changes of function. This is sometimes referred to as the sociolinguistic profile of a language. In the course of this chapter, we shall be attempting to sketch such profiles for the languages that came into contact with English until the end of the Middle Ages; also, of course, seeing how the profile of English itself changed, partly as a result of these contacts.

We have already referred to two of the most important factors: standardisation and literacy. These are so central to the sociolinguistic history and description of a language that in this book they are accorded a chapter to themselves. To recognise their importance, however, is not to say that a standardised, written language is in any way better or more important than its unwritten, unstandardised counterpart. Nor would it be true to say that languages of the latter type are inferior or handicapped. It means, rather, that the demands of speakers on their language are no more than those associated with the customary, local needs of small, technologically simple societies.

A larger, more centralised society will make new demands on its language or languages, as specialised institutions-administrative, legal, religious, educational-are created. The adaptation of a language to such demands is closely bound up with the cultivation of standardised varieties and the written word.

We can see, then, that the range and kinds of functions that a language serves must be borne in mind when we describe its sociolinguistic profile. In general, languages that function in the domains of a centralised state have been described as developed, while the term oral vernacular has been used to denote languages with the alternative characteristics we have outlined. Both developed and vernacular languages can function in societies where they are the only languages their speakers need to know; and where this is the case, we can further describe them as autonomous. Thus, as a standardised, literate language of a modern state, English is autonomous today within England; but no less autonomous was the oral vernacular of the Germanic tribes who first settled here.

The notion of autonomy is important, since it enables us to describe the difference between a vernacular and a dialect. The term dialect is used in many different ways. Our description of a vernacular language may remind us of the characteristics usually associated with dialects, in that these are not normally written; neither are they used in the 'higher' domains of the centralised state. In fact, the term dialect has been used, confusingly, to refer to languages of this type: people have written of 'the myriad dialects of Africa'. In contemporary England, however, we think of dialects as regional variants of a language which also has a standardised, and therefore non-regional form. The use of dialect in this sense is limited to certain 'everyday' domains-for instance, it is spoken among family and peer-group-but the standard variety can, in theory, be used for all purposes in all circumstances: it is fully developed, or omnifunctional. In general, then, the dialects in such a society are dominated by the existence of the more prestigious standard and are not, therefore, autonomous.

Dialects, then, can be described as undeveloped, oral varieties of a language that are heteronomous with respect to a standardised one. Unfortunately, different scholars at different times have used the term to denote different combinations of criteria, some social or functional, others more directly linguistic. In French usage, the term dialecte refers to a regional variety that has a written form, in opposition to a patois, which does not (we shall see the usefulness of this distinction throughout this book). Also, speech-varieties have been called dialects on the basis of purely linguistic similarities among them, such as shared words, similar sound-systems, grammatical patterns, and so on. Some scholars, therefore, have used the term to relate varieties that most of us would consider separate languages, and they have done this because they have drawn their lines on different parts of the linguistic continuum, as described in the Introduction.

Thus, it has been said that the earliest speakers of English used a dialect of Germanic, similar in terms of linguistic structure to the other kinds of speech used by other, related, Germanic tribes. The term Germanic here denotes a kind of parent language. And in principle there is no knowing where to stop applying the term dialect, since it can be used, it seems, to relate any varieties that have some perceived linguistic feature in common. More often the line is drawn according to some notion of mutual intelligibility: when people stop understanding each other, they can be said to be speaking different languages. But this criterion is not nearly as useful as it seems. Unintelligibility can be total, or only partial; and it also depends very much on the motivation of speakers to understand each other. Indeed, some would argue that there are enough problems of intelligibility between different dialects in contemporary England to justify calling them separate languages.

Another crucial dimension in the sociolinguistic description of a language is the value placed on its different varieties by its speakers. Greater prestige tends to be attached to the notion of the standard, since it can function in higher domains, and has a written form. Developed languages, therefore, tend to be more prestigious than vernaculars. We shall see throughout this book that when developed languages come into contact with vernaculars, the latter tend to be influenced by the former. This is partly a reflection of power: developed languages tend to be used by societies that are more centralised politically, and these are usually better equipped to fight and survive in conflicts with less centralised ones. But it is also a reflection of attitudes to language.

People who use a language with traditions of standardisation and literacy may develop a sense of historicity, a pride in their language's past, and its continuity with the present. They tend to be more keenly aware of their language's difference from other languages. They do not see their language as being under threat, and in danger of dying out: rather, they are aware of its vitality. These factors are extremely important in the modern world, when oppressed languages, such as the Celtic ones of Britain and France, and languages such as Pennsylvania German in the United States of America are being kept alive by their speakers. We shall bear all this in mind when we come to consider the status of Latin during the Roman Empire.

The prestige attached to standardised, written varieties of language is associated with the belief that they are the most correct forms of the language, and that they are perhaps the most 'beautiful'. Aesthetic judgments of this kind are even shared by people who may be illiterate, and who have little access to the prestige variety. This is most likely to happen where a classical variety, enshrining a literature either sacred or secular, develops in a language spoken over a very wide area, and where literacy is the preserve of an elite. In such conditions, the everyday spoken varieties of such a language may diverge quite sharply from the classical one. The consequences of this divergence may be seen today in the case of Arabic. This language, to put it rather simply, has two forms: one based on an ancient, classical variety, the other on the colloquial usage of the present.

No contemporary speaker of Arabic uses the form deriving from the ancient literary variety as a medium of everyday conversation. In fact, the two varieties are functionally differentiated, just as they are evaluated differently by their users. The classical form, which is considered more correct and beautiful than the colloquial forms, is used in the prestigious domains like law, religion and education, and has therefore been called the High variety of the language. The Low variety-which uses many words, grammatical constructions, and sounds that are different from the High one-is subject to great regional variation (as distinct from the 'fixed' classical form codified in dictionaries and grammars) and is used in more informal contexts.

The situation just described is known as diglossia and it demonstrates the value of describing languages or linguistic varieties according to the ways in which they function in society. We shall return to diglossia later, in our consideration of Latin, which, like Arabic, was once the official language of a large empire.

Bilingualism

People will readily acquire a second language if they need one, and if they have access to its speakers. This is particularly common when speakers of different languages intermarry, and their children grow up bilingual. In some circumstances, a first, or 'native' language, may not be as useful to an individual's daily needs as a second language: this often happens when people migrate to other countries to work. And in some conditions people learn a simplified version of another language when contact with its speakers is only intermittent; and they use it for very limited purposes, such as trade. These simplified languages are known as pidgins.

Bilingualism can be of various kinds. Where one person commands more than one language, we can speak of individual bilingualism. But this need not mean that both languages are actually spoken: scholars, for instance, can be fluent only in the written form of another language, and translation from one language to another can introduce linguistic changes that are far-reaching. Such cultural bilingualism, as we shall call it, is of great importance in the early history of English.

Where a society regularly uses two or more languages to carry out its affairs, we can speak of societal bilingualism. The restriction of each language to certain areas is referred to as geographical bilingualism. In parts of Belgium for instance, French is spoken as a first language, whereas Flemish is natively spoken elsewhere; and both languages have official status. Some people, of course, will be bilingual; and in most bilingual societies, one language-group is more bilingual, at the individual level, than the other.

This is particularly so in the very common cases where one language is the official one, used in High domains, and the other is relegated to functions that can be described as unofficial, where it is merely tolerated (as in the case of immigrant languages in English cities) or actually proscribed. The speakers of the Low language are much more likely to be bilingual than those whose first language is the High one. In such situations one language is clearly the dominant one, and we can adapt the term diglossia to describe them, and speak of diglossic bilingualism.

Latin as the Language of Empire

To anyone acquainted with the roles and status of English in the world today, a sociolinguistic profile of Latin at the time of the Roman Empire would make familiar reading. Latin was a developed, omnifunctional, autonomous, urbanised, highly standardised language. It had a classical variety which was codified by grammarians, and a writing system that could provide a model for other languages when it was their turn to require orthographies. This imperial language of a vast empire also became the language of an international religion, Christianity.

At first, the imposition of Roman rule over areas of ethnic, cultural, and linguistic heterogeneity would have led to the kind of bilingualism we have described as diglossic. Latin was the official language of High domains, while diverse local vernaculars served the everyday needs of many different subject populations. Thus, ordinary people would have been controlled in a language unfamiliar to them, as in so many parts of the world today. But it seems that this kind of societal bilingualism did not remain stable for long. The spread of Latin came to be not only geographical, but social as well. Subject peoples gradually, over the generations, acquired it as a second language, and subsequently as a first language. In short, the Roman Empire witnessed a process known to sociolinguists as language shift. The evidence for this is demonstrated by the fact that Latin formed the base of French, Spanish, Italian, Portuguese, and Romanian as they are spoken today.

There are a number of reasons why a process of language shift took place. The Romans conquered, but also administered; and their centralised rule lasted so long-several hundred years in many places-that Latin had the chance to take root. Since it was imposed over areas of great linguistic diversity, it could also function as a lingua franca for subject peoples. And finally, there were material advantages in learning it. The characteristic instrument of Roman rule was the town (supported by the agricultural economy of the villa), and to play any part in the life of the towns, it was necessary to learn Latin. Urbanisation, then, brought new influences, practices, and opportunities to people interested in exploiting them.

The successful spread of Latin over a vast area had much in common with the extension of other international languages in the ancient and early medieval worlds. The Hellenic Empire had spread Greek in the eastern Mediterranean, where Latin never displaced it. Later, over much of the Levant and parts of Africa, Islam extended the use of Arabic, religion being a powerful agency in its spread. And it has been argued that all three languages at different points in their history have exhibited the features associated with diglossia.

When today we speak of Latin we tend to think of the literary Latin used by writers like Cicero about two thousand years ago. This is because Classical Latin, as we usually call it, is the variety most often studied: it derives prestige from the great writers who used it, and it enjoys the air of regulation and fixity conferred upon it by the scholars who codified it in grammars. But we must not forget that Latin, like any language, had different varieties, just as many Classical writers themselves could not overlook the differences that were emerging between their metropolitan written usage (described as urbanus, which later came to denote refinement) and the local (rusticus) or popular (vulgaris) Latin which was to provide the basis for Christian writings in the following centuries. Classical Latin is certainly of great importance in the history of English, but it is on the spoken Latin, not of Rome, but of the Imperial provinces, that we must now concentrate.

We have already mentioned the significance of towns to the imposition of Roman rule. In the major Imperial cities, a small elite of Roman citizens used the Latin of Rome as the official language, teaching it in schools to the nobility of the conquered peoples. A major function of all towns was to raise enough cash to pay for the standing armies that were so essential to the maintenance of the Empire. It is in these armies that we can see the conditions for the genesis of new, local varieties of Latin.

Drawing their complements from speakers of many different languages, the armies fostered Latin as a lingua franca: and it is likely that the spoken Latin of the soldiery bore the imprints of numerous mother-tongues, as a process of pidginisation occurred. Similar conditions existed among the trading sectors of the towns. As centres of commerce, the provincial towns attracted a mercantile element almost as multilingual in character as that of the army, and this would have assisted the spread of a local variety of Latin among the neighbouring population.

The spread of Latin was not as even, however, as the above account might suggest. In at least two parts of the Empire, its position was to prove tenuous. In the provinces of the east, Latin did not displace Greek, the prestigious language of an earlier Empire, as an official language. And in the western province known as Britain, and especially among the highland population, it seems unlikely that the language was widely learned at all.

The Collapse of the Empire in the North

The subject populations of both Britain and Gaul were farming peoples known as Celts. Their society was a tribal one, and their language an undeveloped vernacular. The Celts were not literate (although they had an alphabet which they used for inscriptions) and it is probable that the British variety of the language could be understood in Gaul, and vice versa; hence, they could be said to have spoken different dialects of Celtic, if we use dialect in the sense of 'related language', discussed above. Under the Romans, Celtic would have been the Low language, though the pattern of individual bilingualism may have varied widely.

Thus, in the remoter, less urbanised areas, monoglot speakers of Celtic may have predominated, while in the towns Latin may have been the only language used. In the areas influenced by the towns bilingualism was probably quite common. It is impossible to gauge the extent to which Latin displaced Celtic in either Gaul or Britain. But as one of its most enduring and valued possessions, Gaul is more likely to have been the more thoroughly Romanised.

In Britain, however, bilingualism may have had a strongly geographical character. Throughout the more inaccessible northern and western regions, including much of what is now called England, Celtic customs, organisation, and language remained to threaten Roman rule; whereas it is at least conceivable that in certain areas Latin had displaced Celtic.

Unfortunately, we can do little more than speculate on these matters; and, as we shall see, the oblique and even contradictory nature of what evidence exists is very much bound up with the subsequent fortunes of these two outposts of Roman rule. By the fifth century AD, both had fallen to invading Germanic tribespeople; among them, the Angles and Saxons, the speakers of a language that was later to be called English.

Of these Germanic tribes little is known. Like the Celts, they had developed none of the social, political, and economic institutions which demand the cultivation of a standardised language. They were farming peoples, locally organised on the principle of personal loyalty to a chieftain; tribal kings were only elected in times of crisis. Unlike the Celts, however, they had managed to keep the Romans out of their homelands north of the Rhine and Danube.

But in their sustained defence of these areas, many of the tribes came into contact with the Romans, siding with them in campaigns against other tribes, and enlisting in the Roman legions. Such contact had its linguistic consequences: the word cheese was probably adapted from Latin caseus at this time, its pronunciation changing to fit the sound-patterns of the Angles and Saxons.

During the period of the Roman Empire, it seems that the inclination of the Germanic tribes was to expand, generally towards the south and west; but the organisational superiority of Rome kept them bottled up. As Roman rule faltered, however, it came to depend on some of the more Romanised tribes for its survival, and these often had imperial ambitions of their own. The Visigoths of the lower Danube area, for instance, were originally employed to regain what is now Spain from other Germanic adventurers; but as the collapse of Roman rule became imminent, they created their own Empire there.

But Roman ways lived on. The Visigoths were rapidly Christianised. Above all, they adopted Latin; at first for writing, later in speech. It is their version of spoken Latin that forms the basis of the Spanish language. Even those tribes who had not been caught in the Imperial net seem to have been impressed by the apparatus of the Empire when they encountered it in their invasions of the fifth century.

At least, this is true of mainland Europe. The spectacularly successful Franks, who overran Gaul from their homelands by the lower Rhine in less than half a century, seemed content to respect the institutions of Roman rule and leave them intact. Quickly united under one leader, the Franks had been baptised before the end of the fifth century.

With Christianity came Latinisation. Latin remained the language of administration and religion, and soon became the language of law. In the end the Franks, like the Visigoths, discarded their Germanic speech and adopted the spoken Latin of Gaul, the language that was to become French. It is probable that these two cases of language shift were led from above, by each ruling group.

The Germanic Invasion of Britain

The rapidity with which the Franks settled Gaul and embraced the trappings of Latin civilisation contrasts markedly with the slow, less co-ordinated progress of the Germanic invaders of Britain. The groups of Angles, Saxons, Frisians, and Jutes who left their north German homelands for Britain in the course of the fifth century were not united under one leader; neither did they so swiftly secure military success. While the Franks seemed content to allow the town-and-villa economy of Gaul to continue untouched, the Angles and Saxons found resistance from Celtic chieftains, to whom authority had now passed after the withdrawal of the standing army had left Roman institutions undefended.

The Germanic invaders of Britain might well have been content to co-exist peaceably with the Celts, as appears to have happened in Gaul; but naturally enough, British resistance was met with force. This resistance is likely, however, to have been relatively uncentralised and sporadic, so the pattern of Anglo-Saxon invasion would have varied in different places. Some Celts would have been killed in battle; others fled west, and some perhaps into what is now Brittany; some may have been enslaved; many would probably have carried on much as before.

But without the possibility of a military response, those Celts who remained would have been gradually absorbed through intermarriage into the Anglo-Saxon hegemony. We know very little about the early relations between Anglo-Saxons and Celts. Although the Germanic tribes possessed a runic alphabet for purposes of inscription, they had no use for written history, and have bequeathed us no contemporary account of their invasion. But we are left with one striking fact. The Anglo-Saxons did not abandon their language.

The Celtic language was displaced, and English developed not from a local variety of spoken Latin, but from the Germanic language of the invaders. Unfortunately, much of the speculation about Anglo-Celtic relations at this time is based on linguistic evidence, which, as we shall see, is of uncertain value when other crucial information is missing.

One problem concerns the extent to which Latin was spoken in the south and east of Britain. Since the Anglo-Saxons landed on the eastern shores, they would first have encountered Latin-speaking Celts, if that language had taken root. The fact that the Germanic invaders did not then learn Latin may have two possible explanations. First, the Celtic resistance may have been long and bloody enough to have embittered relations with the invaders.

Alternatively, it may have been the case that the Anglo-Saxons were simply unimpressed by what remained of Latin civilisation in Britain. Either the economy of town and villa was less flourishing than in Gaul, or the Anglo-Saxons had no desire to ape or adopt the institutions and language of Imperial Rome. As we shall see, Christianity, which was a potent force for Latinisation, came only slowly and gradually, like the process of settlement itself.

It is more commonly assumed that the Anglo-Saxons encountered a Celtic-speaking population rather than one speaking Latin. If this is the case, it is difficult to know how to interpret the linguistic evidence that exists. When we examine the origins of place-names, we find that Celtic elements are not uncommon in the west of what we now call England, suggesting that Celtic communities co-existed alongside sparser Anglo-Saxon ones.

River-names (such as Axe and Avon) are often of Celtic origin, but this evidence conflicts with the extremely low incidence of Celtic loan-words into Anglo-Saxon. The place-name evidence has been taken to show that Celts and Anglo-

Saxons co-existed peaceably, at least in some areas, while the dearth of loan-words might suggest wholesale slaughter, expulsion, or enslavement of a dominated people.

The only conclusion we may be justified in drawing here is that we do not know how to evaluate these different kinds of linguistic evidence in the absence of other kinds of data. There are in any case great difficulties involved in making predictions or projections about the language-habits of a particular community on the basis of comparisons with situations elsewhere. It would be wrong, for instance, to argue that because the Anglo-Saxons did not learn Latin, as the Franks did in Gaul, the British Celts must have remained Celtic-speaking.

In trying to specify the vital factors which influence the adoption of new languages by conquering peoples and subjugated populations, we need to bear in mind the numerical strength of the invaders, the degree of centralisation of their political organisation, their intentions (the establishment of a ruling caste, for instance, or the settlement of land for farming), the extent to which intermarriage occurs, and so on.

We might also need to know something about the degree of resistance put up by the defending inhabitants, and their own degree of centralisation and military strength, as well as the extent to which they, and the invaders, share an international written culture or religion. Even if we were to have detailed knowledge of this kind, it would still be impossible to predict which language would prevail in any given case. On the available evidence, it seems likely that any comparison between the linguistic histories of Britain and Gaul would need to bear in mind the differing degrees of Romanisation, and the different aims of the Germanic invaders.

Whatever languages the British Celts spoke, the Anglo-Saxons successfully imposed their own undeveloped, oral vernacular. But this case of language imposition is very different from that of Latin as the language of an empire.

While Anglo-Saxon was almost certainly the dominant language, its relationship with either Celtic or Latin could not be described as diglossic: each Anglo-Saxon kingdom took generations to establish. At first, too, bilingualism would have been societal, in that language use was determined by ethnic background, and was to a large extent geographical, since Celtic would have been stronger in the west.

This pattern is likely to have been replaced by individual bilingualism on the part of Celts and in some areas Celtic survived, perhaps for several centuries. It has been claimed that a vestige of it may even have survived into the nineteenth century, particularly in the area of the northern Pennines, in the numeral systems associated with counting sheep, stitches in knitting, and perhaps children's games: a Cumbrian version has pedera (four) and pump (five); the equivalent numerals in modern Welsh are pedwar and pump. But while the Celtic language was preserved in Wales and Cornwall-only to experience a further attack from English in later centuries-it was eventually displaced from most of England altogether.

The Anglo-Saxon Settlement

The fact that the Angles and Saxons had to cross the sea before reaching their chosen territory greatly influenced the process and pattern of their settlement. It is likely that their tribal organisation was disrupted by the voyages: a charismatic leader might attract a boatload of adventurers drawn from different tribal units. The boats would sail up the major rivers like the Thames and the Humber and establish the first settlements-probably strongly fortified-at places on the banks, and then wait for the next boatloads before advancing further.

It seems likely that the invaders largely took over existing agricultural practices. Archaeological and place-name evidence suggests that the settlers used Roman roads and sites when it suited them: but it seems that the AngloSaxons preferred to take over the kind of site called in Latin a vicus, where civilians had settled outside the walls of military centres (giving place-names ending in -wich, -wicham, etc.). This contrasts markedly with the pattern in Gaul, where Roman villa sites became villages, and where towns remained intact and flourishing.

It seems to have been the Anglo-Saxon settlers who largely established the structure of villages in the territory we now call England. An overwhelming proportion of these villages have Anglo-Saxon names, many incorporating the names of local leaders, others the vocabulary of wood management, drainage, and cultivation. In many places, the relatively undisturbed character of village life, and a largely immobile population, created over the centuries the conditions for sharp divergences in local speech. But in parts of the more strongly Celtic west, Anglo-Saxon settlement was often later, and less dense.

The settlers did not venture into Wales or Cornwall (although a heavy 'buffer' settlement occurred in parts of Devon, where Anglo-Saxon boundaries are still a dominant feature in the landscape), and it seems they found the Cumbrian hills uninviting. Here, pockets of Celts remained, and in other parts of the northwest their presence may be attested by the Celtic place-name Eccles, an adoption from Latin ecclesia, which denotes a place of worship.

In these areas the Celtic language may have influenced the local Germanic speech in ways that are no longer recoverable, accounting, perhaps, for characteristic pronunciations of words like boot and soon in the local accent of both Devon and Lancashire; the vowel has a fronted quality, rather like that in French tu, which is unusual elsewhere in England.

The small communities of Angles and Saxons, with their oral culture, were gradually organised into larger political units under petty kings. At one point there seem to have been at least seven kings in different parts of England, often warring amongst themselves. The most important were those of Northumbria (the land north of the River Humber), Mercia (the land with a march or border with Wales), Wessex (the land of the West Saxons, who lived to the south of the western part of the Thames), and Kent; but there were also kingdoms of East Anglia, Essex, and Sussex. We shall see the importance of these separate kingdoms in establishing regional varieties of English in the following paragraphs.

With the institution of kingship came the gradual introduction of Christianity. And with Christianity came literacy. But for the AngloSaxon kings, unlike their Germanic counterparts on the European mainland, Christianity was not synonymous with the use of Latin in both speech and writing. Conversion in early English society was often the work of Irish missionaries, and Ireland, never part of the Roman Empire although influenced by it, developed as well as its own style of Christianity a tradition of writing in its own language.

Rather than use Latin, they adapted its alphabet in Ireland for their own purposes, and this knowledge they shared with the Anglo-Saxons. Each Anglo-Saxon kingdom eventually developed its own traditions of writing, using the local variety of English. Perhaps the finest examples of Germanic poetry, like the epic Beowulf and the elegiac Seafarer, are recorded in Anglo-Saxon. But it is significant that much early writing in English was prose, used for laws, charters, chronicles, and also for sermons.

The development of any literary tradition at this time could not, however, escape the influence of Latin. Christianity and Latin were virtually inseparable over much of Europe, just as the Church was the stablest and most highly structured political institution. The traditions of philosophical, theological, legal, and administrative writing in Latin were so long, pervasive, and prestigious that for Anglo-Saxon scholars like Bede in the eighth century and Aelfric in the tenth, it would almost have been the instinctive choice.

Thus, while Latin was a spoken medium at this time in the monasteries, its use is most directly associated with writing, and it is on this level that the language comes into contact with English. Anglo-Saxon scholars would have been bilingual in English and Latin, but it was a bilingualism that was cultural in character, the preserve of an educated elite. And contact with Latin meant exposure to ideas, practices, and concepts that were Christian. The pagan tradition in poetry, as it was written down, was reinterpreted in Christian terms, and loan-words from Latin in the period of early Anglo-Saxon literacy were often associated with religion *(abbot, apostle, choir, mass).*

The fact that Latin was a model and an inspiration for the first writers in Anglo-Saxon England does not mean that it was in any way superior to the language of the English. Any language, or dialect for that matter, has the potential for use in any domain, and for any purpose. But if the speakers of a vernacular come into contact with a developed language, they will often interpret traditions of use within certain domains as evidence of linguistic superiority. The Anglo-Saxon scholars may well have thought that Latin was the natural and most suitable vehicle for, say, philosophical writing (just as many people think, or used to think, that French is particularly suited to theoretical argument).

What was happening in Anglo-Saxon England was a process of language development, under the influence of another language. Latin may have continued as a High language, but English ceased to be an oral vernacular, as it came to be cultivated in the other's shadow. As English was made to serve some of the functions of the developing monarchies, and as it came to be written down, we can describe its profile as that of a partially developed, literate language. As yet, however, it was unstandardised.

What scanty records remains show that distinctive regional varieties of English were emerging in the different kingdoms. And in time these varieties were to diverge to a point where we should need to describe them as different languages if the criterion of mutual intelligibility were to be the only one applied. It is more usual, however, to refer to these varieties as dialects. If this term is to be used, it should be remembered that each dialect of English at this time was, from a sociolinguistic point of view, a partially developed language.

In that they established centres of influence in different parts of England, the Anglo-Saxon kingdoms have often been seen as highly significant in the history of English. Recent research into English dialects shows that these ancient divisions continue to underpin the traditional regional varieties of English, nine centuries or more after the demise of the monarchies themselves. More recently, however, it has been suggested that the Church, with its superior administration and regional diocese structure, may have been more influential.

Unfortunately, we do not know very much about the Anglo-Saxon dialects, since very few texts have survived from the period, and we do not know anything about the relationship of written Anglo-Saxon to the spoken usage of the ordinary families as they toiled in the fields. A great deal of writing has been lost over the last thousand years. But the indifference, or vandalism, of subsequent centuries is not the only reason for the dearth of records.

More Germanic settlers, this time from Scandinavia, very nearly overturned the few institutions of centralised monarchy that existed in the different kingdoms. Hostile to the developing Christian culture of monasteries and books, at least if contemporary accounts are to be believed, it was the Vikings who, ironically enough, succeeded in pushing the Anglo-Saxons into taking the first steps towards centralisation under *one* monarch.

The Vikings

The pattern of Germanic expansion which we have described above was continued into the eighth and following centuries by the Scandinavian tribes of the north. For nearly two centuries and a half, Anglo-Saxons and Vikings came into contact of one kind or another. A period of piracy was followed by military campaigns. One after another the Anglo-

Saxon kingdoms were overturned, until Wessex was the only source of English resistance. Extensive settlement in much of northern and eastern England was followed by a further round of armed incursions, culminating in the accession to the English throne of the kings of Denmark themselves.

It is the period of settlement that chiefly concerns us here. As great traders, the Scandinavians were interested in securing footholds in the urban centres of Europe; and as farmers, they wanted new land, like the Anglo-Saxons before them. While Norwegians colonised Ireland, the Scottish Islands, the Isle of Man, and parts of England's northwest, Danes settled thickly in the north and east.

The place-name evidence for Yorkshire, Lincolnshire, and Leicestershire suggests that Danes here outnumbered the earlier settlers: the Danish form Ingleby, 'settlement of the English', in north Yorkshire, suggests that AngloSaxons were scattered enough to have a settlement named after them. Wherever they settled, the Scandinavians brought with them their leaders, laws, and their own language.

Very little is known about the relations between the English and the newcomers. While at times these must have been bitter, it appears from recent research into place-names and settlement sites that on many occasions the Scandinavians did not displace the Anglo-Saxons from their own settlements, but grouped themselves near them, often in less fertile places. And although a third of England was occupied by speakers of Danish and Norse, the newcomers did not, and could not, impose an alien set of customs and institutions; nor could they impose their language even if, for a time, it may have been socially dominant.

The independence of the area of Danish settlement, known as Danelaw, was undermined by the baptising of the Danish leaders, who knew that Christianity was a useful form of control over their subjects. And it was further undermined by the resurgent dynasty of Wessex. Alfred checked the Danes militarily and defined the limits of the Danelaw, while his progeny, Edward and Athelstan, carried the authority of Wessex throughout England during the tenth century. Finally, the period of Danish kingship under Svein and Cnut in the early eleventh century was short-lived. Danish could not, therefore, become the official language of England-unlike Norn, which persisted in Orkney and Shetland for nearly a thousand years, during a period of unbroken Norwegian hegemony.

The language that the Scandinavians spoke was an undeveloped, oral vernacular. Similar in sociolinguistic profile to the language of the Anglo-Saxons four centuries earlier, it was also similar in its linguistic structure. It is not improbable that the Anglo-Saxon smallholders were able to follow the speech of their Scandinavian neighbours. The records suggest that differences between the languages might have been akin to those characterising, say, the dialect of Devon compared to that of Aberdeenshire today.

There would have been some predictable variations: the word for 'bone' in Anglo-Saxon might have sounded like ban, but with a longer vowel sound; in Scandinavian, like bane. But there may have been as many differences among the dialects of English as there were between English and Scandinavian (as in the relationship between British English and American English today).

At any rate, similarity in language, as in custom and social organisation, facilitated the absorption of the newcomers in many parts of England, although some distinctive Scandinavian practices, such as land-measurement, survived in what was formerly the Danelaw.

Contact between the languages occurred at the oral level, in those areas where ordinary English people encountered, in face-to-face interaction, their Danish counterparts. In situations such as this, where the communication of basic information is at a premium, we are likely to find a process similar to pidginisation. Language is reduced to bare essentials, as it is when we send a telegram; and one of the clearest means of achieving this is to delete, or simplify, some of the patterns in our grammar. It is probable that grammatical re-structuring, took place wherever contacts were made, and the new forms gradually spread, at the spoken level, beyond the area of Scandinavian influence. As in the case of Anglo-Celtic contact, such innovations will have taken place in conditions where exact evidence is almost entirely lacking.

More obvious evidence of linguistic contact is the massive borrowing into English of loan-words. Not only have numerous words like angry, awkward, get, and take been borrowed into the core of our everyday usage, but indispensable pronoun forms such as they and she derive either directly or indirectly from Scandinavian. These words are now no longer regional; but in much of northern England, local dialect is still heavily 'Scandinavianised'. Forms such as kirk (church), steg (gander), laik (play), as well as pronunciations and grammatical forms are still part of traditional usage, or were until very recently.

We do not know how long an 'unmixed' Scandinavian language survived in England. But the presence in Cumbria of Norse runic inscriptions from the eleventh century confirms the impression given by recent dialect research, that it was the area associated with part of the ancient kingdom of Northumbria that best preserved the Scandinavian culture. With York an important centre of Viking trade, Northumbria stood aloof from the rest of England.

The strongly regional character of Scandinavian influence means that if we are to speak of Anglo/ Scandinavian bilingualism, we should describe it as geographical in nature. The Anglo-Saxons could not dominate the newcomers as they dominated the Celts. Perhaps the linguistic relations between the two languages can best be described as a continuum, ranging from a relatively unmixed Scandinavian at one end of the scale to a relatively uninfluenced English speech at the other. In between, the languages co-existed, and then merged, with English forms and structures competing at first with the Scandinavian ones, then gradually spreading northwards.

At the other end of the country from Northumbria, a concept of 'Englishness' was kept alive by the kings of Wessex. Alfred doggedly maintained the tradition of writing in Anglo-Saxon, particularly in prose; and his desire to translate works from Latin into English makes him one of the first vernacularisers in education. Winchester became the important centre for English writing, and the West Saxon dialect became a kind of literary standard.

Works written in different dialects at earlier times were copied into it, giving us a somewhat indirect insight into the output of the other Anglo-Saxon kingdoms. The influence of the Winchester scriptoria long outlived the period of West Saxon power.

Later kings of Wessex introduced political changes that also had farreaching linguistic consequences. Athelstan instituted the system of shires, political boundaries that by establishing new centres of power could influence the usage of surrounding areas. But the West Saxon dynasty itself was fragile. After further Scandinavian invasions and depredations had brought a Danish king, Cnut, to the English throne, another foreign dynasty was to be imposed on England; Scandinavian in origin, but speaking another language.

The Normans

The Viking adventurers who settled in Normandy in northern France during the early tenth century were also baptised and ceded territory like their counterparts in England. Again, they did not impose their oral vernacular, but were gradually assimilated to the customs and language of the more centralised lands they colonised. In France, however, they had to learn a language that was structurally very different from their own. That they did this, within about four or five generations, is evidenced by the fact that it was a variety of French that they imposed on England when, as Normans, they added this territory to their possessions by the military Conquest of 1066. For the next three centuries or so, French was to be a living force in England, and its influence continued to be felt, though less directly, for centuries after that.

The Norman invaders were few in number, but well-organised. Their intentions were not those of their colonising ancestors, nor of the Anglo-Saxons before them. The Normans were interested in territorial annexation, and they overcame the English by means of efficient military campaigns. The superstructure of political and economic power based on the ownership of land-was then almost exclusively wrested from English hands and given to Norman friends of William the Conqueror.

The positions of power, in respect to both king and Church, were thus in the hands of French speakers, who spent the next 150 years 'commuting' between their possessions on both sides of the Channel. It was only when this ruling class lost its possessions in Normandy at the beginning of the thirteenth century that it could begin to think of itself as English. By that time, French had become firmly established in England as the High language of law, government, administration, and also, to some extent, courtly literature and religion. It was not until the fourteenth century that English was re-developed within these domains.

We need to distinguish, therefore, two phases of contact with French. The first involves the Scandinavianised French of the Norman elite. This language would not have been more developed or more prestigious than that of the English; neither was Norman culture more international or more literate in character: probably the only technical advantages it enjoyed were military organisation and the wider use of stone as a building material.

Norman French was imposed by a ruling caste; but since Latin continued in its spoken form in the Church, and as the written language of scholarship, the linguistic situation after

1066 may be described as triglossic. There has been some controversy about the extent to which this state of societal bilingualism was realised at the individual level. Some have argued that French was very widely learned throughout English society; others, that its use was very limited.

One thing that we can be sure about is that French did not displace English. Unlike Latin in the age of Empire, Norman French did not offer linguistic unity or a prestigious, literate language to linguistically diverse, uncentralised tribes people. Neither is it apparent that the Normans took much trouble to encourage English people to learn their language, still less to offer them material advantages. Norman French was exclusive, the property of the major, and often absent, land owner.

While no wholesale language shift took place, it is probable that individual bilingualism came to exist among certain social groups. The motivation for learning a second language, however, may have been different in each case. Some groups would need to be bilingual, whereas for others opportunities for contact with the other language would have been minimal. Certain domains of usage would make different demands on people's linguistic repertoire. Moreover, we should not assume that language-learning was always in one direction.

About the social extremes there is some agreement. We know that the first language of the English monarchs was French until the end of the fourteenth century-long after the Norman dynasty. It is also probable that the upper aristocracy were monolingual French-speakers for a considerable time after the Conquest. It seems too that the upper aristocracy continued to use French for a considerable time after 1066, although there is also evidence that some of them began to learn English quite soon after that date.

At the other end of the social scale, there is no reason to believe that the ordinary people who worked the land spoke any language other than their local variety of English. In a society overwhelmingly agrarian, this class would constitute the vast majority of the population. During the period of French dominance, then, the regional variation of the Anglo-Saxon era was intensified.

Not all the Normans were aristocrats, however. They brought with them people who could administer their feudal estates; and these would have needed to be bilingual in their role as mediators between overlord and land-labourers. There were also adventurers who became lesser landowners: these were thinly spread in the countryside, and it is likely they would have adapted to local ways and language, just as many of those who went on to settle in Ireland eventually learned Gaelic. Norman craftsmen, merchants, and artisans settled in English towns in greater numbers, but they were never more than a small minority of the urban population.

It is questionable whether they ever dominated trade, or even particular crafts, and it is not certain whether French was ever institutionalized as the language of commerce. The garrisons of Norman soldiers may have retained their language, as a marker of the male peer-group (so that bread-and-butter transactions with local people took place in a kind of Anglo-French pidgin), but in general it may well have been the Normans in the towns who learned a second language, rather than the English.

If at this time bilingualism was at all common, it was perhaps quite unremarkable, as it is in so many parts of the world today. We do know that many Normans married English women, so it is likely that children in the towns grew up as bilinguals. French was also less strongly institutionalised in the domain of religion. Writings in English emanated from the monasteries throughout the period of French dominance: the Anglo-Saxon Chronicle was continued for nearly a century after the Conquest, and in following centuries didactic religious texts circulated from mainly west midland sources. Sermons continued to be delivered in English, although there is some evidence for French.

It has been argued that most of the lesser clergy were monoglot speakers of English, and that even in the monasteries newly founded by the Normans, bilingualism, rather than French, was expected. As an institution of learning, then, the Church tended to promote fluency in more than one language, as it had done in AngloSaxon times.

At the top of the social pyramid, however, Norman French was secure, with Latin, as the language of official transactions and decrees, and of diversions for the powerful: a great deal of Norman French literature was produced in England. About one hundred years after the Conquest, the first loan-words into English show how the language was associated with the instruments and offices of power: prison and castle, cardinal and prior. But the full weight of loan-words comes later, during the second phase of contact with French, this time with another variety of the language.

Cultural Contact with the French of Paris

In 1204, the dukedom of Normandy was won by the king of France. While the kings of England still retained possessions in more southerly parts of France, the descendants of the Norman conquerors lost the sense of their ancestry. The ruling class of England became increasingly Anglicised, but it maintained its contacts with the French of the kings of France, a monarchy which by the end of the thirteenth century had become the strongest and most centralised in Europe.

From a sociolinguistic point of view, this second phase of contact with French is probably more interesting than the first. We see language come to be regarded as a social symbol, as it is identified with social groups of declared interests. The old Norman French is seen as provincial and unfashionable, while the language of the French court is seen as the emblem of the most sophisticated and prestigious culture in the contemporary world.

To use this French, then, is to impress. In the eyes of many, English had perhaps the aura of a peasant language, much like that of Gaelic in nineteenth-century Ireland. But among others, it became a marker of what today we might call ethnicity.

Individual bilingualism would have been extensive during this phase. While the court retained its devotion to French language and culture, the ruling class gradually acquired English. By the fourteenth century, we begin to see the linguistic consequence of this process. English is saturated with French loan-words, some of which have become such common currency that we tend to forget their ancestry-words like pass, join, butcher, large.

Some, like chase and guarantee, had even been borrowed earlier, in the forms catch and warranty, from Norman French. The taste of the Francophile court was reflected in much of the English poetry of this phase, which borrows French themes, techniques, and language; and in so far as the English poet was brought up in this atmosphere, we can best describe this period of contact as one of cultural bilingualism. It is also the case that many English people learned French.

The prestige of French as a marker of high social status meant that some people learned it for its snob value. Since the Conquest, French had been the medium of education, and schools were a means of acquiring the language. A fourteenth-century writer, Higden, records that even people from the country busied themselves 'to speke Freynsh', so they could sound like 'gentil men'. If there was a demand for the language, people who could teach it had a vested interest in its continuance.

Thus, we see in the same century edicts enforcing French in the domains of education and religion. That a similar entrenchment existed in the domain of law can be seen by the fact that 'Law French' was still in use, for some purposes, in the seventeenth century. For a lawyer, the possession of a special language is a powerful weapon, as can be seen in many multilingual societies today. The 'professionalisation' of law in the course of the twelfth and thirteenth centuries meant that its practitioners could exploit the advantages of knowing a special language: they could become parasitic on the people they were meant to serve.

If for some the French language meant social advancement, for others it aroused antagonisms. Cultural contacts with France were an increasing source of tension in English life. The monarchy of France came to be seen as a foreign power, whose interests often clashed with those of the people of England. Moreover, while some kings of England waged long, costly, and fruitless wars against France, others lavished the wealth of England on French favourites. Either was likely to upset baron, lesser landowner, and merchant alike. Frenchmen, and the French language, were increasingly disparaged.

From its position as a tolerated language under the Normans, English became what sociolinguists might call a promoted language, a mark of 'Englishness'. The promotion of English was associated with gradual changes that had been taking place in English society. The old feudal structure so successfully sustained by the Norman kings, the system of obligations between king and aristocracy, was giving way to an economy based, not on land, but on money.

We see the emergence of new bases of power, new feelings of group loyalty. Alliances were made between lesser landowners, who were making money out of raising sheep for wool, and the rising merchant class in the towns, a pact institutionalised in the thirteenth century by the assembly that came to be called Parliament. The founding of universities stimulated mobility, both geographical and social, among certain sections of the population; and by the fourteenth century mobility had even spread to the land-labourers, who could bargain for wages now that labour was scarce. By that time, the balance of forces was beginning to favour an increasingly articulate, English speaking merchant class. It was this class, with London as its base, that spoke the basis of what came to be called standard English.

Chapter 5

The Imposition of English

IN THE BRITISH ISLES

It is possible to argue that in the course of the last four centuries the minority languages of the British Isles have been undermined by English political and economic power, the policies of English governments, and English attitudes, both official and unofficial. The opprobrium cast on the regional dialects of England has been visited, on a grander scale, and with far-reaching consequences, on the speech of regions diverse in language and culture, and situated far away from the metropolitan south-east.

In this chapter we shall trace the long and complicated history of English as a dominant language throughout the British Isles. We shall see how a northern variety of English was developed as the language of an independent Scottish state, and how that variety was displaced in official domains by metropolitan English after the union of parliaments in 1707. Next, we shall consider how the Celtic languages have been maintained, and even promoted, despite generations of linguistic domination. In Ireland, we see a version of English colonialism, and the only territory where a Celtic tongue has become an official language. We shall then consider the maintenance, first of Gaelic in the Scottish Highlands, and then of Welsh, the object of a recent and vigorous campaign of promotion. Finally, we shall discuss two cases of what has been termed language death, the abandoning of Cornish and Manx as the first languages of the local Celtic communities. With one important exception, the languages with which we are dealing are Celtic, and therefore structurally distant from English.

They represent two branches of the Celtic language-family. The Gaelic of Ireland, and its implantations in the Scottish Highlands and the Isle of Man, form one branch. Welsh and Cornish, together with the Breton of north-west France, are more closely related to the British Celtic that was displaced during the Anglo-Saxon settlement. While the two branches had diverged considerably, rather as, say, Swedish, Norwegian, and Danish have done, there was contact between the languages of each branch, at least until English domination severed the links. Such contacts ensured a degree of mutual intelligibility between Gaelic-speaking Irish and Scottish Highlander, and between Welsh and Cornish; but since the imposition of English, the absence of a centre in either branch of Celtic has precluded any tendencies towards standardisation and hastened the proliferation of regional varieties.

However hard it may be to speak of a 'standard' English, it is even harder to speak of a standard Welsh, or a standard Scottish Gaelic. Before we deal with the one exception mentioned above, it is necessary to point out that the story as outlined in this chapter so far represents a particular point of view. It has been told from the perspective of the Celtic communities themselves; more particularly, from the perspective of Celtic nationalism. In the sense adopted here, nationalism is based on the premises that the most potent symbol of cultural uniqueness and political autonomy is the possession of a distinctive 'native' language.

So that any weakening of the bond between people and language-a bond nationalists see as natural-is seen as an erosion of self-esteem and communal integrity. It should already be clear that this view of language may be difficult to square with what we have seen elsewhere in this book of actual behaviour in bi- or multilingual communities. In origin a variant of the Northumbrian dialect of the Anglo-Saxons, Scots has been spoken in south-eastern Scotland almost as long as in England. But outside Scotland, it has rarely been accorded the status of a separate language, partly because attitudes to it have been governed by purely linguistic criteria, and partly because English people have often found it convenient to forget that Scotland was not politically united with England until 1707. This political factor inevitably complicates assessment of the current status of Scots; in fact, it constitutes one of the best examples of the difficulty of drawing the line between a dialect and a language. As we shall see, our stance on this issue will depend on the relative weight we attach to different kinds of criteria.

Whatever status we accord Scots, we must acknowledge that English has most successfully been imposed throughout the British Isles.

Aggression and expansionism have emanated from England since Norman times. This stance was part of a wider European process known as internal colonisation, in which peripheral areas of Europe were increasingly dominated and exploited by the centre. Thus, by the twelfth century, Norman nobles had buttressed southern and eastern Wales with great castles, and had established a presence in Ireland. The Welsh aristocracy was finally defeated in the thirteenth century; and in time, Ireland was to become the first English colony, its land confiscated for the benefit of outsiders. Scotland alone withstood military conquest; but by the early eighteenth century English domination had been achieved through political ingenuity.

Thus, though their language has never figured in census returns like the Celtic ones, many speakers of Scots have felt, and still feel, that they themselves are a linguistic minority whose linguistic traditions have suffered at the hands of the

English Unlike the imposition of Latin in Europe, the spread of English was not dependent on military victories. Nor did it confront oral vernaculars; Wales and Ireland both had developed languages and traditions of literacy as old as the English, and Scots, in the later Middle Ages, was also used for literary and legal purposes. But in other respects, the story is familiar. English in most cases has had a long time to take root; it has acted, and still acts, as a lingua franca. And, there have been obvious material advantages in learning it: industrialisation, and the consequent disruption of life in rural areas, has meant that many people have had to learn English to get employment.

As an imposed language, English has had a symbolic value clearly different from that of the minority languages. On the one hand, as the official language of a power often regarded as alien and remote, it has often been redolent of authority and high social status. It also became of course, the language of social aspiration and economic advancement. On the other hand, it has often been felt to lack those virtues of warmth, sincerity, and local dignity associated with the minority languages. We see here a replication of the symbolic values accorded to those varieties perceived in England as local, versus that perceived as 'standard'. Throughout the British Isles, therefore, the latter has often been seen as useful, but impersonal; effective, but neutral and cold.

The history of English outside England has two major strands. We must first describe how varieties of English-often local ones-were established in the early Plantations of English settlers such as those in Wales and Ireland, and how those varieties developed in the relative isolation of their new locations. Second, we must trace the imposition of metropolitan English as the language of administration, law, and education, a process associated with the Tudors but in the case of Ireland begun in the late Middle Ages. This task is impossible to do without reference to the sociolinguistic history of the minority languages themselves. Thus, we must know something about the functions of those languages in the past, how they have been maintained, and how they are being promoted, just as we needed to explore the factors involved in language imposition, maintenance, and shift in the period of Anglo-Saxon settlement, and beyond.

The history of *relationships* between speakers of different languages, then, cannot just involve the history of the dominant language. So far, we have used the term *minority* in reference to the languages under discussion. Logically a minority language should be one spoken by only a minority of the population in a given area. Here we are using it differently, in the sense of a language quite widely spoken, but subordinated to a *dominant* language, in this case English. Only in Eire has the minority language been declared a 'national', official one-but there we need to distinguish between its declared status and its actual use among the mass of the population. The other surviving Celtic languages have varying functions and sociolinguistic profiles. Formerly discouraged by England, their status in recent years has been at best that of tolerated languages, although governments in London tended to ignore their existence. More recently still, they have sometimes been *promoted,* not by central government, but by local agencies often concerned to advance the cause of nationalism.

Interest in the languages has been kindled, especially among the middle class, and increasingly they have been learned as second, or additional languages. The best known instance of such newly engendered language-loyalty is the recent campaign to promote Welsh, a language which has also, like Gaelic in Ireland and the Highlands of Scotland, been maintained as the first language of some small, isolated local communities. But interest in minority languages has also occurred in the absence of any native speakers at all, as in Cornwall and the Isle of Man. And it has affected the attitudes of speakers of Scots. During the past three decades in particular, Scots has become a focus for language-loyalty, particularly in Scotland's universities.

The imposition of English throughout the British Isles is a process of such length and complexity that it is difficult to make generalisations that are valid for all territories. Nor is it always possible to respect national boundaries and sensitivities. Scotland, for instance, has been split culturally, ethnically, and linguistically for well over a thousand years; this means that we must deal with its Scots-speaking community quite separately from its Gaelic one, for the simple reason that linguistic history only indirectly follows the history of nation-states. In addition, the special relationship between English and Scots must be explored within a framework different from that of contact between English and the Celtic languages.

Two broad generalisations about the process of imposition may perhaps be made. First, we shall see the significance of the Tudors-who were, ironically enough, of Welsh descent-in helping to shape official attitudes towards minority languages in the rest of the British Isles. Although the Tudor monarchs, like some of their Continental counterparts, clearly saw the importance of language as an instrument of political and social control, it is unlikely that they had a coherent policy of language suppression, even though that may ultimately have been an *effect* of their actions.

This, incidentally, had profound consequences for Scots, even though neither the Tudors nor their successors were likely to have seen it as a separate language. Second, it was the educational system that everywhere was instrumental in disseminating a taught variety of English. And after the introduction in 1870 of universal primary education, no other language was even recognised in the schools. Significantly enough, in the twentieth century it is in education that campaigns to promote the minority languages have found both a focus, and some notable successes.

The split in the cultural traditions of Scotland goes back at least as far as the seventh century AD. By then, the Anglo-

Saxons of Northumbria had extended their kingdom to roughly where Edinburgh now stands, adding to the original Celtic population. From the west, Gaels from Ireland had established a kingdom over most of Scotland north of the Forth. By the eleventh century, Scotland had a Gaelic dynasty, its kingdom stretching from the north-west Highlands to the area of the present border with England, although the Outer Isles and parts of the extreme north-east had yet to be wrested from the Norwegians.

But the Northumbrian dialect of south-east Scotland was still spoken; and links with England were strengthened by the arrival of refugees from the Norman Conquest. The court and church were Anglicised; land was granted to men from England (some of whom spoke Norman-French) and many English-speaking people settled in Scottish towns.

Gradually the influence of Gaelic contracted to the Highland area while southern Scotland, with its Northumbrian admixture developed a culture that was partly Germanic, partly Celtic. Scotland was at first successful in resisting the territorial ambitions of the English kings. After Bannockburn in 1314, Scotland enjoyed some form of independence from its expansionist neighbour for nearly 400 years. During this period, the Scottish court cultivated contacts with France, and developed its own educational institutions, parliament, law, and literature. And in the opinion of many, the Scottish variant of the Northumbrian dialect was developed as the language of these institutions, to the point where we can speak of Scots as a language separate from, though related to, English.

The centuries of independence saw Scots emerge as a developed vernacular. We see a process of functional elaboration, similar to that described in relation to English, except that it was Latin, not French that was replaced in official domains. In 1390, Scots was first used for parliamentary records; and the laws were translated into it in 1425. Moreover, an impressive literature was written from the fourteenth century onwards.

The cultivation of Scots was not, it seems, accompanied by a consciousness that it was, or should be, different from English. Such language-consciousness dates from the late eighteenth century, with the origins of modern nationalist thought. Even though a section of the Scottish nobility purported, like modern nationalists, to speak on behalf of the entire population, patriotism in medieval Scotland was based on antipathy to England, much like the anti-French patriotism of the English themselves. Sections of the Scottish bourgeoisie probably also favoured greater contact with England for economic reasons. The replacement of Latin by Scots was probably seen as a question of vernacularisation rather than of the explicit promotion of a 'national' language. Although contemporary observations are almost entirely lacking, the process of standardisation is most clearly seen, perhaps, in literature: a literary norm was emerging, for poetry, and more crucially, for prose. To sum up: by the end of the sixteenth century Scots may be seen as the language of an independent Scottish state and a large section of Scotland's population. It could have become what today is called a national language if its subsequent development had not been dominated by the imposition of English.

The undermining of Scots was not the result of decrees and proscriptions, but of the gradual weakening of independent Scottish institutions. The Reformation, which played such a key part in Tudor policy, had its strong adherents among sections of the Scottish bourgeoisie, so there was no need for the English to impose it. Elsewhere in the British Isles, the language of religion has often proved an important factor in language maintenance; but in southern Scotland, it does not seem to have been an issue. Scots accordingly never became the language of prayer books and Bible in Scotland, and this seems to have been vital in exposing Scottish people to the metropolitan language of

England. This variety was also disseminated in a great deal of printed literature at this time. Scotland had its own presses, but these printed English forms alongside those of Scots. Other Scottish institutions were soon to be eroded. In 1603, the Union of Crowns meant that a Scottish king was on the throne of England; but it was at London that he held his court. Gradually the most privileged and powerful class in Scotland adopted the language of England.

Finally, the Act of Union in 1707 ensured that Scotland's laws and administrative arrangements were determined in London, and therefore in English. By the eighteenth century Scots had become the Low language, and metropolitan English was now the medium of law, administration, education, and religion. And in language, as well as politically, it was 'the end of an auld sang', as was said in Scotland at the time.

From the eighteenth century onwards, the gentry of Scotland tended to receive an English education. This meant that all ideas about the best or most correct usage were articulated with respect to English; no variety of Scots was codified. Scots, therefore, came to be seen as a dialect, to be disparaged; there was a proliferation of books listing Scotticisms to be avoided in polite company. The first Scottish Members of Parliament, finding their accents derided in the English parliament, strove to sound like Englishmen. Like the dialects of England, Scots lost all social status, and its use in school was punished after the 1872 Education Act.

Unlike the dialects of England, however, Scots was never reduced to a patois. A literary tradition was maintained, by people such as Burns; and in the nineteenth century Scots was used to record versions of ballads and folk-songs as they were found by assiduous Scottish collectors. In the twentieth century, attempts have been made by poets like Hugh MacDiarmid to promote Scots as the medium for a serious and tough-minded poetry that was international in character without losing its Scottishness, but which was unencumbered by the traditional associations of Burns. The maintenance or re-creation of a literary prose tradition has been more problematic, since continuity was interrupted in the sixteenth century. There are few models for serious, expository prose, and even in the novel, Scots has gone the way of English dialects in that writers have tended to use it in depictions of regional or lower-class dialogue only.

Outside imaginative literature, however, a Scots prose tradition was maintained in popular Scottish newspapers, particularly those of the north-east, where there is a strong loyalty to the local form of Scots. And in 1983 a Scots translation of the New Testament appeared, a work hailed as a monument of prose style and literary achievement, even as a turning-point in the fortunes of Scots. Since then there have been numerous experiments with written Scots within what has become a vigorous literary culture in Scotland.

The notion that Scots is at most a dialect of English has been communicated to most Scottish people. With no census returns to remind them of the number of speakers of Scots, and no classical texts to give them a sense of historicity-save, perhaps, the *New Testament*-many Scottish people, like some speakers of English-based creoles, may feel that their tongue is not different enough from English to justify calling it a separate language. In other words, it is linguistic criteria that are uppermost in their minds (as they are in the minds of most English people in their attitude to Scots): Scots sounds, grammar, and vocabulary are close to those of English in a way that those of Gaelic, say, are not. But purely linguistic criteria are not enough in settling demarcation disputes of this kind.

Speakers of Dutch dialects, say, on the border with Germany, may understand speakers of neighbouring German dialects better than they can the speakers of Dutch dialects on the other side of Holland; but the conventional wisdom is that people who live in Holland speak Dutch, and that

Germans speak German. To call Scots a dialect of English is to ignore its development during Scottish independence, and to reduce its status to that of the regional dialects of England, unless we use the term *dialect* in a more specialised sense, to refer to regional varieties with their own traditions of writing (as we speak of the dialects of English in medieval times). In sum, the terms *dialect* and *language* are not fine enough to apply unequivocally to Scots.

Opponents of the view that Scots and English are separate languages are likely to argue that many alleged Scots usages can be found in northern dialects of English. Boundaries between usages, for instance, do not by any means always run parallel with the border. Even if they do at present, it can be shown that certain usages alleged to be Scots, like *gaed* (went) and bellies being *sair* (sore) instead of aching, used to be heard either in Northumberland or Cumbria and have only recently been replaced by a less localised English form. Geographical patterns of usage are often complex: sometimes areas on each side of the border share a form unknown outside dialectal English, such as the Anglo-Saxon word *heck* (hay-rack), and occasionally the border divides forms that are also dialectal, like Scots *pook* (to pluck) beside northern English *ploat*. Relationships of this kind are typical of the border areas between dialects; but so they are between different though related languages.

Differences between Scots and English are often therefore not absolute, but may be expressed in terms of general tendencies and frequencies of items. But we can still point to some items that seem characteristic Scots usages. We find a different selection of loan-words north of the border, as in *gar* (make), *gowk* (cuckoo) from Scandinavian. Many Scots loans from French, such as *dote* (endow), *vivers* (victuals), *howtowdie* (young hen) are not found in England because they were adopted during the early sixteenth century, at a time of close political contact with France. Some Gaelic words, such as *tocher* (dowry) and *clarsach* (harp) are not well-known in England. Modal verbs are sometimes used differently: *will I push it?* instead of the usual English use of *shall.*

Other, more well-known features of Scots pronunciation we have already noted in our description of northern dialect sounds. The stereotypes *there's a moose loose aboot the hoose* and *it's a braw bricht moonlicht nicht the nicht* testify to the retention of the undiphthongised vowel in words like *house,* and of the fricative in *night.* Other pronunciations, such as the unrounded vowel in words like *hame* (home) are reflected in traditional Scots spellings. But within Scotland, many of these pronunciations are regarded as broad, and often stigmatised, just as other features (including words and grammatical patterns) are marked regionally, and stylistically. It is for this reason that the study of Scots in many Scottish universities has tended to promote the idea that it is a language separate from English, with its own history, its own dimensions of regional, social, and stylistic variation, and to some extent its own norms.

In pronunciation, therefore, it is helpful to distinguish between Scots, which itself exists in regional dialectal variety in different parts of Scotland, and which is characterised by those features, among others, listed earlier, and a so-called educated Scottish accent, which is much closer to RP. The latter is one of the most prestigious regional accents of English. Scots usages are most consistently found among working-class speakers. While a middle-class Scot may say *I'll not be going home*-a construction not uncommon in the north of England also-a farm worker might say *I'll no be gaun hame.* But in the big industrial cities, usage is changing, just as it is in England: and sometimes it may be described as moving away from a base in Scots.

Thus, while a recent recording of an Edinburgh schoolboy shows the retention of the traditional vowel in *house,* research in the same city shows that among the working class, especially young men, pronunciation of *r* is very different from the 'trilled' or 'tapped' variants stereotypical of Scots, and is so weakly articulated that the accent of this group has actually been described as *r*-less. Whatever linguistic changes are under way in Scotland, commitment to Scots has increased in recent years. In part this is a reflection of growing nationalism, seen in the electoral successes of the Scottish National Party (although that party has shown little interest in Scots, as distinct from Gaelic).

Language-loyalty has also been inspired by the example of the Welsh Language Society's vigorous campaign. Nationalism, however, tends to obscure divisions of class and ethnic group but those issues surface, in rather subtle ways, when commitment to a particular language is espoused. Many younger, middle-class Scots resent what they see as the Anglicisation of their culture, and their loyalty to Scots may be a belated assertion of ethnicity. They want to see themselves as Scots, not citizens of the United Kingdom; and within the last decade, there has been a widespread demand for political autonomy. But since it has in general been the lower class that has maintained the minority languages, commitment to those languages is also, in part, a commitment to the values of that class. Similar motivations, incidentally, may underlie attitudes to Welsh.

It has been persuasively argued that the group most loyal to that language is the heirs to the Welsh tradition of political radicalism that earlier in this century manifested itself in trade unionism and Labour Party politics. University- and college-educated sons and daughters of miners and steelworkers see their national identity as an emblem of class, and of the older, cooperative and collective values of the community. Feelings of language-loyalty must be taken into account in any consideration of the sociolinguistic profile of Scots today. Many Scottish people feel justifiably bitter at finding their linguistic inheritance relegated to a paragraph or two in histories of English, and dismissed as just another dialect of English.

The current status of Scots may accordingly be defined in two different ways. If we accept the view that English is an international language, the property of no single nation, then we can view Scots as the first *national* variety of English outside England, just as American English is a later one. This view respects national sensitivities, and also the linguistic similarities between all varieties of English. Alternatively, we can see Scots as a *deposed* language, which would have enjoyed the kind of relationship to English as, say, Portuguese to Spanish, if the dominant language had not been imposed in Scotland. Our choice between these alternatives may depend to a large extent on which side of the border we happen to live!

LANGUAGE IMPOSITION IN THE CELTIC TERRITORIES

We have mentioned the importance of the Tudors in the formulation of policy towards England's neighbours. It was they who took the first steps towards formal unification with other territories, and therefore towards the imposition of English as the official language throughout the British Isles. Religious uniformity was one instrument of hegemony, and this meant carrying the Reformation to the linguistic minorities. But supremacist attitudes towards minority languages could undermine the ideal of religious conversion: an effective way of achieving the latter was to make translations of the Prayer Book and Bible into the minority languages, and populate the Church in those lands with priests who could preach in them.

Ironically enough, the survival of Scottish Gaelic and Welsh may have depended, to a large extent, on this 'historic blunder': those languages gained prestige by remaining the parlance of the Church. The ambitions of the Tudors, and in particular of subsequent governments, may be compared in this respect with those of the other centralising European monarchies, particularly France and Spain. It is noteworthy that nations where power is devolved on a federal basis generally have a more tolerant attitude to linguistic minorities, as in Switzerland. But in France, the Celtic-speaking Bretons have been subjected to centuries of oppression; and in Spain, the Catalans in the east of the country suffered under the dominant Castilians until power was devolved to the regions following democratisation in the late 1970s.

Wherever we find this linguistic imperialism, we find a similar ideology expressed by the dominant power: bi- or multi-lingualism is incompatible with a unified 'nation' and a free people, therefore the minority languages are associated with 'the enemy'-either secular, or religious; therefore to use them is to identify with the opponents of the State.

Spuriously benign arguments are often advanced to justify the process of suppression. Gaelic in Scotland, after all, was in the eighteenth century the language of 'savages'; English was therefore a civilising force. And in nineteenth-century Wales, it was even suggested that the use of Welsh was a *cause* of poverty: if people would only learn the right language, they could better themselves.

A number of techniques, of varying degrees of subtlety, were used by the English to impose their language. The various Celtic communities have therefore felt different effects at different times. The Cornish were an early casualty of Tudor centralisation: their language ceased to function as a community medium by the end of the eighteenth century. In Wales Anglicisation was begun in the sixteenth century by weaning the sons of noblemen away from their subjects by educating them in England. This removed the source of patronage for vernacular poetry and song, which subsequently became a culture of the lower class. Furthermore, the introduction of English as the language of government and law broke local traditions of prose.

By the early seventeenth century, a similar process of weaning had begun among the Gaels of the Scottish

Highlands; and by then, the Irish chieftains had been defeated. This broke the cultural and linguistic links between Gaelic speakers in Scotland and Ireland, just as contacts between speakers of Welsh, Cornish, and Breton had already been destroyed. In the case of the Scottish Highlands, however, the full force of linguistic oppression was not felt until after the middle of the eighteenth century.

In Ireland, the picture is complicated by religious division. The Tudors encountered great difficulties in extending the Reformation to Ireland, and the Irish chieftains proved resilient in defence of their lands. Since England was at war with Catholic Spain, it could not afford to have an unreformed Church on its doorstep. Treatment of Ireland and the Irish, therefore, was characterised by brutality and paranoia. Ireland became England's first colony, its ancient local culture overlaid by a Protestant English-speaking one. Settlers from England and Scotland were planted on land confiscated from the Irish, and merchant companies in London were given a free hand to plunder its resources.

Like Wales, Ireland had been colonised by small numbers of English-speakers during the twelfth century; but unlike Wales, Ireland was to endure a further, much more significant plantation under the Tudors and Stuarts. Irish Gaelic has therefore had eight centuries of contact with English of one kind or another; yet alone of the Celtic languages, it has become the official language of an independent nation-state. We shall accordingly be treating Ireland in more detail than the other Celtic communities. Throughout the Celtic British Isles, the education system was a powerful agent in the imposition of English. One result of the processes discussed above was that standardisation in any Celtic language had been difficult to maintain, and the breaking of links among Celtic peoples had undermined the sense of historicity that plays such an important part in forming people's attitudes to their own language.

Even if opportunities had been given, the use of the Celtic languages even as media of instruction would have been accompanied by great problems. But the education system overwhelmingly favoured English. Even before the Education Acts of the 1870s, schools in Ireland had been used to promote English, although Wales had maintained traditions of Welsh teaching in the Circulating Schools of the eighteenth century. But after the introduction of compulsory schooling in the last quarter of the nineteenth century, teachers punished children if they spoke their first language, and denied them opportunities of reading and writing in them. Older, first-language speakers of Welsh, for instance, today often cannot write a letter in their own language.

Not only was education often punitive from a linguistic point of view, it was also Anglocentric, in that children learned about the history and culture, not of their own societies, but of the English and their empire, in the English language. The role of the education system was summed up very well in the nineteenth century by the MP who said: 'a band of efficient schoolmasters is kept up at much less expense than a body of police or soldiery'. The survival of the Celtic languages was also threatened by economic factors. In general, the Celtic communities are situated well away from the centres of technological development: for this reason they are often insultingly referred to as the Celtic fringe.

They have tended to be over-dependent on a small number of traditional industries, such as farming, crofting, and fishing, and therefore offer limited opportunities for employment today. In the past, the local economy in two areas has been especially vulnerable to upheavals which have had profound and lasting effects on demographic structure. In the Scottish Highlands, massive depopulation followed the unsuccessful Rising of 1745. By the early nineteenth century, the Highland lairds had been so successfully weaned away from their subjects that they preferred the profits from sheep, and later, deer, to the overseeing of the local communities.

Gaelic speakers were evicted in their thousands, many emigrating to the industrialised cities of southern Scotland and also to Canada (where today, in places like Cape Breton Island, Gaelic is still spoken). Land once cultivated yielded to the wilderness.

In Ireland, the potato famines of the 1840s hit hardest the Gaelic speakers of the west: death or emigration reduced Ireland's population by one-quarter. Such population movements have tended to unbalance many communities with regard to sex and age: it was often the young, able-bodied men who were lost to the large towns. And where urbanisation has occurred, such as in south Wales, the Celtic tongues have failed to compete as first languages with English, the language of commerce, and of the employing class. The psychological effects of centuries of cultural and linguistic imperialism on speakers of the minority languages have been severe. The processes of government and law, enshrined in an alien language, have often been disorientating, if not totally mystifying, to the community.

A sense of powerlessness undermined the feeling of local identity. This has often been exacerbated by the education system, where success at first was equated with proficiency in English, and later with working far away; discouraged and demoralised, those who remained in the local community often awaited and expected initiative and leadership from 'incomers'. At the more personal level, many speakers of each minority tongue were often made to feel ashamed of their first language. Linguistically insecure, and therefore nervous, if not sullenly defiant in their use of English, children in the schools of Scotland and Wales were often judged 'inarticulate', like their Black counterparts in the USA. It is not surprising that there has been a substantial language shift towards English in the Celtic areas over the last century and a half. Indeed, some pessimistic observers have predicted extinction for some Celtic languages by the end of the next century.

The census returns to some extent speak for themselves. First-language speakers of Scottish Gaelic amounted to about 5 per cent of Scotland's population ninety years ago; today, it is only about one-third of that figure. In Ireland, native speakers of Gaelic were estimated at about 23 per cent in 1851; forty years on, the figure was 14 per cent. Welsh proved more durable: the period of language shift is the present century. But in 1900 perhaps half of the population of Wales could speak Welsh; since 1971 the figure has stabilised at around one-fifth. And in the course of the present century, Manx has been abandoned as a first language altogether. Yet in some important respects, these figures do not speak for themselves.

How do they relate to different social functions, differences of age and sex, and of town and country? Can people read and write in the minority languages? Data on these issues is often lacking for the past. Today, however, we know that the figures quoted for Scottish Gaelic need to be balanced against the fact that in Harris, in the Outer Isles, over 75 per cent of the population can speak the minority language. We need to know about the users of these languages, since the symbolic value of a language derives in part from its association with certain social groups and contexts. Such knowledge can also help explain how languages are maintained and promoted and how, why, and where English is learned. The census figures also obscure another important fact. At first, native speakers of Celtic languages would have learned English as a second language.

Such bilingualism would be diglossic, with English as the High language. Since the end of the nineteenth century, however, nationalist campaigns have been mounted in Ireland, the Scottish Highlands, and later Wales to arrest the decline of the Celtic languages by teaching them as second languages. In the course of the present century, therefore, English has become the first language of increasing numbers of people in Celtic areas, while it is the Celtic tongues that have been learned as second languages. So knowledge of Scottish Gaelic has risen; and in the Republic of Ireland, Gaelic is generally taught in school. But there, first-language speakers are outnumbered by ten to one; and as we shall see, the second-language speakers of all the Celtic tongues tend to be different kinds of people from those who maintain Celtic as first languages in the more remote, less fertile areas. A minority language can be maintained as the first language of the local community if there is little incentive to replace it with the dominant one.

In the Outer Hebrides, and parts of the west of Ireland, isolated communities that are dependent on traditional industries, such as crofting, have maintained Gaelic as a community language. While emigration from these areas has been constant, it has still been possible for a small number of people to continue living much as their ancestors did. But since job opportunities for young people remain scarce in such a limited economy, the pull of English has been strong. In such an environment Gaelic has been maintained among the crofting class despite the absence of overt expressions of language-loyalty on the part of its speakers. All the same, Gaelic is seen by them as a symbol of group identity, even if it is rarely articulated in these terms. The language binds the community together in defiance of the values associated with the wider, urban, commercial world where English is spoken. While the towns and cities have generally been the bastions of the English language, they have also been the only refuge for people unable to find subsistence in the countryside.

In what often seem inhospitable and alien surroundings, immigrants from the Celtic-speaking areas have sometimes retained and subsequently promoted the minority language, as a symbol of their identity and their past. It has been said that Glasgow-which in 1971 for instance had 12,000 Gaelic speakers-is the place to hear Gaelic spoken in Scotland, and in Ireland, Belfast. Thus, it is among such emigrés that the potential for feelings of language-loyalty, of expressions of commitment to the minority language, have normally developed. It is in the towns and cities too, that people have been stimulated to learn minority tongues as second or additional languages. This trend is most noticeable among younger people, often from middle-class backgrounds.

The most vociferous expressions of language-loyalty have perhaps been those of the Welsh Language Society; but such activism has also spread to Scotland in more recent years. The campaign on behalf of Gaelic has intensified, and as we have seen, Scots has also been involved. The intellectual origins of such campaigns are complex, but stem in part from the notion that language is the crucial symbol of nationality. From the end of the eighteenth century, but especially after the 1840s, struggles for independence in Europe and beyond have often been inspired, or justified, by the fact that a particular group speaks a language different from that of a dominant or conquering power.

It is unlikely, however, that this language-loyalty was ever much in evidence amongst the first-language speakers of the Celtic tongues during the nineteenth century, such as the Irish peasantry of the west or the working class in newly-industrialised South Wales. Amongst these, language attitudes were probably much more instrumentalist, a matter of *choosing* English for its usefulness, and of gradually abandoning the Celtic languages which for them lacked a positive symbolic value. The long-term survival of the minority languages will depend on more than just the declarations of language-loyalty among college-educated activists. Such attitudes are not uncommon when a language is under threat, even among monolingual speakers of English.

Neither are these languages likely to survive if their only speakers are situated on the depopulated, infertile peripheries. The decisive factor may be their ability to function as community languages in the towns and cities, where most people live and work. Also important may be the presence of a communal hostility to central authority, especially if the latter is clearly associated with the English language. And at the very least, sustained and active support in a number of official institutions may be necessary. Experience has shown that it is one thing to pass laws to promote a minority language, and quite another to implement them.

An issue facing minority languages everywhere is that of standardisation. If, say, Gaelic is to be learned in Highland schools, which variety is to be taught? In general, there are no varieties which approach that of a spoken standard, and when particular *written* varieties are promoted as standards learners have to face the problem of too narrow and too archaic a range of texts. In particular, minority languages must be cultivated as media for serious and functional prose. Language activists maintain, however, that none of these problems are insuperable. They were overcome in Belgium, Switzerland, Finland, and many other European nations.

Chapter 6

English Present and Future

THE ENGLISH LANGUAGE A CULTURAL SUBJECT

It was observed by that remarkable twelfth-century chronicler, Henry of Huntington, that an interest in his past was one of the distinguishing characteristics of man as compared with the other animals. And in these days when the cultivated man or woman is conscious of deficiencies in his education without some knowledge of economics, medieval history, recent advances in the basic natural sciences, so also he may discover a desire to know something of the nature and development of his mother tongue.

The medium by which he communicates his thought and feelings to his fellow men, the tool with which he conducts his business or the government of millions of people, the vehicle by which have been transmitted to him the science, the philosophy, the poetry of the race is surely worthy of study. It is not to be expected that every one should be a philologist or should master the technicalities of linguistic science.

But it is reasonable to assume that the liberally educated man should know something of the structure of his language, its position in the world and its relation to other tongues, the wealth of its vocabulary together with the sources from which that vocabulary has been and is being enriched, and in general the great political, social, and cultural influences which have combined to make his language what it is.

The purpose, then, of the present book is to treat the history of the English language not alone as of interest to the special student but as a cultural subject within the view of all educated people, while including enough references to technical matters to make clear the scientific principles involved in linguistic evolution.

INFLUENCES AT WORK ON LANGUAGE

The English language of today reflects many centuries of development. The political and social events that have in the course of English history so profoundly affected the English people in their national life have generally had a recognizable effect on their language. The Christianizing of Britain in 597 brought England into contact with Latin civilization and made significant additions to our vocabulary. The Scandinavian invasions resulted in a considerable mixture of the two races and their languages.

The Norman Conquest made English for two centuries the language mainly of the lower classes, while the nobles and those associated with them used French on almost all occasions. And when English once more regained supremacy as the language of all elements of the population it was an English greatly changed in both form and vocabulary from what it had been in 1066.

In a similar way the Hundred Years' War, the rise of an important middle class, the Renaissance, the development of England as a maritime power, the expansion of the British Empire, and the growth of commerce and industry, of science and literature, have, each in its way, contributed to make the English language what it is today. In a word, the English language reflects in its entire development the political, social, and cultural history of the English people.

Growth and Decay

Moreover, English, like all other languages, is subject to that constant growth and decay which characterizes all forms of life. It is a convenient figure of speech to speak of languages as living and as dead. While we cannot think of language as something that possesses life apart from the people who speak it, as we can think of plants or of animals, we can observe in speech something like the process of change that characterizes the life of living things. When a language ceases to change, we call it a dead language. Classical Latin is a dead language because it has not changed for nearly two thousand years.

The change that is constantly going on in a living language can be most easily seen in the vocabulary. Old words die out, new words are added, and existing words change their meaning. Much of the vocabulary of Old English has been lost, and the development of new words to meet new conditions is one of the most familiar phenomena of our language. Change of meaning can be illustrated from any page of Shakespeare. Nice in Shakespeare's day meant foolish; rheumatism signified a cold in the head. Less familiar but no less real is the change of pronunciation.

A slow but steady alteration, especially in the vowel. sounds, has characterized English throughout its history. Old English stan has become our stone; cu has become cow. Most of these changes are so regular as to be capable of classification under what are called 'sound laws. Changes likewise occur in the grammatical forms of a language. These may be the result of gradual phonetic modification, or they may result from the desire for uniformity commonly felt where similarity of function or use is involved.

The man who says I knowed is only trying to form the past tense of this verb in the same way that he forms the past tense of so many verbs in English. This process is known as the operation of analogy, and it may affect the sound and meaning as well as the form of words. Thus it will be part of our task to trace the influences that are constantly at work tending to alter a language from age to age as spoken and written, and that have brought about such an extensive alteration in English as to make the language of 900 quite unintelligible to the people of 1900.

The Importance of a Language

So intimate is the relation between a language and the people who speak it that the two can scarcely be thought of apart. A language lives only so long as there are people who speak it and use it as their native tongue, and its greatness is only that given to it by these people. A language is important because the people who speak it are important – politically, economically, commercially, socially, culturally.

English, French, and German are great and important languages because they are the languages of great and important peoples; for this reason they are widely studied outside the country of their use. But Roumanian and Serbian and Malay are seldom learned by any save the native populations. Sometimes the cultural importance of a race or nation has at some former time been so great that their language remains important among cultivated people long after it has ceased to represent political, commercial, or other greatness.

Greek, for example, is studied in its classical form because of the great civilization which its literature preserves the most complete record of; but in its modern form as spoken in Greece today the Greek language is wholly neglected by the outside world. The importance of the English language is naturally very great. English is the language not only of England but of the extensive dominions and colonies associated in the British Empire, and it is the language of the United States. Spoken by over 260 million people, it is in the number who speak it the largest of the occidental languages.

English-speaking people constitute about one tenth of the world's population. English, however, is not the largest language in the world. The more conservative estimates of the population of China would indicate that Chinese is spoken by about 450 million people. But the numerical ascendancy of English among European languages can be seen by a few comparative figures. Russian, next in size to English, is spoken by about 140 million people; Spanish by

135 millions; German by 90 millions; Portuguese by 63 millions; French by 60 millions; Italian by 50 millions.

Thus at the present time English has the advantage in numbers over all other western languages. But the importance of a language is not alone a matter of numbers or territory; as we have said, it depends also on the importance of the people who speak it.

The importance of a language is inevitably associated in the mind of the world with the political role played by the nations using it and their influence in international affairs; with the confidence people feel in their financial position and the certainty with which they will meet their obligations — i.e., pay their debts to other nations, meet the interest on their bonds, maintain the gold or other basis of their currency, control their expenditures; with the extent of their business enterprise and the international scope of their commerce; with the conditions of life under which the great mass of their people live; and with the part played by them in art and literature and music, in science and invention, in exploration and discovery — in short, with their contribution to the material and spiritual progress of the world.

English is the mother tongue of nations whose combined political influence, economic soundness, commercial activity, social well-being, and scientific and cultural contributions to civilization give impressive support to its numerical precedence.

The Future of the English Language

The extent and importance of the English language today are such as to make it reasonable to ask whether we cannot attempt an intelligent speculation as to the probable position which it will occupy in the future. It is admittedly hazardous to predict the future of nations; there are individuals who doubt even the permanence of our present civilization. But, assuming that a people's past is to some extent an index of its future, at least over a moderate period of time, and that the future development of Europe (and its colonial extensions) will continue more or less along the lines which that development has pursued in recent centuries, some speculation seems justifiable at least concerning the growth and possible spread of the European languages.

Growth in language is primarily a matter of population. Consequently the most important question affecting the future size of a language is, how much undeveloped territory does it have in which to expand? A second and almost equally important consideration is the climate and fertility of that territory. Civilization today thrives best in the temperate zones. It would obviously be of little value to a language to possess vast territory at the North Pole.

What then is the territorial position of the principal European languages? Of the seven languages mentioned above, English, Russian, and Spanish possess the largest areas. As a result of the colonial expansion of England in the seventeenth and eighteenth centuries, the English-speaking nations today control about a quarter of the earth's surface, while Russian controls a sixth and Spanish a ninth. French in the colonial possessions of France and Belgium, and Portuguese as the language of Brazil, have opportunities, though more limited, for growth.

On the other hand, any growth in German or Italian will apparently now be confined chiefly to the areas in which these languages are spoken in Europe. It would seem then that, numerically speaking, the three great languages of the future should be English, Russian, and Spanish. Among the English-speaking territories, those offering the greatest opportunity for growth of population are the United States and Canada, Australia, New Zealand, and South Africa.

The political changes in India and Egypt since World War II are not favorable to the expansion of English in these areas. Russia is capable of great increase in population, and at the present time the Slavic race shows a fairly rapid rate of growth. On the other hand, a considerable part of Russian territory in Asia is in or near the Arctic zone, obviously an unfavorable factor.

The opportunities for growth which Spanish has centre in Spanish America, and not a little of this territory is in the tropics. All in all, we may conclude that the English language is best provided with the facilities for expansion. Such expansion will come partly from the natural growth of the present population, partly from immigration. Between 1901 and 1910 over thirteen million people emigrated from Europe.

While the world wars have brought about important changes in this movement of people, both in the countries from. which and the areas to which population is flowing, humanity still seeks and will probably continue to seek the opportunities and advantages offered by those districts in which a favorable soil and climate, abundance of natural resources, and populations of lesser density prevail.

English, Russian, and Spanish are, in varying degrees, in a position to benefit by this transfer. On the basis of territorial control it is probable that at no very distant time the English language will be spoken by a fifth, perhaps even a quarter, of the population of the world. The probable extension of English in the future, thus indicated, leads many people to wonder whether English will some day become the language of the entire world, or at least its civilized portions.

In many cases the wish is father to the thought, and the wish springs partly from considerations of national pride, partly from a consciousness of the many disadvantages that result from a multiplicity of tongues. How much pleasanter travel would be if we did not have to contend with the inconveniences of a foreign language. How much more readily we could conduct our business abroad if there were but a single language of trade.

How greatly would the problem of the scientist and the scholar be simplified if there were one universal language of learning. And how many of the misunderstandings and prejudices that divide nations would be avoided, how much the peace of the world would be promoted if there were free interchange of national thought and feeling – if only we could make effective the French proverb, Tout comprendre, c'est tout pardonner.

That the world is fully alive to the need for an international language is evident from the number of attempts that have been made to supply that need artificially. Between 1880 and 1907 fifty-three universal languages were proposed. Some of these enjoyed an amazing, if temporary, vogue. In 1889 Volapuk claimed nearly a million adherents. Today it is all but forgotten. A few years later Esperanto experienced a similar vogue, but interest in it now is kept alive largely by local groups and organizations.

Apparently the need has not been filled by any of the laboratory products so far created to fill it. And it is doubtful if it ever can be filled in this way. An artificial language might serve sufficiently the needs of business and travel, but no one has proved willing to make it the medium of political, historical, or scientific thought, to say nothing of the impossibility of making it serve the purposes of pure literature, involving sustained emotion and creative imagination.

It would seem as though the hope of the world for intellectual community lay in the eventual employment of one or a few widely known languages whose importance is universally recognized. Less than a century ago French would have appeared to have attained an undisputed claim to such employment. It was then widely cultivated throughout Europe as the language of polite society, it was the diplomatic language of the world, and it enjoyed considerable popularity in literary and scientific circles.

During the nineteenth century its prestige, though still great, gradually declined. The prominence of Germany in all fields of scientific and scholarly activity made German a serious competitor. And the rapid expansion of English and its growing influence in political and commercial affairs have raised a second great competitor. Today it would seem as though English were in the ascendant. Its pre-eminence in commercial use is undoubted.

Its employment for purposes of science and research has increased notably of late, especially in Scandinavian countries and among the smaller nationalities of Europe. Its influence is dominant in the East; cultivated Chinese and Japanese have adopted it as a second language. It is nowhere a question of substituting English for the native speech. Nothing is a matter of greater patriotic feeling than the mother tongue. The question simply concerns the use of English, or some other widely known idiom, for international communication.

And as John Galsworthy remarked, "any impartial scrutiny made at this moment of time must place English at the head of all languages as the most likely to become, in a natural, unforced way, the single intercommunicating tongue." Since English seems likely to occupy an increasingly prominent place in international communication, it is worth pausing to inquire into its qualifications for so important a mission. We may assume without argument that it shares with the other highly developed languages of Europe the ability to express the multiplicity of ideas and the refinements of thought that demand expression in our modern civilization. The question is rather one of simplicity.

How readily can it be learned by the foreigner? Does it possess characteristics of vocabulary and grammar that render it easy or difficult of acquirement? To attain a completely objective view of one's own language is no simple matter. It is so easy to assume that what we have in infancy acquired without sensible difficulty will seem equally simple to those attempting to learn it in maturity. What virtues can we honestly attribute to English and what shortcomings must we recognize as handicaps to be acknowledged and, where possible, overcome?

Cosmopolitan Vocabulary

Prominent among the assets of the English language must be considered the mixed character of its vocabulary. English is classified as a Teutonic language. That is to say, it belongs to the group of languages to which German, Dutch, Flemish, Danish, Swedish, and Norwegian also belong. It shares with these languages similar grammatical structure and many common words. On the other hand, more than half of its vocabulary is derived from Latin. Some of these borrowings have been direct, a great many through French, some through the other Romance languages.

As a result, English also shares a great number of words with those languages of Europe which are derived from Latin, notably French, Italian, Spanish, and Portuguese. All of this means that English presents a somewhat familiar appearance to any one who speaks either a Germanic or a Romance language. There are parts of the language which he feels he does not have to learn, or learns with little effort.

To a lesser extent the English vocabulary contains borrowings from many other languages. Instead of making new words chiefly by the combination of existing elements, as German does, English has shown a marked tendency to go outside her own linguistic resources and borrow from other languages.

In the course of centuries of this practice English has built up an unusual capacity for assimilating outside elements. We do not feel that there is anything 'foreign' about the words chipmunk, hominy, moose, raccoon, skunk, all of which we have borrowed from the American Indian. We are not conscious that the words *brandy, cruller, golf, duck* (light canvas), *isinglass, measles, selvage, wagon, uproar* are from Dutch. And so with many other words in daily use.

From Italian come balcony, canto, duet, granite, opera, piano, umbrella, volcano; from Spanish alligator, cargo, contraband, cork, hammock, mosquito, sherry, stampede, tornado, vanilla; from Greek, directly or indirectly, acme, acrobat, anthology, barometer, catarrh, catastrophe, chronology, elastic, magic, tactics, tantalize, and a host of others; from Russian steppe, drosky, vodka, ruble; from Persian caravan, dervish, divan, khaki, mogul, shawl, sherbet, and ultimately from Persian jasmine, paradise, check, chess, lemon, lilac, turban, borax, and possibly spinach.

A few minutes spent in the examination of any good etymological dictionary will show that English has borrowed from Hebrew and Arabic, Hungarian, Hindustani, Bengali, Malay, Chinese, the languages of Java, Australia, Tahiti, Polynesia, West Africa, and from one of the aboriginal languages of Brazil. And it has assimilated these heterogeneous elements so successfully that only the professional student of language is aware of their origin.

Even a commercial coinage like Kodak has probably lost its exotic look for most people. So cosmopolitan a vocabulary is an undoubted asset to any language that seeks to attain international use. A second asset which English possesses to a pre-eminent degree is inflectional simplicity. The evolution of language, at least within the historical period, is a story of progressive simplification. The farther back we go in the study of the languages to which English is most closely allied, the more complex we find them.

Sanskrit, Greek, and Latin, for example, as classical languages of early date, have inflections of the noun, the adjective, the verb, and to some extent the pronoun that are no longer found in Russian or French or German. In this process of simplification English has gone further than any other language in Europe. Inflections in the noun as spoken have been reduced to a sign of the plural and a form for the possessive case. The elaborate Teutonic inflection of the adjective has been completely eliminated except for the simple indication of the com parative and the superlative degrees.

The verb has been simplified by the loss of practically all the personal endings, the almost complete abandonment of any distinction between the singular and the plural, and the gradual discard of the subjunctive mood. The complicated agreements that make German difficult for the foreigner are absent from English. However compensated for, such a reduction of inflections can hardly be considered anything but an advantage. In the third place, English enjoys an exceptional advantage over all other major European languages in having adopted natural in place of grammatical gender.

In studying other European languages the student labors under the heavy burden of memorizing, along with the meaning of every noun, its gender. In the Romance languages, for example, there are only two genders, and all nouns which would be neuter in English are there either masculine or feminine. Some help in these languages is afforded by distinctive endings which at times characterize the two classes. But even this aid is lacking in the Germanic languages, where the distribution of the three genders appears to the English student to be quite arbitrary.

Thus in German Sonne (sun) is feminine, Mond (moon) is masculine, but Kind (child), Mädchen (maiden), and Weib (wife) are neuter. The distinction must be constantly kept in mind, since it affects not only the reference of pronouns but determines the form of inflection and the agreement of adjectives. In the English language all this was stripped away during the Middle English period, and today the gender of every noun in the dictionary is known instantly. Gender in English is determined by meaning.

All nouns naming living creatures are masculine or feminine according to the sex of the individual, and all other nouns are neuter. Attributive gender, as when we speak of a ship as feminine, sun and moon as masculine or feminine, is personification and a matter of rhetoric, not grammar. The three features just described are undoubtedly of great advantage in facilitating the acquisition of English by foreigners. On the other hand, it is equally important to recognize the difficulties which the foreign student encounters in learning our language.

One of these difficulties is the result of that very simplification of inflections which we have considered among the assets of English. It is the difficulty, of which foreigners often complain, of expressing themselves not only logically but idiomatically. An idiom is a form of expression peculiar to one language, and English is not alone in possessing such individual forms of expression. All languages have their special ways of saying things.

Thus a German says was *fur ein Mann* (what for a man) where in English we say what kind of man; the French say *il fait froid* (it makes cold) where we say it is cold. The French visitor who had learned the English idiom to press a person to do something was making a natural mistake when he said *Can we not squeeze the young lady to sing*? His substitution was in a way logical but not idiomatic. Now languages with a minimum of inflection are very likely to depend more than others on stereotyped expressions or idioms.

Their mastery depends largely on memory. The distinction between My husband isn't up yet and My husband isn't down yet, or the quite contradictory use of the word fast in go fast and stand fast seems to the foreigner to be without reasonable justification. It is doubtful whether such idiomatic expressions are so much commoner in English than in other languages — for example, French — as those learning our language believe, but they undoubtedly bulk large in the mind of foreigners.

A more serious criticism of English by those attempting to master it is the chaotic character of our spelling and the frequent lack of correlation between spelling and pronunciation. Writing is merely a mechanical means of recording speech. And theoretically the most adequate system of spelling is that which best combines simplicity with consistency.

In alphabetic writing an ideal system would be one in which the same sound was regularly represented by the same character and a given character always represented the same sound. None of the European languages fully attains this high ideal, although many of them, such as Itahan or German, come far nearer to it than English.

In English the vowel sound in be*lieve*, re*ceive*, *leave*, ma*chine*, *be*, *see* is in each case represented by a different spelling. Conversely the symbol *a* in *father*, *hate*, *hat*, and many other words has nearly a score of values. The situation is even more confusing in our treatment of the consonants. We have fourteen spellings for the sound of *sh*: *shoe*, *sugar*, *issue*, *mansion*, *mission*, *nation*, *suspicion*, *ocean*, *nauseous*, *conscious*, *chaperon*, *schist*, *fuchsia*, *pshaw*. And although the *s* and *ss* of *mansion* and *mission* are really the same as in *sugar* and *issue*, there remain a full dozen completely different spellings to testify to our lack of uniformity.

This is an extreme case, but there are many others only less disturbing, and it serves to show how far we are at times from approaching the ideal of simplicity and consistency. We shall consider in another place the causes that have brought about this diversity. We are concerned here only with the fact that one cannot tell how to spell an English word by its pronunciation or how to pronounce it by its spelling.

The English speaking child undoubtedly wastes much valuable time during the early years of his education in learning to spell his own language, and to the foreigner our spelling is appallingly difficult. To be sure, it is not without its defenders. There are those who lay stress on the useful way in which the spelling of an English word often indicates its etymology.

Again, a distinguished French scholar has urged that since we have preserved in thousands of borrowed words the spelling which those words have in their original language, the foreigner is thereby enabled more easily to recognize the word. And it has been further suggested that the very looseness of our orthography makes less noticeable in the written language the dialectal differences that would be revealed if the various parts of the English-speaking world attempted a more phonetic notation on the basis of their local pronunciation.

But in spite of these considerations, each of which is open to serious criticism, it seems as though some improvement might be effected without sacrificing completely the advantages claimed. That such improvement has often been felt to be desirable is evident from the number of occasions on which attempts at reform have been made.

In the early part of the present century a movement was launched, later supported by Theodore Roosevelt and other influential men, to bring about a moderate degree of simplification. It was suggested that since we wrote *has* and *had* we could just as well write *hav* instead of *have*, and in the same way *ar* and *wer* since we wrote *is* and *was*.

But though logically sound, these spellings seemed strange to the eye, and the advantage to be gained from the proposed simplifications was not sufficient to overcome human conservatism or indifference or force of habit. It remains to be seen whether the extension of English in the future will some day compel us to consider the reform of our spelling from an impersonal and, indeed, international, point of view. For the present, at least, we do not seem to be ready for simplified spelling.

CHANGES THROUGH PHONETIC

The English phonetic laws involved in the rise of the words *foot, feet, mouse* and *mice* from their early West-Germanic prototypes *fot, foti, mus, musi* may be briefly summarized as follows:

In *foti* "feet" the long *o* was colored by the following *i* to long *ö*, that is, *o* kept its lip-rounded quality and its middle height of tongue position but anticipated the front tongue position of the *i*; *ö* is the resulting compromise. This assimilatory change was regular, i.e., every accented long *o* followed by an *i* in the following syllable automatically developed to long *ö*; hence *tothi* "teeth" became *töthi, fodian* "to feed" became *födian*. At first there is no doubt the alternation between *o* and *ö* was not felt as intrinsically significant. It could only have been an unconscious mechanical adjustment such as may be observed in the speech of many to-day who modify the *"oo"* sound of words like *you* and *few* in the direction of German *ü* without, however, actually departing far enough from the "oo" vowel to prevent their acceptance of *who* and *you* as satisfactory rhyming words. Later on the quality of the *ö* vowel must have departed widely enough from that of *o* to enable *ö* to rise in consciousness as a neatly distinct vowel. As soon as this happened, the expression of plurality in *föti, töthi,* and analogous words became symbolic and fusional, not merely fusional.

In *musi* "mice" the long *u* was colored by the following *i* to long *ü*. This change also was regular; *lusi* "lice" became *lüsi, kui* "cows" became *küi* (later simplified to *kü;* still preserved as *ki-* in *kine), fulian* "to make foul" became *fülian* (still preserved as *-file* in *defile*).

The old drift toward reducing final syllables, a rhythmic consequence of the strong Germanic stress on the first syllable, now manifested itself. The final *-i,* originally an important functional element, had long lost a great share of its value, transferred as that was to the symbolic vowel change (*o: ö*). It had little power of resistance, therefore, to the drift. It became dulled to a colorless *-e; föti* became *föte.*

The weak *-e* finally disappeared. Probably the forms *föte* and *föt* long coexisted as prosodic variants according to the rhythmic requirements of the sentence, very much as *Füsse* and *Füss'* now coexist in German.

The *ö* of *föt* became "unrounded" to long *e* (our present *a* of *fade*). The alternation of *fot: foti,* transitionally *fot: föti, föte, föt,* now appears as *fot: fet.* Analogously, *töth* appears as *teth, födian* as *fedian,* later *fedan.* The new long *e*-vowel "fell together" with the older *e-* vowel already existent (e.g., *her* "here," *he* "he"). Henceforward the two are merged and their later history is in common. Thus our present *he* has the same vowel as *feet, teeth,* and *feed.* In other words, the old sound pattern *o, e,* after an interim of *o, ö, e,* reappeared as *o, e,* except that now the *e* had greater "weight" than before.

Fot: fet, mus: müs (written *mys*) are the typical forms of Anglo-Saxon literature. At the very end of the Anglo-Saxon period, say about 1050 to 1100 A.D., the *ü*, whether long or short, became unrounded to *i*. *Mys* was then pronounced *mis* with long *i* (rhyming with present *niece*). The change is analogous but takes place several centuries later.

In Chaucer's day (circa 1350–1400 A.D.) the forms were still *fot: fet* (written *foot, feet*) and *mus: mis* (written very variably, but *mous, myse* are typical). About 1500 all the long *i*-vowels, whether original (as in *write, ride, wine*) or unrounded from Anglo-Saxon *ü* (as in *hide, bride, mice, defile*), became diphthongized to *ei* (i.e., *e* of *met* + short *i*). Shakespeare pronounced *mice* as *meis* (almost the same as the present Cockney pronunciation of *mace*).

About the same time the long *u*- vowels were diphthongized to *ou* (i.e., *o* of present Scotch *not* + *u* of *full*). The Chaucerian *mus: mis* now appears as the Shakespearean *mous: meis*. This change may have manifested itself; all English dialects have diphthongized old Germanic long *i*. but the long undiphthongized *u* is still preserved in Lowland Scotch, in which *house* and *mouse* rhyme with our *loose*.

Some time before 1550 the long *e* of *fet* (written *feet*) took the position that had been vacated by the old long *i*, now diphthongized, i.e., *e* took the higher tongue position of *i*. Our (and Shakespeare's) "long *e*" is, then, phonetically the same as the old long *i*. *Feet* now rhymed with the old *write* and the present *beat*.

About the same time the long *o* of *fot* (written *foot*) took the position that had been vacated by the old long *u*, now diphthongized, i.e., *o* took the higher tongue position of *u*. Our (and Shakespeare's) "long *oo*" is phonetically the same as the old long *u*. *Foot* now rhymed with the old *out* and the present *boot*. Shakespeare pronounced *meis, mous, fit, fut*, of which *meis* and *mous* would affect our ears as a rather "mincing" rendering of our present *mice* and *mouse*, *fit* would sound practically identical with (but probably a bit more "drawled" than) our present *feet,* while *foot,* rhyming with *boot,* would now be set down as "broad Scotch."

Gradually the first vowel of the diphthong in *mice* was retracted and lowered in position. The resulting diphthong now varies in different English dialects, but *ai* (i.e., *a* of *father,* but shorter, + short *i*) may be taken as a fairly accurate rendering of its average quality. What we now call the "long *i*" (of words like *ride, bite, mice*) is, of course, an *ai*-diphthong. *Mice* is now pronounced *mais.*

The first vowel of the diphthong in *mouse* was unrounded and lowered in position. The resulting diphthong may be phonetically rendered *au,* though it too varies considerably according to dialect. *Mouse,* then, is now pronounced *maus.*

The vowel of *foot* became "open" in quality and shorter in quantity, i.e., it fell together with the old short *u*-vowel of words like *full, wolf, wool.*

This change has taken place in a number of words with an originally long *u* (Chaucerian long close *o*), such as *forsook, hook, book, look, rook, shook,* all of which formerly had the vowel of *boot.* The older vowel, however, is still preserved in most words of this class, such as *fool, moon, spool, stoop.* It is highly significant of the nature of the slow spread of a "phonetic law" that there is local vacillation at present in several words.

One hears *roof, soot,* and *hoop,* for instance, both with the "long" vowel of *boot* and the "short" of *foot.* It is impossible now, in other words, to state in a definitive manner what is the "phonetic law" that regulated the change of the older *foot* (rhyming with *boot*) to the present *foot.* We know that there is a strong drift towards the short, open vowel of *foot,* but whether or not all the old "long *oo*" words will eventually be affected we cannot presume to say.

If they all, or practically all, are taken by the drift, phonetic law will be as "regular," as sweeping, as most of the twelve that have preceded it. If not, it may eventually be possible, if past experience is a safe guide, to show that the modified words form a natural phonetic group, that is, that the "law" will have operated under certain definable limiting conditions, e.g., that all words ending in a voiceless consonant (such as *p, t, k, f*) were affected (e.g., *hoof, foot, look, roof*), but that all words ending in the *oo*-vowel or in a voiced consonant remained unaffected (e.g., *do, food, move, fool*).

Whatever the upshot, we may be reasonably certain that when the "phonetic law" has run its course, the distribution of "long" and"short" vowels in the old *oo-* words will not seem quite as erratic as at the present transitional moment. We learn, incidentally, the fundamental fact that phonetic laws do not work with spontaneous automatism, that they are simply a formula for a consummated drift that sets in at a psychologically exposed point and gradually worms its way through a gamut of phonetically analogous forms.

It will be instructive to set down a table of form sequences, a kind of gross history of the words *foot, feet, mouse, mice* for the last 1500 years:

I. *fot: foti; mus: musi* (West Germanic)

II. *fot: föti; mus: müsi*

III. *fot: föte; mus: müse*

IV. *fot: föt; mus: müs*

V. *fot: fet; mus: müs* (Anglo-Saxon)

VI. *fot: fet; mus: mis* (Chaucer)

VII. *fot: fet; mous: meis*

VIII. *fut* (rhymes with *boot*: *fit; mous: meis* (Shakespeare)

IX. *fut: fit; maus: mais*

X. *fut* (rhymes with *put*): *fit; maus: mais* (English of 1900)

It will not be necessary to list the phonetic laws that gradually differentiated the modern German equivalents of the original West Germanic forms from their English cognates. The following table gives a rough idea of the form sequences in German:

I. *fot: foti; mus: musi* (West Germanic)

II. *foss: fossi; mus: musi*

III. *fuoss: fuossi; mus: musi* (Old High German)

IV. *fuoss: füessi; mus: müsi*

V. *fuoss: füesse; mus: müse* (Middle High German)

VI. *fuoss: füesse; mus: müze*

VII. *fuos: füese; mus: müze*

VIII. *fuos: füese; mous: möüze*

IX. *fus: füse; mous: möüze* (Luther)

X. *fus: füse; maus: moize* (German of 1900)

We cannot even begin to ferret out and discuss all the psychological problems that are concealed behind these bland tables. Their general parallelism is obvious. Indeed we might say that to-day the English and German forms resemble each other more than does either set the West Germanic prototypes from which each is independently derived.

Each table illustrates the tendency to reduction of unaccented syllables, the vocalic modification of the radical element under the influence of the following vowel, the rise in tongue position of the long middle vowels (English *o* to *u*, *e* to *i;* German *o* to *uo* to *u, üe* to *ü*), the diphthongizing of the old high vowels (English *i* to *ei* to *ai;* English and German *u* to *ou* to *au;* German *ü* to *öü* to *oi*). These dialectic parallels cannot be accidental. They are rooted in a common, pre-dialectic drift. Phonetic changes are "regular." All but one (English table, X.), and that as yet uncompleted, of the particular phonetic laws represented in our tables affect all examples of the sound in question or, if the phonetic change is conditional, all examples of the same sound that are analogously circumstanced.

An example of the first type of change is the passage in English of all old long *i*-vowels to diphthongal *ai* via *ei*. The passage could hardly have been sudden or automatic, but it was rapid enough to prevent an irregularity of development due to cross drifts. The second type of change is illustrated in the development of Anglo-Saxon long *o* to long *e,* via *ö,* under the influence of a following *i.* In the first case we may say that *au* mechanically replaced long *u,* in the second that the old long *o* "split" into two sounds—long *o,* eventually *u,* and long *e,* eventually *i.*

The former type of change did no violence to the old phonetic pattern, the formal distribution of sounds into groups; the latter type rearranged the pattern somewhat. If neither of the two sounds into which an old one "splits" is a new sound, it means that there has been a phonetic leveling, that two groups of words, each with a distinct sound or sound combination, have fallen together into one group. This kind of leveling is quite frequent in the history of language. In English, forinstance, we have seen that all the old long *ü*-vowels, after they had become unrounded, were indistinguishable from the mass of long *i*-vowels. This meant that the long *i*-vowel became a more heavily weighted point of the phonetic pattern than before.

It is curious to observe how often languages have striven to drive originally distinct sounds into certain favourite positions, regardless of resulting confusions. In Modern Greek, for instance, the vowel *i* is the historical resultant of no less than ten etymologically distinct vowels (long and short) and diphthongs of the classical speech of Athens. There is, then, good evidence to show that there are general phonetic drifts toward particular sounds.

More often the phonetic drift is of a more general character. It is not so much a movement toward a particular set of sounds as toward particular types of articulation. The vowels tend to become higher or lower, the diphthongs tend to coalesce into monophthongs, the voiceless consonants tend to become voiced, stops tend to become spirants.

As a matter of fact, practically all the phonetic laws enumerated in the two tables are but specific instances of such far-reaching phonetic drifts. The raising of English long *o* to *u* and of long *e* to *i,* for instance, was part of a general tendency to raise the position of the long vowels, just as the change of *t* to *ss* in Old High German was part of a general tendency to make voiceless spirants of the old voiceless stopped consonants.

A single sound change, even if there is no phonetic leveling, generally threatens to upset the old phonetic pattern because it brings about a disharmony in the grouping of sounds. To reestablish the old pattern without going back on the drift the only possible method is to have the other sounds of the series shift in analogous fashion. If, for some reason or other, *p* becomes shifted to its voiced correspondent *b,* the old series *p, t, k* appears in the unsymmetrical form *b, t, k.* Such a series is, in phonetic effect, not the equivalent of the old series, however it may answer to it in etymology.

The general phonetic pattern is impaired to that extent. But if *t* and *k* are also shifted to their voiced correspondents *d* and *g,* the old series is reestablished in a new form: *b, d, g.* The pattern as such is preserved, or restored. *Provided that* the new series *b, d, g* does not become confused with an old series *b, d, g* of distinct historical antecedents. If there is no such older series, the creation of a *b, d, g* series causes no difficulties. If there is, the old patterning of sounds can be kept intact only by shifting the old *b, d, g* sounds in some way. They may become aspirated to *bh, dh, gh* or spirantized or nasalized or they may develop any other peculiarity that keeps them intact as a series and serves to differentiate them from other series.

And this sort of shifting about without loss of pattern, or with a minimum loss of it, is probably the most important tendency in the history of speech sounds. Phonetic leveling and "splitting" counteract it to some extent but, on the whole, it remains the central unconscious regulator of the course and speed of sound changes.

The desire to hold on to a pattern, the tendency to "correct" a disturbance by an elaborate chain of supplementary changes, often spread over centuries or even millennia—these psychic undercurrents of language are exceedingly difficult to understand in terms of individual psychology, though there can be no denial of their historical reality. What is the primary cause of the unsettling of a phonetic pattern and what is the cumulative force that selects these or those particular variations of the individual on which to float the pattern readjustments we hardly know.

Many linguistic students have made the fatal error of thinking of sound change as a quasi-physiological instead of as a strictly psychological phenomenon, or they have tried to dispose of the problem by bandying such catchwords as "the tendency to increased ease of articulation" or "the cumulative result of faulty perception" (on the part of children, say, in learning to speak). These easy explanations will not do. "Ease of articulation" may enter in as a factor, but it is a rather subjective concept at best. Indians find hopelessly difficult sounds and sound combinations that are simple to us; one language encourages a phonetic drift that another does everything to fight.

"Faulty perception" does not explain that impressive drift in speech sounds which I have insisted upon. It is much better to admit that we do not yet understand the primary cause or causes of the slow drift in phonetics, though we can frequently point to contributing factors. It is likely that we shall not advance seriously until we study the intuitional bases of speech. How can we understand the nature of the drift that frays and reforms phonetic patterns when we have never thought of studying sound patterning as such and the "weights" and psychic relations of the single elements (the individual sounds) in these patterns?

Every linguist knows that phonetic change is frequently followed by morphological rearrangements, but he is apt to assume that morphology exercises little or no influence on the course of phonetic history. I am inclined to believe that our present tendency to isolate phonetics and grammar as mutually irrelevant linguistic provinces is unfortunate. There are likely to be fundamental relations between them and their respective histories that we do not yet fully grasp.

After all, if speech sounds exist merely because they are the symbolic carriers of significant concepts and groupings of concepts, why may not a strong drift or a permanent feature in the conceptual sphere exercise a furthering or retarding influence on the phonetic drift? I believe that such influences may be demonstrated and that they deserve far more careful study than they have received.

This brings us back to our unanswered question: How is it that both English and German developed the curious alternation of unmodified vowel in the singular (*foot, Fuss*) and modified vowel in the plural (*feet, Füsse*)? Was the pre-Anglo-Saxon alternation of *fot* and *föti* an absolutely mechanical matter, without other than incidental morphological interest? It is always so represented, and, indeed, all the external facts support such a view. The change from *o* to *ö,* later *e,* is by no means peculiar to the plural. It is found also in the dative singular (*fet*), for it too goes back to an older *foti.*

Moreover, *fet* of the plural applies only to the nominative and accusative; the genitive has *fota,* the dative *fotum.* Only centuries later was the alternation of *o* and *e* reinterpreted as a means of distinguishing number; *o* was generalized for the singular, *e* for the plural. Only when this reassortment of forms took place was the modern symbolic value of the *foot: feet* alternation clearly established. Again, we must not forget that *o* was modified to *ö (e)* in all manner of other grammatical and derivative formations.

Thus, a pre-Anglo-Saxon *hohan* (later *hon*) "to hang" corresponded to a *höhith, hehith* (later *hehth*) "hangs"; to *dom* "doom," *blod* "blood," and *fod* "food" corresponded the verbal derivatives *dömian* (later *deman*) "to deem," *blödian* (later *bledan*) "to bleed," and *födian* (later *fedan*) "to feed." All this seems to point to the purely mechanical nature of the modification of *o* to *ö* to *e.* So many unrelated functions were ultimately served by the vocalic change that we cannot believe that it was motivated by any one of them.

The German facts are entirely analogous. Only later in the history of the language was the vocalic alternation made significant for number. And yet consider the following facts. The change of *foti* to *föti* antedated that of *föti* to *föte, föt*. This may be looked upon as a "lucky accident," for if *foti* had become *fote, fot* before the *-i* had had the chance to exert a retroactive influence on the *o,* there would have been no difference between the singular and the plural. This would have been anomalous in Anglo-Saxon for a masculine noun. But was the sequence of phonetic changes an "accident"? Consider two further facts. All the Germanic languages were familiar with vocalic change as possessed of functional significance.

Alternations like *sing, sang, sung* (Anglo-Saxon *singan, sang, sungen*) were ingrained in the linguistic consciousness. Further, the tendency toward the weakening of final syllables was very strong even then and had been manifesting itself in one way and another for centuries. I believe that these further facts help us to understand the actual sequence of phonetic changes. We may go so far as to say that the *o* (and *u*) could afford to stay the change to *ö* (and *ü*) until the destructive drift had advanced to the point where failure to modify the vowel would soon result in morphological embarrassment. At a certainmoment the *-i* ending of the plural (and analogous endings with *i* in other formations) was felt to be too weak to quite bear its functional burden.

The unconscious Anglo-Saxon mind, if I may be allowed a somewhat summary way of putting the complex facts, was glad of the opportunity afforded by certain individual variations, until then automatically canceled out, to have some share of the burden thrown on them. These particular variations won through because they so beautifully allowed the general phonetic drift to take its course without unsettling the morphological contours of the language. And the presence of symbolic variation (*sing, sang, sung*) acted as an attracting force on the rise of a new variation of similar character. All these factors were equally true of the German vocalic shift.

Chapter 7

Foreign Influences on Old English

ENGLISH WITH OTHER LANGUAGES

The language which has been described in the preceding chapter was not merely the product of the dialects brought to England by the Jutes, Saxons, and Angles. These formed its basis, the sole basis of its grammar and the source of by far the largest part of its vocabulary. But there were other elements which entered into it. In the course of the first seven hundred years of its existence in England it was brought into contact with three other languages, the languages of the Celts, the Romans, and the Scandinavians. From each of these contacts it shows certain effects, more especially additions to its vocabulary.

Nothing would seem more reasonable than to expect that the conquest of the Celtic population of Britain by the Teutons and the subsequent mixture of the two races should have resulted in a corresponding mixture of their languages; that consequently we should find in the Old English vocabulary numerous instances of words which the Teutons heard in the speech of the native population and adopted. For it is apparent that the Celts were by no means exterminated except in certain areas, and that in most of England large numbers of them were gradually absorbed by the new inhabitants. The AngloSaxon Chronicle reports that at Andredesceaster or Pevensey a deadly struggle occurred between the native population and the newcomers and that not a single Briton was left alive. The evidence of the place-names in this region lends support to the statement.

But this was probably an exceptional case. In the east and southeast, where the Teutonic conquest was fully accomplished at a fairly early date, it is probable that there were fewer survivals of a Celtic population than elsewhere. Large numbers of the defeated fled to the west. Here it is apparent that a considerable Celtic-speaking population survived until fairly late times. Some such situation is suggested by a whole cluster of Celtic place-names in the northeastern corner of Dorsetshire. It is altogether likely that many Celts were held as slaves by the conquerors and that many of the Teutons married Celtic women. In parts at least of the island, contact between the two races must have been constant and in some districts intimate for several generations.

Celtic Place-names

When we come, however, to seek the evidence for this contact in the English language investigation yields very meager results. Such evidence as there is survives chiefly in place-names. The kingdom of *Kent*, for example, owes its name to the Celtic word *Canti* or *Cantion*, the meaning of which is unknown, while the two ancient Northumbrian kingdoms of *Deira* and *Bernicia* derive their designations from Celtic tribal names. Other districts, especially in the west and southwest, preserve in their present-day names traces of their earlier Celtic designations.

Devonshire contains in the first element the tribal name *Dumnonii*, *Cornwall* means the 'Cornubian Welsh', and Cumberland is the 'land of the Cymry or Britons'. Moreover, a number of important centres in the Roman period have names in which Celtic elements are embodied. The name *London* itself, although the origin of the word is somewhat uncertain, most likely goes back to a Celtic designation. The first syllable of *Winchester*, *Salisbury*, *Exeter*, *Gloucester*, *Worcester*, *Lichfield*, and a score of other names of cities is traceable to a Celtic source, while the earlier name of Canterbury (*Durovernum*) and the name *York* are originally Celtic.

But it is in the names of rivers and hills and places in proximity to these natural features that the greatest number of Celtic names survive. Thus the *Thames* is a Celtic river name, and various Celtic words for river or water are preserved in the names *Avon, Exe, Esk, Usk, Dover,* and *Wye.* Celtic words meaning 'hill' are found in place-names like *Barr* (cf. Welsh *bar,* 'top, summit'), *Bredon* (cf. Welsh *bre,* 'hill'), *Bryn Mawr* (cf. Welsh *bryn* 'hill' and *mawr* 'great'), *Creech, Pendle* (cf. Welsh *pen* 'top'), and others.

Certain other Celtic elements occur more or less frequently such as *cumb* (a deep valley) in names like *Duncombe, Holcombe, Winchcombe; torr* (high rock, peak) in *Torr, Torcross, Torhill; pill* (a tidal creek) in *Pylle, Huntspill;* and *brocc* (badger) in *Brockholes, Brockhall,* etc. Besides these purely Celtic elements a few Latin words such as *castra, fontana, fossa, portus,* and *vicus* were used in naming places during the Roman occupation of the island and were passed on by the Celts to the English.

These will be discussed later. It is natural that Celtic place-names should be commoner in the west than in the east and southeast, but the evidence of these names shows that the Celts impressed themselves upon the Teutonic consciousness at least to the extent of causing the newcomers to adopt many of the local names current in Celtic speech and to make them a permanent part of their vocabulary.

Other Celtic Loan-words

Outside of place-names, however, the influence of Celtic upon the English language is almost negligible. Not over a score of words in Old English can be traced with reasonable probability to a Celtic source. Within this small number it is possible to distinguish two groups: (1) those which the Anglo-Saxons learned through everyday contact with the natives, and (2) those which were introduced by the Irish missionaries in the north. The former were transmitted orally and were of popular character; the latter were connected with religious activities and were more or less learned.

The popular words include *binn* (basket, crib), *bratt* (cloak), and *brocc* (brock or badger); a group of words for geographical features which had not played much part in the experience of the AngloSaxons in their continental home — *crag*, *luh* (lake), *cumb* (valley), and *torr* (outcropping or projecting rock, peak), the two latter chiefly as elements in place-names; possibly the words *dun* (dark colored), and *ass* (ultimately from Latin *asinus*). Words of the second group, those that came into English through Celtic Christianity, are likewise few in number.

In 563 St. Columba had come with twelve monks from Ireland to preach to his kinsmen in Britain. On the little island of Iona off the west coast of Scotland he established a monastery and made it his headquarters for the remaining thirty-four years of his life. From this centre many missionaries went out, founded other religious houses, and did much to spread Christian doctrine and learning. As a result of their activity the words *ancor* (hermit), *drȳ* (magician), *cine* (a gathering of parchment leaves), *cross*, *clugge* (bell), *gabolrind* (compass), *mind* (diadem), and perhaps *star* (history) and *cursian* (to curse) came into at least partial use in Old English.

It does not appear that many of these Celtic words attained a very permanent place in the English language. Some soon died out and others acquired only local currency. The relation of the two races was not such as to bring about any considerable influence on English life or on English speech. The surviving Celts were a submerged race. Had they, like the Romans, possessed a superior culture, something valuable to give the Teutons, their influence might have been greater. But the Anglo-Saxon found little occasion to adopt Celtic modes of expression and the Celtic influence remains the least of the early influences which affected the English language.

Three Latin Influences on Old English

If the influence of Celtic upon Old English was slight, it was doubtless so because the relation of the Celt to the Teuton was that of a submerged race and, as suggested above, because the Celt was not in a position to make any notable contribution to Anglo-Saxon civilization.

It was quite otherwise with the second great influence exerted upon English – that of Latin – and the circumstances under which they met. Latin was not the language of a conquered people. It was the language of a race with a higher civilization, a race from which the Teutons had much to learn. Contact with that civilization, at first commercial and military, later religious and intellectual, extended over many centuries and was constantly renewed. It began long before the Anglo-Saxons came to England and continued throughout the Old English period.

For several hundred years, while the Teutons who later became the English were still occupying their continental homes, they had various relations with the Romans through which they acquired a considerable number of Latin words. Later when they came to England they saw the evidences of the long Roman rule in the island and learned from the Celts a few additional Latin words which had been acquired by them.

And a century and a half later still, when Roman missionaries reintroduced Christianity into the island, this new cultural influence resulted in a really extensive adoption of Latin elements into the language. There were thus three distinct occasions on which borrowing from Latin occurred before the end of the Old English period, and it will be of interest to consider more in detail the character and extent of these borrowings.

Chronological Criteria

In order to form an accurate idea of the share which each of these three periods had in extending the resources of the English vocabulary it is first necessary to determine as closely as possible the date at which each of the borrowed words entered the language. This is naturally somewhat difficult to do and in the case of some words impossible. But in a large number of cases it is possible to assign a word to a given period with a high degree of probability and often with certainty. It will be instructive to pause for a moment to inquire how this is done.

The evidence which can be employed is of various kinds and naturally of varying value. Most obvious is the appearance of the word in literature. If a given word occurs with fair frequency in texts such as *Beowulf*, or the poems of Cynewulf, such occurrence indicates that the word has had time to pass into current use and that it came into English not later than the early part of the period of Christian influence. But it does not tell us how much earlier it was known in the language since the earliest written records in English do not go back beyond the year 700.

Moreover the late appearance of a word in literature is no proof of late adoption. The word may not be the kind of word that would naturally occur very often in literary texts, and so much of Old English literature has been lost that it would be very unsafe to argue about the existence of a word on the basis of existing remains. Some words which are not found recorded before the tenth century (e.g.,*pi* + *pē* pipe', *ci* + *ēse* cheese') can be assigned confidently on other grounds to the period of continental borrowing.

The character of the word sometimes gives some clue to its date. Some words are obviously learned and point to a time when the church had become well established in the island. On the other hand, the early occurrence of a word in several of the Teutonic dialects points to the general circulation of the word in the Teutonic territory and its probable adoption by the ancestors of the English on the continent. Testimony of this kind must of course be used with discrimination. A number of words, for example, found in Old English and in Old High German can hardly have been borrowed by either language before the Teutons migrated to England but are due to later independent adoption under conditions more or less parallel, brought about by the introduction of Christianity into the two areas.

But it can hardly be doubted that a word like *copper*, which is rare in Old English, was nevertheless borrowed on the continent when we find it in no less than six Teutonic languages. Much the most conclusive evidence of the date at which a word was borrowed, however, is to be found in the phonetic form of the word. The changes which take place in the sounds of a language can often be dated with some definiteness and the presence or absence of these changes in a borrowed word constitutes an important test of age.

A full account of these changes would carry us far beyond the scope of this book, but one or two examples may serve to illustrate the principle. Thus there occurred in Old English, as in most of the Teutonic languages, a change known as *i-umlaut*.

This change affected certain accented vowels and diphthongs (æ, *ɑ*+τ+˘, ō+˘, ū+˘, ē+˘a, ē+˘o, and ι +¯ = ˘o) when they were followed in the next syllable by an ι+¯+˘ or *j*. Under such circumstances æ and *ɑ* + ˘became ḝ and ō + ˘became ḝ+˘*ɑ*+τ became ǣ, and ū+˘ became ȳ+˘. The diphthongs ē + ˘a, ē + ˘o, ι + ¯ + ˘o became ι + ¯ + ˘e, later ι +¯+˘, ȳ+˘. Thus *bankiz* > *benc* (bench), *mūsiz* > *mȳs*, plural of *mûs* (mouse), etc. The change occurred in English in the course of the seventh century, and when we find it taking place in a word borrowed from Latin it indicates that the Latin word had been taken into English by that time. Thus Latin *monēta* (which became *munit* in Prim. O.E.) > *mynet* (a coin, Mod. E. *mint*) and is an early borrowing. Another change (even earlier) that helps us to date a borrowed word is that known as palatal *diphthongization*.

By this sound-change an ǣ+˘ or ē+˘ in early Old English was changed to a diphthong (ē+˘a and ι+¯˘e respectively) when preceded by certain palatal consonants (*c*, *g*, *sc*). O.E.

cı+ ēse (L.*ca* + *τseus*, cheese), mentioned above, shows both *i-umlaut* and palatal diplithongization (*ca* + *τseus* > *cǣsi* > **cēasi* > *cı* + *ēse*). In many words evidence for date is furnished by the sound-changes of Vulgar Latin.

Thus, for example, an intervocalic *p* (and *p* in the combination *pr*) in the late Latin of northern Gaul (seventh century) was modified to a sound approximating a v, and the fact that L. *cuprum, coprum* (copper) appears in O.E. as *copor* with the *p* unchanged indicates a period of borrowing prior to this change (cf. F. *cuivre*). Again Latin ı+ᵕ changed to e before A.D. 400 so that words like O.E. *biscop* (L. *episcopus*), *disc* (L. *discus*), *sigel*, 'brooch' (L. *sigillum*), etc., which do not show this change, were borrowed by the English on the continent. But enough has been said to indicate the method and to show that the distribution of the Latin words in Old English among the various periods at which borrowing took place rests not upon guesses, however shrewd, but upon definite facts and upon fairly reliable phonetic inferences.

Latin Influence of the Zero Period

The first Latin words to find their way into the English language owe their adoption to the early contact between the Romans and the Germanic tribes on the continent. Several hundred Latin words found in the various Teutonic dialects at an early date – some in one dialect only, others in several – testify to the extensive intercourse between the two races. The number of Germans living within the empire by the fourth century is estimated at several million.

They are found in all ranks and classes of society, from slaves in the fields to commanders of important divisions of the Roman army. While they were scattered all over the empire, they were naturally most numerous along the northern frontier. This stretched along the Rhine and the Danube and bordered on German territory. Close to the border was Treves, in the third and fourth centuries the most flourishing city in Gaul, already boasting Christian churches, a focus of eight military roads, where all the luxury and splendor of Roman civilization were united almost under the gaze of the Teutons on the Moselle and the Rhine. Traders, German as well as Roman, came and went, while German youth returning from within the empire must have carried back glowing accounts of Roman cities and Roman life. Such intercourse between the two races was certain to carry words from one language to the other.

The frequency of the intercourse may naturally be expected to diminish somewhat as one recedes from the borders of the empire. Roman military operations, for example, seldom extended as far as the district occupied by the Angles or the Jutes. But after the conquest of Gaul by Caesar, Roman merchants quickly found their way into all parts of the Germanic territory, even into Scandinavia, so that the Teutons living in these remoter sections were by no means cut off from Roman influence.

Moreover, intercommunication between the different Teutonic tribes was frequent and made possible the transference of Latin words from one tribe to another. In any case some fifty words from the Latin can be credited with a considerable degree of probability to the ancestors of the English in their continental homes.

The adopted words naturally indicate the new conceptions which the Teutons acquired from this contact with a higher civilization. Next to agriculture the chief occupation of the Germans in the empire was war, and this experience is reflected in words like *camp* (battle), *segn* (banner), *pı + ¯l* (pointed stick, javelin), *weall* (wall), *pytt* (pit), *strǣt* (road, street), *mı + ¯l* (mile), and *miltestre* (courtesan). More numerous are the words connected with trade. The Teutons traded amber, furs, slaves, and probably certain raw materials for the products of Roman handicrafts, articles of utility, luxury, and adornment.

The words *cēap* (bargain; cf. Eng., *cheap*, *chapman*) and *mangian* (to trade) with its derivatives *mangere* (monger), *mangung* (trade, commerce), and *mangung-hūs* (shop) are fundamental, while *pund* (pound), *mydd* (bushel), *sēam* (burden, load), and *mynet* (coin) are terms likely to be employed. From the last word Old English formed the word *mynetian* (to mint, or coin) and *mynetere* (money-changer). One of the most important branches of Roman commerce with the Teutons was the wine trade: hence such words in English as *wı* + *n̄* (wine), *must* (new wine), *eced* (vinegar), and *flasce* (flask, bottle).

To this period are probably to be attributed the words *cylle* (L. *culleus*, leather bottle), *cyrfette* (L. *curcurbita*, gourd), and *sester* (jar, pitcher). A number of the new words relate to domestic life and designate household articles, clothing, etc.: *cytel* (kettle; L. *catillus*, *catı* + *n̄us*), *mēse* (table), *scamol* (L. *scamellum*, bench, stool; cf. modern *shambles*), *teped* (carpet, curtain; L. *tapçtum*), *pyle* (L. *pulvé* + *n̄us*, pillow), *pilece* (L. *pellicia*, robe of skin), and *sigel* (brooch, necklace; L. *sigillum*). Certain other words of a similar kind probably belong here although the evidence for their adoption thus early is not in every case conclusive: *cycene* (kitchen; L. *co- quı* + *n̄a*), *cuppe* (L. *cuppa*, cup), *disc* (dish; L. *discus*), *cucler* (spoon; L. *cocleQ* + *ōrium*), *mortere* (L. *mortQ* + *ôrium*, a mortar, a vessel of hard material), *linen* (cognate with or from L. *lı* + *n̄um*, flax), *lı* + *ne* (rope, line; L. *lı* + *nea*), and *gimm* (L. *gemma*, gem).

The Teutons adopted Roman words for certain foods, such as *cı* + ēse (L. *ca* + *τseus*, cheese), *spelt* (wheat), *pipor* (pepper), *senep* (mustard; L. *sina* + *τpi*), *popig* (poppy), *cisten* (chestnut-tree; L. *castanea*), *cires*(*bēam*) (cherry-tree; L. *cerasus*), while to this period are probably to be assigned *butere* (butter; L. *būtȳrum*), *ynne*(*lēac*) (L. *ūnio*, onion), *plūme* (plum), *pise* (L. *pisum*, pea), and *minte* (L. *mentha*, mint). Roman contributions to the building arts are evidenced by such words as *cealc* (chalk), *copor* (copper), *pic* (pitch), and *tigele* (tile), while miscellaneous words such as *mûl* (mule), *draca* (dragon), *pa* + *τwa* (peacock), the adjectives sicor (L. *sēcūrus*, safe) and *calu* (L. *calvus*, bald), *segne* (seine), *pı* + *p̄e* (pipe, musical instrument), *cirice* (church), *biscop* (bishop), c*a* + τsere (emperor), and *Sæternesdæg* (Saturday) may be mentioned.

In general, if we are surprised at the number of words acquired from the Romans at so early a date by the Teutonic tribes that came to England, we can see nevertheless that the words were such as they would be likely to borrow and such as reflect in a very reasonable way the relations that existed between the two peoples.

Latin through Celtic Transmission (Latin Influence of the First Period)

The circumstances responsible for the slight influence which Celtic exerted on Old English limited in like manner the Latin influence that sprang from the period of Roman occupation. From what has been said above about the Roman rule in Britain, the extent to which the country was Romanized, and the employment of Latin by certain elements in the population, one would expect a considerable number of Latin words to have remained in use and to appear in the English language today. But this is not the case.

It would be hardly too much to say that not five words outside of a few elements found in place-names can be really proved to owe their presence in English to the Roman occupation of Britain. It is probable that the use of Latin as a spoken language did not long survive the end of Roman rule in the island and that such vestiges as remained for a time were lost in the disorders that accompanied the Teutonic invasions. There was thus no opportunity for direct contact between Latin and Old English in England, and such Latin words as could have found their way into English would have had to come in through Celtic transmission.

The Celts, indeed, had adopted a considerable number of Latin words — over six hundred have been identified — but the relations between the Celts and the English were such, as we have already seen, that these words were not passed on. Among the few Latin words that the Teutons seem likely to have acquired upon settling in England one of the most likely, in spite of its absence from the Celtic languages, is *ceaster*. This word, which represents the Latin *castra* (camp) is a common designation in Old English for a town or enclosed community. It forms a familiar element in English placenames such as *Chester*, *Colchester*, *Dorchester*, *Manchester*,

Winchester, Lancaster, Doncaster, Gloucester, Worcester, and many others. Some of these refer to sites of Roman camps, but it must not be thought that a Roman settlement underlies all the towns whose names contain this common element.

The English attached it freely to the designation of any enclosed place intended for habitation, and many of the places so designated were known by quite different names in Roman times. A few other words are thought for one reason or another to belong to this period: *port* (harbor, gate, town) from L. *portus* and *porta, munt* (mountain) from L. *mōns, montem, torr* (tower, rock) possibly from L. *turris,* possibly from Celtic, *wı* + $\bar{c}$ (village) from L. *vı* + $\bar{c}$*us.*

All of these words are found also as elements in place-names. It is possible that some of the Latin words which the Teutons had acquired on the continent, such as *street* (L. *strQ* + *ôta via*), *wall, wine,* etc., were reinforced by the presence of the same words in Celtic. At best, however, the Latin influence of the First Period remains much the slightest of all the influences which Old English owed to contact with Roman civilization.

Latin Influence of the Second Period

The greatest influence of Latin upon Old English was occasioned by the introduction of Christianity into Britain in 597. The new faith was far from new in the island, but this date marks the beginning of a systematic attempt on the part of Rome to convert the inhabitants and make England a Christian country. According to the well-known story reported by Bede as a tradition current in his day, the mission of St. Augustine was inspired by an experience of a man who later became Pope Gregory the Great.

Walking one morning in the market-place at Rome, he came upon some fair-haired boys about to be sold as slaves and was told that they were from the island of Britain and were pagans. " 'Alasl what pity,' said he, 'that the author of darkness is possessed of men of such fair countenances, and that being remarkable for such a graceful exterior, their minds should be void of inward grace?' He therefore again asked, what was the name of that nation and was answered, that they were called Angles. 'Right,' said he, 'for they have an angelic face, and it is fitting that such should be co-heirs with the angels in heaven. What is the name,' proceeded he, 'of the province from which they are brought?' It was replied that the natives of that province were called Deiri. 'Truly are they *de ira*," said he, 'plucked from wrath, and called to the mercy of Christ.

How is the king of that province called?' They told him his name was *Ælla*; and he, alluding to the name, said 'Alleluia, the praise of God the Creator, must be sung in those parts.' The same tradition records that Gregory wished himself to undertake the mission to Britain, but could not be spared. Some years later, however, when he had become pope, he had not forgotten his former intention, and looked about for some one whom he could send at the head of a missionary band. Augustine, the person of his choice, was a man well known to him.

The two had lived together in the same monastery, and Gregory knew him to be modest and devout, and thought him well suited to the task assigned him. With a little company of about forty monks Augustine set out for what seemed then like the end of the earth. It is not easy to appreciate the difficulty of the task which lay before this small band. Their problem was not so much to substitute one ritual for another as to change the philosophy of a nation.

The religion which the Anglo-Saxons shared with the other Teutonic tribes seems to have had but a slight hold on the people at the close of the sixth century; but their habits of mind, their ideals, and the action to which these gave rise were often in sharp contrast to the teachings of the New Testament. Teutonic philosophy exalted physical courage, independence even to haughtiness, loyalty to one's family or leader that left no wrong unavenged.

Christianity preached meekness and humility, patience under suffering, and said that if a man struck you on one cheek you should turn the other. Clearly it was no small task which Augustine and his forty monks faced in trying to alter the age-old mental habits of such a people. They might even have expected difficulty in obtaining a respectful hearing. But they seem to have been men of exemplary lives, appealing personality, and devotion to purpose, and owed their ultimate success as much to what they were as to what they said. Fortunately, upon their arrival in England one circumstance was in their favour.

There was in the kingdom of Kent, in which they landed, a small number of Christians. But the number, though small, included no less a person than the queen. Æthelberht, the king, had sought his wife among the powerful nation of the Franks, and the princess Bertha had been given to him only on condition that she be allowed to continue undisturbed in her Christian faith.

Æthelberht set up a small chapel near his palace in Kentwarabyrig (Canterbury), and there the priest who accompanied Bertha to England conducted regular services for her and the numerous dependents whom she brought with her. The circumstances under which Æthelberht received Augustine and his companions are related in the extract from Bede. Æthelberht was himself baptized within three months, and his example was followed by numbers of his subjects. By the time Augustine died seven years later the kingdom of Kent had become wholly Christian.

The conversion of the rest of England was a gradual process. In 635 Aidan, a monk from the Scottish monastery of Iona, undertook independently the conversion of Northumbria. He was a man of great sympathy and tact. With a small band of followers he journeyed from town to town and wherever he preached drew crowds to hear him. Within twenty years he had made all Northumbria Christian. There were periods of reversion to paganism, and some clashes between the Celtic and the Roman leaders over doctrine and authority, but England was slowly won over to the faith.

It is significant that the Christian missionaries were allowed considerable freedom in their labors. There is not a single instance recorded in which any of them suffered martyrdom in the cause which they espoused. Possibly the fact that the important nation of the Franks was known to have accepted the new religion was a significant factor in rendering the English more receptive. At all events within a hundred years of the landing of Augustine in Kent all England was permanently Christian.

Effects on English Civilization

The introduction of Christianity meant the building of churches and the establishment of monasteries. Latin, the language of the services and of ecclesiastical learning, was once more heard in England. Schools were established in most of the monasteries and larger churches. Some of these became famous through the possession of great teachers and from them trained men went out to set up other schools at other centres. The beginning of this movement was in 669 when a Greek bishop, Theodore of Tarsus, was made archbishop of Canterbury. He was accompanied by Hadrian, an African by birth, a man described by Bede as "of the greatest skill in both the Greek and Latin tongues."

They devoted considerable time and energy to teaching. "And because," says Bede, "they were abundantly learned in sacred and profane literature, they gathered a crowd of disciples . . . and together with the books of Holy Writ, they also taught the arts of poetry, astronomy, and ecclesiastical arithmetic; a testimony of which is that there are still living at this day some of their scholars, who are as well versed in the Greek and Latin tongues as in their own, in which they were born."

A decade or two later Aldhelm carried on a similar work at Malmesbury. He was a remarkable classical scholar. He had an exceptional knowledge of Latin literature, and he wrote Latin verse with ease. In the north the school at York became in time almost as famous as that of Canterbury. The two monasteries of Wearmouth and Jarrow were founded by Benedict Biscop, who had been with Theodore and Hadrian at Canterbury, and who on five trips to Rome brought back a rich and valuable collection of books. His most famous pupil was the Venerable Bede, a monk at Jarrow. Bede assimilated all the learning of his time. He wrote on grammar and prosody, science and chronology, and composed numerous commentaries on the books of the Old and New Testament.

His most famous work is the *Ecclesiastical History of the English People (731)*, from which we have already had occasion to quote more than once and from which we derive a large part of our knowledge of the early history of England. Bede's spiritual grandchild was Alcuin, of York, whose fame as a scholar was so great that in 782 Charlemagne called him to be the head of his Palace School. In the eighth century England held the intellectual leadership of Europe, and it owed this leadership to the church. In like manner vernacular literature and the arts received a new impetus.

Workers in stone and glass were brought from the continent for the improvement of church building. Rich embroidery, the illumination of manuscripts, and church music occupied others. Moreover the monasteries cultivated their land by improved methods of agriculture and made numerous contributions to domestic economy. In short, the church as the carrier of Roman civilization influenced the course of English life in many directions, and, as is to be expected, numerous traces of this influence are to be seen in the vocabulary of Old English.

The Earlier Influence of Christianity on the Vocabulary

From the introduction of Christianity in 597 to the close of the Old English period is a stretch of over five hundred years. During all this time Latin words must have been making their way gradually into the English language. It is likely that the first wave of religious feeling which resulted from the missionary zeal of the seventh century, and which is reflected in intense activity in church building and the establishing of monasteries during this century, was responsible also for the rapid importation of Latin words into the vocabulary.

The many new conceptions which followed in the train of the new religion would naturally demand expression and would at times find the resources of the language inadequate. But it would be a mistake to think that the enrichment of the vocabulary which now took place occurred overnight. Some words came in almost immediately, others only at the end of our period. In fact it is fairly easy to divide the Latin borrowings of the Second Period into two groups, more or less equal in size but quite different in character.

The one group represents words whose phonetic form shows that they were borrowed early and whose early adoption is attested also by the fact that they had found their way into literature by the time of Alfred. The other contains words of a more learned character first recorded in the tenth and eleventh century and owing their introduction clearly to the religious revival that accompanied the Benedictine Reform. It will be well to consider them separately.

It is obvious that the most typical as well as the most numerous class of words introduced by the new religion would have to do with that religion and the details of its external organization. Words are generally taken over by one language from another in answer to a definite need. They are adopted because they express ideas that are new or because they are so intimately associated with an object or a concept that acceptance of the thing involves acceptance also of the word. A few words relating to Christianity such as church and bishop were, as we have seen, borrowed earlier. The Anglo-Saxons had doubtless plundered churches and come in contact with bishops before they came to England. But the great majority of words in Old English having to do with the church and its services, its physical fabric and its ministers, when not of native origin were borrowed at this time. Since most of these words have survived in only slightly altered form in Modern English, the examples may be given in their modern form.

The list includes *abbot, alms, altar, angel, anthem, ark, Arian, candle, canon, chalice, cleric, cowl, deacon, disciple, epistle, hymn, litany, manna, martyr, mass, minster, noon, nun, offer, organ, pall, palm, pope, priest, provost, psalm, psalter, shrine, shrive, shrift, stole, sub-deacon, synod, relic, rule, temple,* and *tunic*. Some of these were reintroduced later. But the church also exercised a profound influence on the domestic life of the people.

This is seen in the adoption of many words, such as the names of articles of clothing and household use – *cap, sock, silk, purple, chest, mat, sack*; words denoting foods, such as *beet, caul* (cabbage), *lentil* (O.E. *lent*), *millet* (O.E. *mil*), *pear, radish, doe, oyster* (O.E. *ostre*), *lobster, mussel,* to which we may add the noun cook; names of trees, plants, and herbs (often cultivated for their medicinal properties), such as *box, pine, aloes, balsam, fennel, hyssop, lily, mallow, marshmallow, myrrh, rue, savory* (O.E. *sæperige*), and the general word *plant*.

A certain number of words having to do with education and learning reflect another aspect of the church's influence. Such are school, *master, Latin* (possibly an earlier borrowing), *grammatic(al), verse, metre, gloss, notary* (a scribe). Finally we may mention a number of words too miscellaneous to admit of profitable classification, like *anchor, coulter, fan* (for winnowing), *fever, place* (cf. *market place*), *spelter* (asphalt), *sponge, elephant, phoenix, mancus* (a coin) and some more or less learned or literary words, such as *calend, circle, legion, giant, consul,* and *talent*.

The words cited in these examples are mostly nouns, but Old English borrowed also a number of verbs and adjectives such as *a + τspendan* (to spend; L. *expendere*) *bemūtian* (to exchange; L. *mūta + τre*), *dihtan* (to compose; L. *dicta + τre*), *pı + nian* (to torture; L. *poena*), *pinsian* (to weigh; L. *pçnsa + τre*), *pyngan* (to prick; L. *pungere*), *sealtian* (to dance; L. *salta + τre*), *temprian* (to temper; L. *tempera + τre*), *tré + ifolian* (to grind; L. *trı + bula + τre*), *tyrnan* (to turn; L. *torna + τre*), and *crisp* (L. *crispus,* curly). But enough has been said to indicate the extent and variety of the borrowings from Latin in the early days of Christianity in England and to show how quickly the language reflected the broadened horizon which the English people owed to the church.

The Benedictine Reform

The flourishing state of the church which resulted in these significant additions to the English language unfortunately did not continue uninterrupted. One cause of the decline is to be attributed to the Danes, who at the end of the eighth century began their ravages upon the country. Lindisfarne was burnt in 793 and Jarrow, Bede's monastery, was plundered the following year. In the ninth century throughout Northumbria and Mercia churches and monasteries lay everywhere in ruins. By the tenth century the decline had affected the moral fiber of the church. It would seem as though once success had been attained and a reasonable degree of security, the clergy relaxed their efforts.

Wealthy men had given land freely to religious foundations in the hope of laying up spiritual reserves for themselves against the life in the next world. Among the clergy poverty gave way to ease, and ease by a natural transition passed into luxury. Probably a less worthy type was drawn by these new conditions into the religious profession. We hear much complaint about immoderate feasting and drinking and vanity in dress. In the religious houses discipline became lax, services were neglected, monasteries were occupied by groups of secular priests, many of them married, immorality was flagrant. The work of education was neglected and learning decayed.

By the time of Alfred things had reached such a pass that he looked upon the past as a golden age which had gone, "when the Kings who ruled obeyed God and His evangelists", and when "the religious orders were earnest about doctrine, and learning, and all the services they owed to God"; and he laments that the decay of learning was so great at the beginning of his reign "that there were very few on this side of the Humber who could understand their rituals in English, or translate a letter from Latin into English, and I believe not many beyond the Humber.

So few were there that I cannot remember a single one south of the Thames when I came to the kingship." Two generations later Aelfric, abbot of Eynsham, echoes the same sentiment when he says, "Until Dunstan and Athelwold revived learning in the monastic life no English priest could either write a letter in Latin, or understand one." It is hardly likely, therefore, that many Latin words were added to the English language during these years when religion and learning were both at such a low ebb.

But abuses when bad enough have a way of bringing about their own reformation. What is needed generally is an individual with the zeal to lead the way and the ability to set an example that inspires imitation. King Alfred had made a start. Besides restoring churches and founding monasteries, he strove for twenty years to spread education in his kingdom and foster learning. His efforts bore little fruit.

But in the latter half of the tenth century three great religious leaders, imbued with the spirit of reform, arose in the church: Dunstan, archbishop of Canterbury, Athelwold, bishop of Winchester, and Oswald, bishop of Worcester and archbishop of York. With the sympathetic support of King Edgar these men effected a genuine revival of monasticism in England. The true conception of the monastic life was inseparable from the observance of the Benedictine Rule. Almost everywhere in England this had ceased to be adhered to. As the first step in the reform the secular clergy were turned out of the monasteries and their places filled by monks pledged to the threefold vow of chastity, obedience, and poverty. In their work of restoration the reformers received powerful support from the example of continental monasteries, notably those at Fleury and Ghent.

These had recently undergone a similar reformation under the inspiring leadership of Cluny, where in 910 a community had been established on even stricter lines than those originally laid down by St. Benedict. Dunstan had spent some time at the Abbey of Blandinium at Ghent; Oswald had studied the system at Fleury; and Athelwold, although wanting to go himself, had sent a representative to Fleury for the same purpose. On the pattern of these continental houses a number of important monasteries were re-created in England, and Athelwold prepared a version of the Benedictine Rule, known as the Concordia Regularis, to bring about a general uniformity in their organization and observances.

The effort toward reform extended to other divisions of the church, indeed to a general reformation of morals, and brought about something like a religious revival in the island. One of the objects of special concern in this work of rehabilitation was the improvement of education — the establishment of schools and the encouragement of learning among the monks and the clergy. The results were distinctly gratifying. By the close of the century the monasteries were once more centres of literary activity. Works in English for the popularizing of knowledge were prepared by men who thus continued the example of King Alfred, and manuscripts both in Latin and the vernacular were copied and preserved.

It is significant that the four great codices in which the bulk of Old English poetry is preserved date from this period. We doubtless owe their existence to the reform movement. The influence of Latin upon the English language rose and fell with the fortunes of the church and the state of learning so intimately connected with it. As a result of the renewed literary activity just described a new series of Latin importations took place.

These differed somewhat from the earlier Christian borrowings in being words of a less popular- kind and expressing more often ideas of a scientific and learned character. They are especially frequent in the works of Aelfric and reflect not only the theological and pedagogical nature of his writings but his classical tastes and attainments. His literary activity and his vocabulary are equally representative of the movement.

As in the earlier Christian borrowings a considerable number of words have to do with religious matters: *alb, Antichrist, antiphoner, apostle, cantor, canticle, cell, cloister, collect, creed, chrism, dalmatic, demon, dirge, font, idol, nocturn, prime, prophet, sabbath, synagogue, troper*. But we miss the group of words relating to everyday life characteristic of the earlier period. Literary and learned words predominate.

Of the former kind are *accent, brief* (the verb), *decline* (as a term of grammar), *history, paper, pumice, quatern* (a quire or gathering of leaves in a book), *term*(inus), *title*. A great number of plant names are recorded in this period. Many of them are familiar only to readers of old herbals. Some of the better known include *verbena, celandine, centaury, coriander, cucumber, hellebore, ginger, lovage, periwinkle, petersili* (parsley). A few names of trees might be added, such as *cedar, cypress, fig, laurel,* and *magda + da* (almond).

Medical terms, like *cancer, circula + ôdl*(shingles), *paralysis, scrofula, plaster,* and words relating to the animal kingdom, like *aspide* (viper), *camel, lamprey, scorpion, tiger,* belong apparently to the same category of learned and literary borrowings. It would be possible to extend these lists considerably by including words which were taken over in their foreign form and not assimilated. Such words as *epactas, corporale, confessores, columba* (dove), *columne, cathedra, catacumbas, apostata, apocalipsin, acolitus, absolutionem, invitatorium, unguentum, cristalla, cometa, bissexte, bibliothece, basilica, adamans, prologus* show at once by their form their foreign character.

Although many of them were later reintroduced into the language, they do not constitute an integral part of the vocabulary at this time. In general the later borrowings of the Christian period come through books. An occasional word assigned to this later period may have been in use earlier, but there is nothing in the form to indicate it, and in the absence of any instance of its use in the literature before Alfred it is safer to put such borrowings in the latter part of the Old English period.

The Application of Native Words to New Concepts

The words which Old English borrowed in this period are only a partial indication of the extent to which the introduction of Christianity affected the lives and thoughts of the English people. The English did not always adopt a foreign word to express a new concept. Often an old word was applied to a new thing and by a slight adaptation made to express a new meaning. The Anglo-Saxons, for example, did not borrow the Latin word *deus,* since their own word God was a satisfactory equivalent.

Likewise *heaven* and *hell* express conceptions not unknown to Anglo-Saxon paganism and are consequently English words. *Patriarch* was rendered literally by *hçahf¿der* (high father), *prophet* by *wı + tega* (wise one), *martyr* often by the native word *prôwere* (one who suffers pain), and saint by *ha + tlga* (holy one). While specific members of the church organization such as *pope, bishop,* and *priest,* or *monk* and *abbot* represented individuals for which the English had no equivalent and therefore borrowed the Latin terms, they did not borrow a general word for clergy but used a native expression *∂ + æt ga + tstlice folc* (the spiritual folk).

The word *Easter* is a Teutonic word taken over from a pagan festival, likewise in the spring, in honor of Eostre, the goddess of dawn. Instead of borrowing the Latin word *praedica + tre* (to preach) the English expressed the idea with words of their own, such as *lǣran* (to teach) or *bodian* (to bring a message); to pray (L. *preca + tre*) was rendered by *biddan* (to ask) and other words of similar meaning, prayer by a word from the same root, *gebed.*

For *baptize* (L. *baptiza + tre*) the English adapted a native word *fullian* (to consecrate) while its derivative *fulluht* renders the noun *baptism.* The latter word enters into numerous compounds, such as *fulluht-bæp* (font), *fulwere* (baptist), *fulluht-fæder* (baptizer), *fulluht-ha + td* (baptismal vow), *fulluht-nama* (Christian name), *fulluht-stōw* (baptistry), *fulluht-tı + d* (baptism time), and others. Even so individual a feature of the Christian faith as the sacrament of the Lord's Supper was expressed by the Teutonic word *hūsl* (modern *housel*) while *la + τc*, the general word for sacrifice to the gods, was also sometimes applied to the Sacrifice of the Mass.

The term *Scriptures* found its exact equivalent in the English word *gewritu,* and *çvangelium* was rendered by *godspell,* originally meaning good tidings. *Trinity* (L. *trinitas*) was translated *prines* (three-ness), the idea of God the Creator was expressed by *scieppend* (one who shapes or forms), *fruma* (creator, founder), or *metod* (measurer). Native words like *fæder* (father), *dryhten* (prince), *wealdend* (ruler), *pçoden* (prince), *weard* (ward, protector), *hla + τford* (lord) are frequent synonyms. Most of them are also applied to *Christ,* originally a Greek word and the most usual name for the Second Person of the Trinity, but *Hælend* (Savior) is also commonly employed.

The Third Person (Spiritus Sanctus) was translated *Ha + τlig Ga + τst* (Holy Ghost). Latin diabolus was borrowed as *dēofol* (devil) but we find *fēond* (fiend) as a common synonym. Examples might be multiplied. Cross is *rōd* (rood), *trēow* (tree), *gealga* (gallows), etc.; resurrection is *ǣrist,* from *a + τrı + san* (to arise); *peccatum* is *synn* (sin), while other words like *ma + ōn, firen, leahtor, wōh,* and *scyld,* meaning 'vice', 'crime', 'fault', and the like, are commonly substituted. The Judgment Day is *Doomsday.* Many of these words are translations of their Latin equivalents and their vitality is attested by the fact that in a great many cases they have continued in use down to the present day. It is important to recognize that the significance of a foreign influence is not to be measured simply by the foreign words introduced but is revealed also by the extent to which it stimulates the language to independent creative effort and causes it to make full use of its native resources.

To be sure, the extent of a foreign influence is most readily seen in the number of words borrowed. As a result of the Christianizing of Britain some 450 Latin words appear in English writings before the close of the Old English period. This number does not include derivatives or proper names, which in the case of biblical names are very numerous. But about one hundred of these were purely learned or retained so much of their foreign character as hardly to be considered part of the English vocabulary.

Of the 350 words that have a right to be so considered some did not make their way into general use until later — were, in fact, reintroduced later. On the other hand, a large number of them were fully accepted and thoroughly incorporated into the language. The real test of a foreign influence is the degree to which the words that it brought in were assimilated. This is not merely a question of the power to survive; it is a question of how completely the words were digested and 'became indistinguishable from the native wordstock, so that they could enter into compounds and be made into other parts of speech, just like native words.

When, for example, the Latin noun *planta* comes into English as the noun *plant* and later is made into a verb by the addition of the infinitive ending *-ian* (*plantian*) and other inflectional elements, we may feel sure that the word has been assimilated. This happened in a number of cases as in *gentartyrian* (to martyr), *sealmian* (to play on the harp), *culpian* (to humiliate oneself), *fersian* (to versify), *glçsan* (to gloss), and *crispian* (to curl).. Assimilation is likewise indicated by the use of native formative suffixes such as *-dōm, -hα + τd, -ung* to make a concrete noun into an abstract (*martyrdôm, martyrhα + τd, martyrung*).

The use of a foreign word in making compounds is evidence of the same thing. The word *church* enters into more than forty compounds and derivatives (*church-bell, church-book, church-door*, etc.). The Latin influence of the Second Period was not only extensive but thorough and marks the real beginning of the English habit of freely incorporating foreign elements into its vocabulary.

The Scandinavian Influence

The Viking Age

Near the end of the Old English period English underwent a third foreign influence, the result of contact with another important language, the Scandinavian. In the course of history it is not unusual to witness the spectacle of a nation or people, through causes too remote or complex for analysis, suddenly emerging from obscurity, playing for a time a conspicuous, often brilliant, part, and then, through causes equally difficult to define, subsiding once more into a relatively minor sphere of activity.

Such a phenomenon is presented by the Teutonic inhabitants of the Scandinavian peninsula and Denmark, one-time neighbors of the Anglo-Saxons and closely related to them in language and blood. For some centuries the Scandinavians had remained quietly in their northern home. But in the eighth century a change, possibly economic, possibly political, occurred in this area and provoked among them a spirit of unrest and adventurous enterprise. They began a series of attacks upon all the lands adjacent to the North Sea and the Baltic. Their activities began in plunder and ended in conquest.

The Swedes established a kingdom in Russia; Norwegians colonized parts of the British Isles, the Faroes and Iceland, and from there pushed on to Greenland and the coast of Labrador; the Danes founded the dukedom of Normandy and finally conquered England. The pinnacle of their achievement was reached in the beginning of the eleventh century when Cnut, king of Denmark, obtained the throne of England, conquered Norway, and from his English capital ruled the greater part of the Scandinavian world.

The daring sea-rovers to whom these unusual achievements were due are commonly known as Vikings, and the period of their activity, extending from the middle of the eighth century to the beginning of the eleventh, is popularly known as the Viking Age. It was to their attacks upon, settlements in, and ultimate conquest of England that the Scandinavian influence upon Old English was due.

The Scandinavian Invasions of England

In the Scandinavian attacks upon England three well-marked stages can be distinguished. The first is the period of early raids, beginning according to the Anglo-Saxon Chronicle in 787 and continuing with some intermissions until about 850. The raids of this period were simply plundering attacks upon towns and monasteries near the coast. Sacred vessels of gold and silver, jeweled shrines, costly robes, valuables of all kinds, and slaves were carried off.

Noteworthy instances are the sacking of Lindisfarne and Jarrow in 793 and 794. But with the plundering of these two famous monasteries the attacks apparently ceased for forty years, until renewed in 834 along the southern coast and in East Anglia. These early raids were apparently the work of small isolated bands. The second stage is the work of large armies and is marked by widespread plundering in all parts of the country and by extensive settlements.

This new development was inaugurated by the arrival in 850 of a Danish fleet of 350 ships. Their pirate crews wintered in the isle of Thanet and the following spring captured Canterbury and London and ravaged the surrounding country. Although finally defeated by a West Saxon army they soon renewed their attacks. In 866 a large Danish army plundered East Anglian and in 867 captured York. In 869 the East Anglian king, Edmund, met a cruel death in resisting the invaders.

The incident made a deep impression on all England, and the memory of his martyrdom was vividly preserved in English tradition for nearly two centuries. The eastern part of England was now largely in the hands of the Danes, and they began turning their attention to Wessex. The attack upon Wessex began shortly before the accession of King Alfred. Even the greatness of this greatest of English kings threatened to prove insufficient to withstand the repeated thrusts of the

Northmen. After seven years of resistance, in which temporary victories were invariably succeeded by fresh defeats, Alfred was forced to take refuge with a small band of personal followers in the marshes of Somerset.

But in this darkest hour for the fortunes of the English Alfred's courage and persistence triumphed. With a fresh levy of men from Somerset, Wiltshire, and Hampshire, he suddenly attacked the Danish army under Guthrum at Ethandun (now Edington, in Wiltshire). The result was an overwhelming victory for the English and a capitulation by the Danes. The Treaty of Wedmore (near Glastonbury), which was signed by Alfred and Guthrum the same year, marks the culmination of the second stage in the Danish invasions. Wessex was saved. The Danes withdrew from Alfred's territory. But they were not compelled to leave England.

The treaty merely defined the line, running roughly from Chester to London, to the east of which the foreigners were henceforth to remain. This territory was to be subject to Danish law and is hence known as the Danelaw. In addition the Danes agreed to accept Christianity, and Guthrum was baptized. This last provision was important. It might secure the better observance of the treaty, and, what was more important, it would help to pave the way for the ultimate fusion of the two groups. The third stage of the Scandinavian incursions covers the period of political adjustment and assimilation from 878 to 1042.

The Treaty of Wedmore did not put an end to Alfred's troubles. Guthrum was inclined to break faith and there were fresh invasions from outside. But the situation slowly began to clear. Under Alfred's son Edward the Elder and grandson Athelstan the English began a series of counterattacks that put the Danes on the defensive. One of the brilliant victories of the English in this period was Athelstan's triumph in 937 in the battle of Brunanburh, in Northumbria, over a combined force of Danes and Scots, a victory celebrated in one of the finest of Old English poems. By the middle of the century a large part of eastern England, though still strongly Danish in blood and custom, was once more under English rule. Toward the end of the century, however, when England seemed at last on the point of solving its Danish problem, a new and formidable succession of invasions began. In 991 a fleet of ninety-three ships under Olaf Tryggvason and his associates suddenly entered the Thames.

They were met by Byrhtnoth, the valiant earl of the East Saxons, in a battle celebrated in another famous Old English war poem, *The Battle of Maldon.* Here the English, heroic in defeat, lost their leader, and soon the invaders were being bribed by large sums to refrain from plunder. The invasions now began to assume an official character. In 994 Olaf, who shortly became king of Norway, was joined by Svein, king of Denmark, in a new attack on London. The sums necessary to buy off the enemy became greater and greater, rising in 1012 to the amazing figure of £ 48,000. In each case the truce thus bought was temporary, and Danish forces were soon again marching over England, murdering and pillaging. Finally Svein determined to make himself king of the country.

In 1014, supported by his son Cnut, he crowned a series of victories in different parts of England by driving Ethelred, the English king, into exile and seizing the throne. Upon his sudden death the same year his son succeeded him. Three years of fighting established Cnut's claims to the throne, and for the next twenty-five years England was ruled by Danish kings.

The Settlement of the Danes in England

The events here rapidly summarized had as an important consequence the settlement of large numbers of Scandinavians in England. However temporary may have been the stay of many of the attacking parties, especially those which in the beginning came simply to plunder, many individuals remained behind when their ships returned home. Often they became permanent settlers in the island. Some indication of their number may be had from the fact that more than 1400 places in England bear Scandinavian names. Most of these are naturally in the north and east of England, the district of the Danelaw, for it was here that the majority of the invaders settled.

Most of the new inhabitants were Danes, although there were considerable Norwegian settlements in the northwest, especially in what is now Cumberland and Westmoreland, and in a few of the northern counties. The presence of a large Scandinavian element in the population is indicated not merely by place-names but by peculiarities of manorial organization, local government, legal procedure, and the like.

Thus we have to do not merely with large bands of marauders, marching and countermarching across England, carrying hardship and devastation into all parts of the country for upward of two centuries, but with an extensive peaceable settlement by farmers who intermarried with the English, adopted many of their customs, and entered into the everyday life of the community. In the districts where such settlements took place conditions were favorable for an extensive Scandinavian influence on the English language.

The Amalgamation of the Two Races

The amalgamation of the two races was greatly facilitated by the close kinship that existed between them. The problem of the English was not the assimilation of an alien race representing an alien culture and speaking a wholly foreign tongue. The policy of the English kings in the period when they were re-establishing their control over the Danelaw was to accept as an established fact the mixed population of the district and to devise a modus vivendi for its component elements. In this effort they were aided by the natural adaptability of the Scandinavian.

Generations of contact with foreign communities, into which their many enterprises had brought them, had made the Scandinavians a cosmopolitan people. The impression derived from a study of early English institutions is that in spite of certain native customs which the Danes continued to observe they adapted themselves largely to the ways of

English life. That many of them early accepted Christianity is attested by the large number of Scandinavian names found not only among monks and abbots, priests and bishops, but also among those who gave land to monasteries and endowed churches. It would be a great mistake to think of the relation between Anglo-Saxon and Dane, especially in the tenth century, as uniformly hostile.

One must distinguish, as we have said, between the predatory bands that continued to traverse the country and the large numbers that were settled peacefully on the land. Alongside the ruins of English towns – Symeon of Durham reports that the city of Carlisle remained uninhabited for two hundred years after its destruction by the Danes – there existed important communities established by the newcomers. They seem to have grouped themselves at first in concentrated centres, parceling out large tracts of land from which the owners had fled, and preferring this form of settlement to too scattered a distribution in a strange land.

Among such centres the Five Boroughs – Lincoln, Stamford, Leicester, Derby, and Nottingham – became important *foci* of Scandinavian influence. It was but a question of time until these large centres and the multitude of smaller communities where the Northmen gradually settled were absorbed into the general mass of the English population.

The Relation of the Two Languages

The relation between the two languages in the district settled by the Danes is a matter of inference rather than exact knowledge. Doubtless the situation was similar to that observable in numerous parts of the world today where people speaking different languages are found living side by side in the same region. While in some places the Scandinavians gave up their language early. There were certainly communities in which Danish or Norse remained for some time the usual language. Up until the time of the Norman Conquest the Scandinavian language in England was constantly being renewed by the steady stream of trade and conquest. In some parts of Scotland Norse was still spoken as late as the seventeenth century.

In other districts in which the prevailing speech was English there were doubtless many of the newcomers who continued to speak their own language at least as late as 1100 and a considerable number who were to a greater or lesser degree bilingual. The last-named circumstance is rendered more likely by the frequent intermarriage between the two races and by the similarity between the two tongues.

The Anglian dialect resembled the language of the Northmen in a number of particulars in which West Saxon showed divergence. The two may even have been mutually intelligible to a limited extent. Contemporary statements on the subject are conflicting, and it is difficult to arrive at a conviction. But wherever the truth lies in this debatable question, there can be no doubt that the basis existed for an extensive interaction of the two languages upon each other, and this conclusion is amply borne out by the large number of Scandinavian elements subsequently found in English.

The Tests of Borrowed Words

The similarity between Old English and the language of the Scandinavian invaders makes it at times very difficult to decide whether a given word in Modern English is a native or a borrowed word. Many of the commoner words of the two languages were identical, and if we had no Old English literature from the period before the Danish invasions, we should be unable to say that many words were not of Scandinavian origin. In certain cases, however, we have very reliable criteria by which we can recognize a borrowed word. These tests are not such as the layman can generally apply, although occasionally they are sufficiently simple.

The most reliable depend upon differences in the development of certain sounds in the North Teutonic and West Teutonic areas. One of the simplest to recognize is the development of the sound sk. In Old English this was early palatalized to *sh* (written sc), except possibly in the combination *scr*, whereas in the Scandinavian countries it retained its hard *sk* sound. Consequently, while native words like *ship, shall, fish* have *sh* in Modern English, words borrowed from the Scandinavians are generally still pronounced with *sk: sky, skin, skill, scrape, scrub, bask, whisk.* The O.E. *scyrte* has become shirt, while the corresponding O.N. form *skyrta* gives us *skirt.* In the same way the retention of the hard pronunciation of *k* and *g* in such words as *kid, dike* (cf. *ditch*) *get, give, gild, egg,* is an indication of Scandinavian origin. Occasionally, though not very often, the vowel of a word gives clear proof of borrowing.

For example, the Teutonic diphthong *ai* became *ɑ* + τ in Old English (and has becomed in modern English), but became ei or ē in Old Scandinavian. Thus *aye, nay* (beside *no* from the native word), *hale* (cf. the English form *(w)hole*), *reindeer, swain* are borrowed words, and many more examples can be found in Middle English and in the modern dialects. Thus there existed in Middle English the forms *geit, gait,* which are from Scandinavian, beside *gɑ* + *ēt, gōt* from the O.E. word.

The native word has survived in Modern English *goat.* In the same way the Scandinavian word for *loathsome* existed in Middle English as *leip, laip* beside *lɑ* + *τp, lōp.* Such tests as these, based on sound-developments in the two languages are the most reliable means of distinguishing Scandinavian from native words. But occasionally meaning gives a fairly reliable test. Thus our word *bloom* (flower) could come equally well from O.E. *blōma* or Scandinavian *blōm.* But the O.E. word meant an "ingot of iron', whereas the Scandinavian word meant 'flower, bloom'.

It happens that the Old English word has survived as a term in metallurgy, but it is the Old Norse word that has come down in ordinary use. Again, if the initial *g* in *gift* did not betray the Scandinavian origin of this word, we should be justified in suspecting it from the fact that the cognate O.E. word *gift* meant the 'price of a wife', and hence in the plural 'marriage,' while the O.N. word had the more general sense of 'gift, present'.

The word *plow* in Old English meant a measure of land, in Scandinavian the agricultural implement, which in Old English was called a *sulh.* When neither the form of a word nor its meaning proves its Scandinavian origin we can never be sure that we have to do with a borrowed word. The fact that an original has not been preserved in Old English is no proof that such an original did not exist.

Nevertheless when a word appears in Middle English which cannot be traced to an Old English source but for which an entirely satisfactory original exists in Old Norse, and when that word occurs chiefly in texts written in districts where Danish influence was strong, or when it has survived in dialectal use in these districts today, the probability that we have here a bor rowed word is fairly strong. In every case final judgment must rest upon a careful consideration of all the factors involved.

Scandinavian Place-names

Among the most notable evidences of the extensive Scandinavian settlement in England is the large number of places that bear Scandinavian names. When we find more than six hundred places like *Grimsby, Whitby, Derby, Rugby,* and *Thoresby,* with names ending in *-by,* nearly all of them in the district occupied by the Danes, we have a striking evidence of the number of Danes who settled in England. For these names all contain the Danish word *by,* meaning 'farm or 'town', a word which is also seen in our word *by-law* (town law).

Some three hundred names like *Althorp, Bishopsthorpe, Gawthorpe, Linthorpe* contain the Scandinavian word *thorp* (village). An almost equal number contain the word *thwaite* (an isolated piece of land) – *Applethwaite, Braithwaite, Cowperthwaite, Langthwaite, Satterthwaite.* About a hundred places bear names ending in *toft* (a piece of ground, a messuage) – *Brimtoft, Eastoft, Langtoft, Lowestoft, Nortoft.* Numerous other Scandinavian elements enter into English place-names, which need not be particularized here. It is apparent that these elements entered intimately in the speech of the people of the Danelaw.

It has been remarked above that more than 1400 Scandinavian place-names have been counted in England, and the number will undoubtedly be increased when a more careful survey of the material has been made. These names are not uniformly distributed over the Danelaw. The largest number are found in Yorkshire and Lincolnshire. In some districts in these counties as many as 75 per cent of the place-names are of Scandinavian origin.

Cumberland and Westmoreland contribute a large number, reflecting the extensive Norse settlements in the northwest, while Norfolk, with a fairly large representation, shows that the Danes were numerous in at least this part of East Anglia. It may be remarked that a similar high percentage of Scandinavian personal names has been found in the medieval records of these districts. Names ending in *son,* like *Stevenson* or *Johnson,* conform to a characteristic Scandinavian custom, the equivalent Old English patronymic being *-ng,* as in Browning.

The Earliest Borrowing

The extent of this influence on English place-nomenclature would lead us to expect a large infiltration of other words into the vocabulary. But we should not expect this infiltration to show itself at once. The early relations of the invaders with the English were too hostile to lead to much natural intercourse, and we must allow time for such words as the Anglo-Saxons learned from their enemies to find their way into literature. The number of Scandinavian words that appear in Old English is consequently small, amounting to only about two score.

The largest single group of these is such as would be associated with a sea-roving and predatory people. Words like *barda* (beaked ship), *cnearr* (small warship), *scegh* (vessel), *lip* (fleet), *sceghtnann* (pirate), *dreng* (warrior), *ha + τ* (oarlock) and *ha + τ-sǣta* (rower in a warship), *ba + τtswegen* (boatman), *hofding* (chief, ringleader), *orrest* (battle), *ra + ôn* (robbery, rapine), and *fylcian* (to collect or marshal a force) show in what respects the invaders chiefly impressed the English. A little later we find a number of words relating to the law or characteristic of the social and administrative system of the Danelaw. The word law itself is of Scandinavian origin, as is the word *outlaw*. The word *ma + τl* (action at law), *hold* (freeholder), *wapentake* (an administrative district), *hûsting* (assembly), and *riding* (originally *thriding*, one of the three divisions of Yorkshire) owe their use to the Danes.

In addition to these, a number of genuine Old English words seem to be translations of Scandinavian terms: *bôtlças* (what cannot be compensated), *ha + τnsōcn* (attacking an enemy in his house), *lahcēap* (payment for re-entry into lost legal rights), *landcēap* (tax paid when land was bought) are examples of such translations. English legal terminology underwent a complete reshaping after the Norman Conquest, and most of these words have been replaced now by terms from the French. But their temporary existence in the language is an evidence of the extent to which Scandinavian customs entered into the life of the districts in which the Danes were numerous.

Scandinavian Loan-words and their Character

It was after the Danes had begun to settle down peaceably in the island and enter into the ordinary relations of life with the English that Scandinavian words commenced to enter in numbers into the language. If we examine the bulk of these words with a view to dividing them into classes and thus discovering in what domains of thought or experience the Danes contributed especially to English culture and therefore to the English language, we shall not arrive at any significant result.

The Danish invasions were not like the introduction of Christianity, bringing the English into contact with a different civilization and introducing them to many things, physical as well as spiritual, that they had not known before. The civilization of the invaders was very much like that of the

English themselves, if anything somewhat inferior to it. Consequently the Scandinavian elements that entered the English language are such as would make their way into it through the give and take of everyday life. Their character can best be conveyed by a few examples, arranged simply in alphabetical order.

Among nouns that came in are *axle-tree, band, bank, birth, boon, booth, brink, bull, calf* (of leg), *crook, dirt, down* (feathers), *dregs, egg, fellow, freckle, gait, gap, girth, guess, hap, keel, kid, leg, link, loan, mire, race, reindeer, reef* (of sail), *rift, root, scab, scales, score, scrap, seat, sister, skill, skin, skirt, sky, slaughter, snare, stack, steak, swain, thrift, tidings, trust, want, window.*

The list has been made somewhat long in order the better to illustrate the varied and yet simple character of the borrowings. Among adjectives we find *awkward, flat, ill, loose, low, meek, muggy, odd, rotten, rugged, scant, seemly, sly, tattered, tight,* and *weak*. There is also a surprising number of common verbs among the borrowings, verbs like *to bait, bask, batten, call, cast, clip, cow, crave, crawl, die, droop, egg (on), flit, gape, gasp, get, give, glitter, kindle, lift, lug, nag, ransack, raise, rake, rid, rive, scare, scout* (an idea), *scowl, screech, snub, splint, take, thrive, thrust*. Lists such as these suggest better than any explanation the familiar, everyday character of the words which the Scandinavian invasions and subsequent settlement brought into English.

The Relation of Borrowed and Native Words

It will be seen from the words in the above lists that in many cases the new words could have supplied no real need in the English vocabulary. They made their way into English simply as the result of the mixture of the two races. The Scandinavian and the English words were being used side by side, and the survival of one or the other must often have been a matter of chance. Under such circumstances a number of things might happen. Where words in the two languages coincided more or less in form and meaning the modern word stands at the same time for both its English and its Scandinavian ancestors. Examples of such words are *burn, cole, drag, fast, gang, murk(y), scrape, thick.* Where there were differences of form the English word often survived.

Beside such English words as *bench, goat, heathen, yarn, few, grey, loath, leap, flay* corresponding Scandinavian forms are found quite often in Middle English literature and in some cases still exist in dialectal use. We find *screde, skelle, skere* with the hard pronunciation of the initial consonant group beside' the standard Enghsh shred, shell, sheer, wae beside woe, the surviving form except in *welaway, trigg* the Old Norse equivalent of O.E. *trēowe* (true). Again where the same idea was expressed by different words in the two languages it was often, as we should expect, the English word that lived on. We must remember that the area in which the two languages existed for a time side by side was confined to the northern and eastern half of England.

Examples are the Scandinavian words *attlen* beside English *think* (in the sense of *purpose, intend*), *bolnen beside swell, tinen* (O.N. *tȳna*) beside *lose, site* beside *sorrow, roke* (fog) beside *mist, reike* beside *path.* In other cases the Scandinavian word replaced the native word, often after the two had long remained in use concurrently. Our word *awe* from Scandinavian, and its cognate *eye* (*aye*) from Old English are both found in the *Ormulum.* In the earlier part of the Middle English period the English word is commoner, but by 1300 the Scandinavian form begins to appear with increasing frequency, and finally replaces the Old English word. The two forms must have been current in the everyday speech of the northeast for several centuries, until finally the pronunciation *awe* prevailed.

The Old English form is not found after the fourteenth century. The same thing happened with the two words for egg, *ey* (English) and *egg* (Scandinavian). Caxton complains at the close of the fifteenth century that it was hard even then to know which to use. In the words *sister* (O.N. *syster,* O.E. *sweostor*), *boon* (O.N. *bōn,* O.E. *bēn*), *loan* (O.N. *la* + τ*n,* O.E. *laen*), *weak* (O.N. *veikr,* O.E. *wa* + τ*c*) the Scandinavian form lived. Often a good Old English word was lost, since it expressed the same idea as the foreign word.

Thus the verb *take* replaced the O.E. *niman; cast* superseded the O.E. *weorpan,* while it has itself been largely displaced now by *throw; cut* took the place of O.E. *snı* + *∂* + *an* and *ceorfan.* Old English bad several words for *anger* (O.N. *angr*), including *torn, grama,* and *irre,* but the Old Norse word prevailed.

In the same way the Scandinavian word *bark* replaced O.E. *rind, wing* replaced O.E. *fepra, sky* took the place of *ûprodor* and *wolcen* (the latter now being preserved only in the poetical word *welkin*), and *window* (= wind-eye) drove out the equally appropriate English word ē*agpȳrel* (eye-thirl, i.e., eye-hole; cf. *nostril* = nose thirl, nose hole). Occasionally both the English and the Scandinavian words were retained with a difference of meaning or use, as in the following pairs (the English word is given first): *no-nay, whole – hale, rear – raise, from – fro, craft – skill, hide – skin, sick – ill.*

In certain cases a native word which was apparently not in common use was reinforced, if not reintroduced, from the Scandinavian. In this way we must account for such words as *till, dale, rim, blend, run,* and the Scotch *bairn.* Finally, the English word might be modified, taking on some of the character of the corresponding Scandinavian word. *Give* and *get* with their hard g are examples, as are *scatter* beside *shatter,* and *Thursday* instead of the O.E. *Thunresdæg.* Some confusion must have existed in the Danish area between the Scandinavian and the English form of many words, a confusion that is clearly betrayed in the survival of such hybrid forms as *shriek* and *screech.*

All this merely goes to show that in the Scandinavian influence on the English language we have to do with the intimate mingling of two tongues. The results are just what we should expect when two rather similar languages are spoken for upwards of two centuries in the same area. If further evidence were needed of the intimate relation that existed between the two languages, it would be found in the fact that the Scandinavian words that made their way into

English were not confined to nouns and adjectives and verbs, but extended to pronouns, prepositions, adverbs, and even a part of the verb *to be.* Such parts of speech are not often transferred from one language to another. The pronouns they, *their,* and *them* are Scandinavian. Old English used *hie, hiera, him.* Possibly the Scandinavian words were felt to be less subject to confusion with forms of the singular.

Moreover, though these are the most important, they are not the only Scandinavian pronouns to be found in English. A late Old English inscription contains the Old Norse form *hanum* for *him. Both* and *same,* though not primarily pronouns, have pronominal uses and are of Scandinavian origin. The preposition *till* was at one time widely used in the sense of *to,* besides having its present meaning, and *fro,* likewise in common use formerly as the equivalent *of from,* survives in the phrase *to and fro.*

Both words are from the Scandinavian. From the same source comes the modern form of the conjunction *though,* the Old Norse equivalent of O.E. *pçah.* The Scandinavian use of at as a sign of the infinitive is to be seen in the English *ado (at-do)* and was more widely used in this construction in Middle English The adverbs *aloft, athwart, aye* (ever), and *seemly,* and the earlier *hepen* (hence) and *hwepen* (whence) are all derived from the Scandinavian.

Finally the present plural *are* of the verb *to be* is a most significant adoption. While *we àron* was the Old English form in the north, the West Saxon plural was *syndon* (cf. German *sind*) and the form *are* in Modern English undoubtedly owes its extension to the influence of the Danes. When we remember that in the expression *they are* both the pronoun and the verb are Scandinavian we realize once more how intimately the language of the invaders has entered into English.

Scandinavian Influence outside the Standard Speech

We should miss the full significance of the Scandinavian influence if we failed to recognize the extent to which it is found outside the standard speech. Our older literature and the modern dialects are full of words which are not now in ordinary use. The ballads offer many examples. When the *Geste of Robin Hood* begins "*Lythe* and listin, gentilmen" it has for its first word an Old Norse synonym for *listen.* When a little later on the Sheriff of Nottingham says to Little John"Say me nowe, *wight* yonge man, What is nowe thy name?" he uses the O.N. *vigt* (strong, courageous). In the ballad of *Captain Car* the line "*Busk* and *bowne,* my merry men all" contains two words from the same source meaning *prepare.* The word *gar,* meaning *to cause* or *make one do something,* is of frequent occurrence.

Thus, in *Chevy Chace* we are told of Douglas' men that "Many a doughetë the(y) *garde* to dy" – i.e., they made many a doughty man die. In *Robin Hood and Guy of Gisborne* the Virgin Mary is addressed: "Ah, deere Ladyl sayd Robin Hoode, Thou art both mother and *may!*" in which *may* is a Scandinavian form for *maid.* Bessie Bell and Mary Gray, in the ballad of that name, "*bigget* a bower on yon burn-brae", employing in the process another word of Norse origin, *biggen* (to build), a word also used by Burns in *To a Mouse:* "Thy wee bit housie, too, in ruin! . . .

And naething now to big a new ane." In Burns and Scott we find the comparative *worse* in the form *waur:* "A' the warld kens that they maun either marry or do waur" (*Old Mortality*), also an old word (O.N. *verre*) more commonly found in the form used by Chaucer in the *Book of the Duchess:*"Allasl how myghte I fare werre?" Examples could be multiplied, but it is sufficiently evident that there is much Scandinavian material in the dialects besides what has found its way into the standard speech.

Effect on Grammar and Syntax

That the Scandinavian influence not only affected the vocabulary but extended to matters of grammar and syntax as well is less capable of exact demonstration but is hardly to be doubted. Inflections are seldom transferred from one language to another. A certain number of inflectional elements peculiar to the Northumbrian dialect have been attributed to Scandinavian influence, among others the *-s* of the third person singular, present indicative, of verbs and the participial ending *-and* (*bindand*), corresponding to *-end* and *-ind* in the Midlands and South, and now replaced by *-ing*. The words *scant, want, athwart* preserve in the final *t* the neuter adjective ending of Old Norse.

But this is of no great significance. It is much more important to recognize that in many words the English and Scandinavian languages differed chiefly in their inflectional elements. The body of the word was so nearly the same in the two languages that only the endings would put obstacles in the way of mutual understanding.

In the mixed population which existed in the Danelaw these endings must have led to much confusion, tending gradually to become obscured and finally lost. It seems but natural that the tendency toward the loss of inflections, which was characteristic of the English language in the north even in Old English times, was strengthened and accelerated by the conditions that prevailed in the Danelaw, and that some credit must be given the Danes for a development which, spreading to other parts and being carried much further, resulted after the Norman Conquest in so happily simplifying English grammar.

Likewise, the way words are put together in phrases and clauses — what we call syntax — is something in which languages less often influence each other than in matters of vocabulary. The probability of such influence naturally varies with the degree of inti macy that exists between the speakers of two languages. In those parts of Pennsylvania — the ' Pennsylvania Dutch' districts — where German and English have mingled in a jargon peculiar to itself, German turns of expression are frequently found in the English spoken there. It is quite likely that the English spoken in the districts where there were large numbers of Danes acquired certain Danish habits of expression.

A modern Dane like Jespersen notes that the omission of the relative pronoun in relative clauses (rare in Old English) and the retention or omission of the conjunction *that* are in conformity with Danish usage; that the rules for the use of *shall* and *will* in Middle English are much the same as in Scandinavian; and that some apparently illogical uses of these auxiliaries in Shakespeare do not seem strange to a Dane, who would employ the same verb.

Logeman notes the tendency, common to both languages, to put a strong stress at times on the preposition, and the occurrence of locutions such as 'he has some one to work for', which are not shared by the other Teutonic languages. It is possible, of course, that similarities such as these are merely coincidences that the Scandinavian languages and English happened to develop in these respects along similar lines. But there is nothing improbable in the assumption that certain Scandinavian turns of phrase and certain particular usages should have found their way into the idiom of people in no small part Danish in descent and living in intimate contact with the speakers of a Scandinavian tongue.

It is hardly possible to estimate the extent of the Scandinavian influence by the number of borrowed words that exist in Standard English. That number, if we restrict the list to those for which the evidence is fully convincing, is about nine hundred.

These, as the examples given above show, are almost always words designating common every day things and fundamental concepts. To this group we should probably be justified in adding an equal number in which a Scandinavian origin is probable or in which the influence of Scandinavian forms has entered.

Furthermore there are, according to Wright, the editor of the *English Dialect Dictionary,* thousands of Scandinavian words which are still a part of the everyday speech of people in the north and east of England and in a sense are just as much a part of the living language as those that are used in other parts of the country and have made their way into literature. He notes that "if we exclude all *sc-* words of various origins which are common to the standard language and the dialects, it is a remarkable fact that the *English Dialect Dictionary* contains 1,154 simple words beginning with *sc-* (*sk-*)." Locally, at least, the Scandinavian influence was tremendous. The period during which this large Danish element was making its way into the English vocabulary was doubtless the tenth and the eleventh century.

This was the period during which the merging of the two races was taking place. The occurrence of many of the borrowed words in written records is generally somewhat later. A considerable number first make their appearance in the *Ormulum* at the beginning of the thirteenth century. But we must attribute this fact to the scarcity of literary texts of an earlier date, particularly from the region of the Danelaw. Because of its extent and the intimate way in which the borrowed elements were incorporated, the Scandinavian influence is one of the most interesting of the foreign influences that have contributed to the English language.

ENGLISH OF BRITISH AND AMERICAN

In the UK, a student is said to *study* a subject, while in the U.S., a student either *studies* the subject or *majors* in it. Unlike most of the world where university students pursue a single field of study, United States universities often require a variety of courses. *To major* refers only to the student's principal course of study, while *to study* may refer to any class being taken.

At the tertiary level in BrE, a *module* is taught by a *lecturer*, while in AmE, a *class* is taught by a *professor*. At the primary and secondary levels the term "teacher" is used instead in both BrE and AmE. The term "lecturer," in an educational context, would be perceived in AmE as denoting anyone, professor or special guest, giving an actual lecture before a class.

BrE:

"She studied history at Bristol."

"She read history at Oxford."

AmE:

"She majored in history at Yale."

"He majored in Elementary Education at the University of Minnesota."

The word *course* is ambiguous in American usage. It may refer to a student's major (as in the phrase "course of study") but more commonly it refers to the study of a restricted topic (for example, "a course in Early Medieval England", "a course in Integral Calculus") and is equivalent to a *module* at a British University.

In the UK, a student *revises* or *does revision* for an examination, while in AmE, the student *reviews* for it. In the UK, a student is said to *sit* or *take* an exam, while in the U.S., a student *takes* an exam. The expression *he sits for* an exam also arises in BrE, but only rarely in AmE; American lawyers-to-be *sit for* their bar exams, and American master's and doctoral students may *sit for* their comprehensive exams, but in nearly all other instances, Americans *take* their exams. Examinations are supervised by *invigilators* in the UK and *proctors* (or *(exam) supervisors*) in the U.S. In the UK, a teacher *sets* an exam, while in the U.S., a teacher *writes* or *gives* an exam.

BrE:

"I sat my Spanish exam yesterday."

"I plan to set a difficult exam for my students, but I haven't got it ready yet."

AmE:

"I took my exams at Yale."

"I spent the entire day yesterday writing the exam. I'm almost ready to give it to my students."

Another source of confusion is the different usage of the word *college*. (See a full international discussion of the various meanings at college.) In the U.S., this refers to a post-high school institution that grants bachelor's degrees, while in the UK it refers primarily to a tertiary institution between secondary school and university (normally referred to as a *Sixth Form College* after the old name in secondary education for Years 12 and 13, the *6th form*) where intermediary courses such as A Levels or NVQs can be taken and GCSE courses can be retaken, with the interchangeability of college with secondary school being rare but not unknown.

In both the U.S. and UK, *college* can refer to some division within a university such as the "college of business and economics". Institutions in the U.S. that offer two to four years of post-high school education often have the word *college* as part of their name, while those offering more advanced degrees are called a *university*. (There are exceptions, of course: Boston College, Dartmouth College and The College of William and Mary are examples of colleges that offer advanced degrees.) (An obvious sign that an educational institution aspires to a better station in life may be seen when it drops "college" from its name and substitutes "university.")

American students who pursue a *bachelor's degree* (four years of higher education) or an *associate degree* (two years of higher education) are *college students* regardless of whether they attend a college or a university and refer to their educational institutions informally as *colleges*. A student who pursues a master's degree or a doctorate degree in the arts and sciences is in AmE a *graduate student*; in BrE a *post-graduate student* although *graduate student* also sometimes used. Students of advanced professional programmes are known by their field (*business student, law student, medical student*, the last of which is frequently shortened to *med student*). Some universities also have a residential college system, the details of which may vary from school to school but generally involve common living and dining spaces as well as college-organized activities.

"Professor" has different meanings in BrE and AmE. In BrE it is the highest academic rank, followed by Reader, Senior Lecturer and Lecturer. In AmE "Professor" refers to academic staff of all ranks, with (Full) Professor (largely equivalent to the UK meaning) followed by Associate Professor and Assistant Professor.

There is additionally a difference between American and British usage in the word *school.* In British usage "school" by itself refers only to primary (elementary) and secondary (high) schools, and to *sixth forms* attached to secondary schools – if one "goes to school", this type of institution is implied. By contrast, an American student at a university may talk of "going to school" or "being in school". U.S. law students and med students almost universally speak in terms of going to "law school" and "med school," respectively. However, the word is used in BrE in the context of higher education; to describe a division grouping together several related subjects in a university, for example a "School of European Languages" containing *departments* for each language, and also in the term "art school".

Among high school and college students in the United States, the words *freshman* (or the gender-neutral term *frosh* or *first year*), *sophomore, junior* and *senior* refer to the first, second, third, and fourth years, respectively. It is important that the context of either high school or college first be established, or else it must be stated directly (that is, "She is a high school freshman." "He is a college junior."). Many institutions in both countries also use the term *first-year* as a gender-neutral replacement for *freshman,* although in the U.S. this is recent usage, formerly referring only to those in the first year as a graduate **student.**

One exception is the University of Virginia; since its founding in 1819, the terms "first-year", "second-year", "third-year", and "fourth-year" have been used to describe undergraduate university students. At the United States military academies, at least those operated directly by the federal government, a different terminology is used, namely "fourth class", "third class", "second class", and "first class" (note that the order of numbering is the reverse of the number of years in attendance).

In the UK, first year university students are often called *freshers,* especially early in the academic year; however, there are no specific names for those in other years, nor for school pupils. Graduate and professional students in the United States are known by their year of study (a "second-year medical student" or a "fifth-year doctoral candidate"; law students are generally not referred to as "nth-year law students", but rather "1L", "2L", or "3L").

While anyone in the U.S. who finishes studying at any educational institution by passing relevant examinations is said to *graduate* and to be a *graduate,* in the UK only degree and above level students can *graduate. Student* itself has a wider meaning in AmE, meaning any person of any age studying at any educational institution, whereas in BrE it tends to be used for people studying at a post-secondary educational institution.

In the UK, the U.S. equivalent of a *high school* is often referred to as a *secondary school* regardless of whether it is state funded or private. Secondary education in the United States also includes *middle school* or *junior high school,* a two or three year transitional school between elementary school and high school.

A *public school* has opposite meanings in the two countries. In the U.S. this is a government-owned institution supported by taxpayers. In England and Wales, the term strictly refers to a select group of prestigious private independent schools funded by students' fees, although it is often more loosely used to refer to any independent school. Independent schools are also known as *private schools*, and the latter is the correct term in Scotland and Northern Ireland for all such fee-funded schools. Strictly, the term *public school* is not used in Scotland and Northern Ireland in the same sense as in England, but nevertheless, Gordonstoun, the Scottish private school which Charles, Prince of Wales attended, is sometimes confusingly referred to as a *public school*. Government-funded schools in Scotland and Northern Ireland are properly referred to as *state schools* – but are sometimes confusingly referred to as *public schools* (with the same meaning as in the U.S.); whereas in the U.S., where most public schools are administered by local governments, a *state school* is typically a college or university run by one of the states.

Speakers in both the United States and the United Kingdom use several additional terms for specific types of secondary schools. A *prep school* or *preparatory school* is an independent school funded by tuition fees; the same term is used in the UK for a private school for pupils under thirteen, designed to prepare them for fee-paying public schools. An American *parochial school* covers costs through tuition and has affiliation with a religious institution.

In the UK, the state-funded education system grew from parish schools organised by the local established church, the Church of England (C.of E., or C.E.), and many schools, especially primary schools (up to age 11) retain a church connection and are known as *church schools, C.E. Schools* or *C.E. (Aided) Schools*. There are also *faith schools* associated with the Roman Catholic church and other major faiths, with a mixture of funding arrangements.

In the U.S., a *magnet school* receives government funding and has special admission requirements: students gain admission through superior performance on admission tests. The UK has city academies, which are independent privately sponsored schools run with public funding, and which can select up to 10% of pupils by aptitude.

Americans refer to *transportation,* while British people refer to *transport.* As *transportation* in Britain was a penalty for a crime, that is, *deportation,* the British use the word *communication* to include goods and persons, whereas in America the word primarily refers to messages sent by post or electronics. The British devised the term *telecoms* for this last use; it is not quite standard in America.

Differences in terminology are especially obvious in the context of roads. The British term *dual carriageway,* in American parlance, would be a *divided highway. Central reservation* on a *motorway* in the UK would be a *median* on a *freeway, expressway, highway,* or *parkway* in the U.S. The one-way lanes that make it possible to enter and leave such roads at an intermediate point without disrupting the flow of traffic are generally known as *slip roads* in the UK, but U.S. civil engineers call them *ramps,* and further distinguish between *on-ramps* (for entering) or *off-ramps* (for leaving).

When American engineers speak of *slip roads,* or *slip ramps,* they are referring to on-ramps and off-ramps that have been rearranged (through use of a grade separation) to minimize weaving on a freeway segment between two interchanges that are too close together. These last two terms are almost never used by the general public in the U.S. In the UK, the term *outside lane* refers to the higher-speed *overtaking lane* (*passing lane* in the U.S.) closest to the centre of the road, while *inside lane* refers to the lane closer to the edge of the road. These terms have the opposite meanings in AmE, with the *outside lane* being the one near the edge and the *inside lane* being the one closer to the median.

In much of the U.S., *outside lane* is only used in the context of a turn, in which case it depends on which direction the road is turning (i.e. if the road bends right the left lane is the *outside lane,* but if the road bends left the right lane is the *outside lane*). Both also refer to *slow* and *fast* lanes (even though all actual traffic speeds may be at or even above the legal speed limit). UK traffic officials, firefighters, and police officers refer to Lanes 1, 2 and 3, referring to the 'slow', 'middle' and 'fast' lanes respectively. In the U.S. the meanings are exactly reversed with Lane 1 referring to the fast lane and so on.

In the UK, *drink driving* is against the law, while in the U.S. the term is *drunk driving*. The legal term in the U.S. is "driving while intoxicated" (D.W.I.) or "driving under the influence" of alcohol (D.U.I.). The equivalent legal phrase in the UK is to be found "drunk in charge" of a motor vehicle (DIC).

When Christmas is explicitly mentioned in a greeting, the universal phrasing in North America is *Merry Christmas*. In Britain and Ireland, *Happy Christmas* is common, although *Merry Christmas* is often used. It is worth noting, however, that Americans quite often say "Happy Holidays" or "Season's Greetings" when referring to all winter holidays (Christmas, New Year's Day, Hanukkah and Kwanzaa) as a single event.

Punctuation

- *Full stops/Periods in abbreviations:* Americans tend to write "Mr.", "Mrs.", "St.", "Dr." etc., while British will usually, but not always, write "Mr", "Mrs", "St", "Dr", etc., following the rule that a full stop is used only when the last letter of the abbreviation is not the last letter of the complete word. However, many British writers would tend to write other abbreviations without a full stop, such as "Prof", "etc", "eg", and so on (so recommended by some Oxford dictionaries). The rationale behind this usage is that it is typographically more elegant, and that the omitted full stops/periods are essentially superfluous, as the reader recognizes the abbreviation without them. It also removes ambiguity by reserving the period for ending sentences. However, the "American" usage of periods after most abbreviations is also widely used in the UK. Note that in either case it is incorrect to put a period after units such as kg for kilogram or Hz for hertz, as these are considered unit symbols, not abbreviations; however, in non-scientific contexts, the unit for "inch" is often written "in.", as it would be ambiguous without the period.

- It is sometimes believed that BrE does not hyphenate multiple-word adjectives (e.g. "a first class ticket"). The most common form is as in AmE ("a first-class ticket"), but some British writers omit the hyphen when no ambiguity would arise.
- *Quoting:* Americans start with double quotation marks (") and use single quotation marks (') for quotations within quotations. In general this is also true of BrE, but can be the opposite when used in book publishing, for example. In journals and newspapers, quotation mark double/single use depends on the individual publication's house style.
- *Contents of quotations:* Americans are taught to put commas and periods inside quotation marks, whereas British people will put the punctuation inside if it belongs to the quote and outside otherwise. This means that direct speech retains punctuation inside the quotation marks in BrE also, with a full stop changing into a comma if followed by explanatory text.

  – Carefree means "free from care or anxiety." (American style)

  – Carefree means "free from care or anxiety". (British style)

  – "Hello, world," I said. (both styles)

The American style was established for typographical reasons, an historical holdover from the days of the handset printing press. It also eliminates the need to decide whether a period or comma belongs to the quotation. However, many people find the usage counterintuitive. For this reason, the more "logical" British style is increasingly used in America, although formal writing still generally calls for the

"American" style. In fact, the British style is often the *de facto* standard among Americans for whom formal or professional writing is not a part of their daily life; many are in fact unaware that the normative American usage is to place commas and periods within the quotation marks. (This rule of placing all punctuation inside quotation if and only if it belongs to the quotation is expressly prescribed by some American professional organisations such as the American Chemical Society; see *ACS Style Guide*.) According to the Jargon File, American hackers have switched to using "logical" British quotation system, because including extraneous punctuation in a quotation can sometimes change the fundamental meaning of the quotation. More generally, it is difficult for computer manuals, online instructions, and other textual media to accurately quote exactly what a computer user should see or type on their computer if they follow American punctuation conventions.

In both countries, the "British" style is used for quotation around parentheses, so in both nations one would write:

"I am going to the store. (I hope it is still open.)"

But:

"I am going to the store (if it is still open)."

Letter-writing: American students in some areas have been taught to write a colon after the greeting in business letters ("Dear Sir:") while British people usually write a comma ("Dear Sir,") or make use of the so-called *open punctuation* ("Dear Sir"). However, this practice is not consistent throughout the United States, and it would be regarded as a highly formal usage by most Americans.

Chapter 8

Relationship of English to other Languages

THE INDO-EUROPEAN FAMILY

The English language belongs to the Teutonic branch of the Indo-European family of tongues. By a family of languages is meant a group bound together by unmistakable likenesses in words and grammatical forms. A branch indicates a smaller group which has, besides the characteristics of the larger division, a certain similarity in words and forms not known to other members of the family. This similarity within the group is accounted for by original union of all members of the family within a limited area; in other words, by a common home and a common ancestry.

The differences between two members of the same family, or group, are the result of gradual separation from one another, emphasized it may have been by some natural boundary, as a river or mountain range. Under these circumstances began changes in the spoken language, which in time resulted in different dialects.

Completer separation, as by migration, caused greater differences to appear, until the various languages of the group became mutually unintelligible and were no longer recognized by the casual observer as having anything in common. There still remain, however, in all members of the family a body of simple, every-day words easily recognized as cognates by the student of language, together with certain forms of inflection that the philologist is able to trace to a common source. There are in all about one hundred families of languages known to the philologist, although but few of these have been studied with any considerable degree of thoroughness.

The remaining families are made up of the aboriginal dialects of America and Africa, where the lack of literature and the rapid changes constantly going on, prevent the arrangement into determinate groups. The four families that have been most systematically investigated are the Hamitic, the Semitic, the Ural-Altaic, and the IndoEuropean families, in the last of which alone we are specially interested.

The Indo-European family consists of languages of the inflectional type; that is, in all members of the group words are made up of roots and inflectional endings, or modifying parts, united into inseparable wholes. But from this it is clear that we may suppose a time when the IndoEuropean, or parent speech, was not inflectional; that is, when the inflectional suffixes had not become attached to words.

This is sometimes called the root period of the parent speech. Later, words of the inflectional type gradually arose by a union of roots and suffixes, or by a soldering together of words forming a syntactical group. After the inflectional type had been assumed, the Indo-European family gradually split up into many dialects, the differentiation taking place as early as 2000 B.C. This is proved by the fact that we know the history of the languages of India from about 1500 B.C.

The Indo-European family includes eight branches, each of which has several sub-divisions. They are as follows: –

The Aryan Branch

This consists of two groups, the Indian and the Iranian. The Indian is represented by the archaic language of the Brahmanic scriptures, or *Veda*, the oldest portions of which were perhaps written as early as 1500 B.C. Nearest to this is the Sanskrit proper, the representative of a lost dialect very like the Vedic. Sanskrit became the literary language of India, and so has been handed down in a fixed form. Beside it existed a vulgar language, or Prakrit, differing from the Sanskrit as early as the third century B.C. The Prakrit was also adopted as a literary language by the Buddhists, and called Pali, while from it has descended in addition the numerous dialects of India. The Iranian is first represented by the Old Persian, in which cuneiform inscriptions were written from about 520 to 350 B.C. Next comes the Avestic, or Zend, the language of the sacred book of Zoroaster. The modern representatives of Iranian, though

not direct descendants of the Old Persian, or Zend, are the Persian, the Kurdish, and the Afghan.

The Armenian Branch

Armenian was long supposed to be a member of the Iranian group, but it has been recently proved to be an independent member of the IndoEuropean family. It is preserved as a literary language, Old Armenian, which dates from the fifth century A.D. when it was used in the Christian books of the Armenians. There are also modern Armenian dialects.

The Hellenic Branch

The Greek dialects, making up the Hellenic branch, are numerous. There are the Ionic-Attic; the Doric; the northwest Greek of Phocis, Ætolia, Epirus, etc.; the Æ olic; the Elean; the ArcadianCyprian; and the Pamphylian. The literary language, common to all Greeks, sprang from the Attic in the fifth century B.C. This is the form that has come down to us, the dialects being mainly known through inscriptions. There are also many dialects of Modern Greek, although their relation to the older language has not been accurately determined.

The Albanian Branch

This consists of the language of ancient Illyria, which has been known only since the seventeenth century. It is of little importance except to the philologist, who finds in it a connecting link between the Hellenic and the Italic branches.

The Italic Branch

To this branch belong the Latin and the Umbrian-Samnitic dialects. Latin, the literary language of ancient Rome, is known from about 300 B.C. when it sprang from the dialect of Latium. Side by side with this there existed a popular language, the vulgar Latin, which as spoken in the provinces developed into the Modern Romance languages, the most important being Italian, French, Spanish, and Portuguese. Of the Umbrian-Samnitic group, the best known are the Umbrian and the Oscan, with which we are acquainted through inscriptions dating from the last centuries before our era.

The Celtic Branch

The Celtic was originally spoken over Portugal, Spain, France, and England, but was later displaced by the Romance languages and English. This branch includes three groups: the Gallic, the Britannic, and the Gaelic. Gallic is little known except through names quoted by Greek and Latin authors, or through inscriptions and coins. Britannic includes the Cymric, or Welsh, the Cornish, and the Armorican of northwest France. Welsh and Armorican are known from the eighth or ninth centuries, Cornish from a somewhat later period.

The latter also became extinct at the end of the last, or the beginning of the present, century. To the Gaelic belong the Irish, the Scotch-Gaelic, and the Manx now spoken in the Isle of Man. The oldest Gaelic is known from inscriptions of about 500 A.D. Old Irish was a literary language in the eighth century, while Scotch-Gaelic literature begins somewhat later. Manx has been known only in the last few centuries.

The Balto-slavic Branch

This consists of the Prussian which died out in the seventeenth century, the Lithu anian and the Lettic, forming the Baltic group. The Slavonic group falls into two divisions, the southeastern and the western. The first comprises Russian in its varieties, with Bulgarian and Illyrian; the second, Czech, or Bohemian, Sorabian, and Polish. The oldest and most important of these is Old Bulgarian, the language in which the Slavonic apostles Cyril and Methodius wrote in the ninth century. It thus became the language of the Greek church, a somewhat modified form of it being called Church Slavonic.

The Teutonic Branch

This is the branch to which our own language belongs, together with German, Dutch, Flemish, and the Scandinavian languages. Its oldest representative is Gothic, preserved to us in a partial translation of the Bible by Bishop Ulfilas, who lived from 311 to 381 A.D. Norse, or Scandinavian, was a single speech down to the period of the Vikings 800 to 1000 A.D., its oldest records being runic inscriptions dating perhaps from the fourth century.

Other members of the Teutonic branch are Old English, Old Frisian, Old Saxon, Old Low Franconian, and Old High German, the more exact relationships of which will be given hereafter. The earliest records of these languages date from the seventh to the ninth centuries, with the exception of Frisian, which has been known only from the fourteenth century. In order to show the relation of the eight branches here described, the branching stem has been most frequently used.

This, however, fails to emphasize the common inheritance of all the Indo-European languages, besides not well representing the theory of dialectal divergence. A better representation of the more important relations appears in the accompanying diagram. The large oval in this diagram represents the common ground of words and grammatical forms.

The overlapping of the smaller circles indicates the possession of similar forms binding together the minor groups. The latter groups, while based on certain resemblances, take no account of others which might be regarded as important. With certain other characteristics in view, Teutonic and Celtic might be united; Latin and Greek also have some common bonds, and likewise Balto-Slavic and Indo-Iranian.

This indicates that the various branches of the Indo-Europian family are inseparably united by bonds that cross and recross in many ways. But the diagram above probably takes into account the more important relationships of the principal members of the family. The common ancestry of the Indo-European languages implies a common home in the remote past. But when we ask the geographical position of the parent race, we are met with various answers.

The view most commonly held in the past has been that this home was in the table-lands of central Asia. Fifty years ago however, an English scholar, Latham, proposed Europe as the original home of the Indo-European family and more and more this view has found support among scholars. When a European home was first proposed, the region assigned by scholars was that surrounding the southern end of the Baltic Sea; but more recently the tendency has been to place the home of the parent people farther south, until the region more commonly chosen at the present time is about the Black Sea in southern Russia.

The arguments for and against these views are too elaborate for our space, but it may be said in general that the conclusions rest upon a minute study of the culture of the parent people, as shown by the languages and literatures of its descendants. From this survey of the Indo-Eoropean family it will be evident that English is no isolated language, but that it belongs to a widely extended group with ramifications in all parts of Europe and considerable portions of Asia.

To all of these English is related through many common words inherited by all alike, and by many kindred inflectional forms which, though largely lost in our modern speech, can be explained only by a common ancestry with Sanskrit, Greek, Latin, Irish, Russian, and other languages. An extended treatment of these common bonds of union belongs to comparative philology, to which we owe many discoveries in recent years.

The Teutonic Languages

The three main divisions of Teutonic are Norse, or Scandinavian; Gothic; and West Germanic, a term which includes because of certain similarities all the other members of the group. Norse, or Scandinavian, may be divided into West Norse, including Norwegian and Icelandic, and East Norse, comprising Danish and Swedish. Gothic has no modern representative.

The language which Ulfilas used in his translation of the Bible was the speech of the West, or Visi-Goths. An East, or Ostro-Gothic speech remained in the Crimea until modern times, but only a few words of it have been preserved to us through the curiosity of travellers. Gothic and Norse were formerly classed together under the title East Germanic, but it is now more common to consider them as separate members of the Teutonic branch.

West Germanic as used above is a generic term, by which is meant that no such language is preserved to us except in its descendants, the historical representatives of this division. The name implies a theoretical speech, re-established by comparative study of the various members of the group.

It is used, therefore, to embody characteristics common to all the individuals, just as the term genus, applied to plants and animals, includes the characteristics common to all the species. West Germanic has two divisions, High German on the one side and Low German on the other. High German is that spoken in Germany to-day, or originally as the name implies, the language of that part of the Teutonic family which inhabited the highlands of Europe.

The distinguishing feature of High German, however, is owing to a consonant change, or shifting of consonants, which took place among the people dwelling in the highlands of Germany, but not among the people dwelling in the lowlands. The modern representative of High German is called New High German, or simply German, the oldest period of the speech being designated as Old High German, and the intermediate period as Middlle High German.

Low German, again a generic term, is used to designate all the languages not affected by the High German consonant change mentioned above. These are Old English, or Anglo-Saxon; Old Frisian, the descendant of which is still spoken on some of the islands off the coast of North Germany; Old Saxon, now Low German; Old Low Franconian, now Dutch, Flemish, and Low Franconian.

The general relationships of the older divisions of the Teutonic language may be represented by the following diagram similar to that used for the Indo-European family, § 5. The common ground of likeness in words and forms is shown by the large oval, into the circles representing the sub divisions are linked. We have also tried to show some important relationships within the group.

Thus Norse and Gothic may be said to be bound together by certain common characteristics. Old English and Old Frisian are even more completely united by common bonds, so that some scholars set up a theoretic Anglo-Frisian as the parent of both. Next to these come Low Franconian and Old Saxon, Old High German by reason of its consonant system stands alone. But is in the case of the

Indo-European languages, such a division into minor groups leaves out of account some other characteristics, by reason of which a different interlinking is possible. For example, Old Low Franconian may be linked with Old High German, and the latter for certain reasons with Old Norse or

Old Saxon. But this only shows that the union of the Teutonic languages is such as no diagram can fully represent. Some idea of the relative age of the various Teutonic languages, as well as an approximation to the time of their separation, may be gained.

Teutonic

Such a grouping suggests the questions, what are the characteristics on which it rests? In what respects does the Teutonic branch differ from the other branches of the Indo-European family? And since these are as necessary to an understanding of English as of any other Teutonic speech, they rightly belong here.

These characteristics, it should be remembered, are more noticeable in the older periods of the Teutonic languages, although no inconsiderable traces of them are still to be found in all members of the group.

The Great Consonant Shift

The Indo-European consonant system is not perfectly preserved in any language. It is most nearly kept in Sanskrit, and with considerable regularity in all other members of the family except Teutonic. The last therefore stands by itself by reason of characteristic consonantal differences. Even a superficial examination of the classical languages shows, that there are many words which have similar meanings and some resemblances in form, while in other respects they differ from English words.

Examples are Latin *frater*, English *brother*; the Latin roots *ped*, Eng. *foot; ed-*, Eng; *eat;* Latin *tu*, Eng. *thou; duo*, Eng. *two; qui*, Eng. *who* (*hwû*); *collis*, Eng. *hill*; and many others. Examination of many examples led Rask, a Danish scholar, to the discovery that these changes were in great measure regular and that they came about in accordance with a certain law of change. This law was afterwards formulated more completely by a Ger man scholar, Jacob Grimm, and from him it has been more commonly called Grimm's Law.

According to Grimm's statement of the law, certain series of consonant sounds show regular shiftings in the Teutonic languages, as compared with the classical or other IndoEuropean tongues. This statement, however, has been considerably modified by subsequent investigation. The great difficulty with Grimm's statement of the consonant shifting is, that the classical languages do not perfectly preserve the Indo-European consonant system and it is only when we consider this system that the law appears in its perfection.

For example, I-E. *dh* appears as è in Greek, and in Latin as *f* initially, *b* or *d* medially, while some other divergencies in the classical languages, compared with Indo-European, are equally great. For this reason it is necessary to state the law of consonant change, or the great consonant shift, from the standpoint of IndoEuropean. This we shall attempt to do, giving illustrative examples from Sanskrit, Greek, and Latin. The first or great consonant shift affected four series of Indo-European consonants as follows: –

I. a. The Labials *bh, b, p*.

II. a. The Dentals *dh, d, t*.

III. a. The Palatals *gh'2, g'2, k'2* .

IV. a. The Velars *gh, g, k*.

The last series shows a double development in Greek, Latin, Celtic, and Teutonic, so that it becomes necessary to make two divisions, –

1. a. The *gh, g, k* series, and

2. a. The *ghu, gu, ku* series,

in the last of whichu& represents a labialized form of the consonants, which later usually became a consonant + *w* or *u*. For Teutonic, however, series III and division 1 of series IV. have come together by a later development, so that the five divisions noted might again resolve themselves into four. But to prevent confusion, it seems better that the development of each series and subdivision should be considered separately, with some typical examples to illustrate the changes.

The Labial Series

The Indo-European labials *bh, b,* and Þ shifted in early Teutonic to *b,* í, and *f* respectively. It is important to note that I-Ė. *bh* appears only in Sanskrit, its Greek representative being Ô, and its Latin symbols f initially, and b medially. It may also be pointed out that I-E. *b* is a rare sound, its Teutonic equivalent í probably not occurring initially and seldom medially.

Chapter 9

The History of English Inflections

INFLECTIONAL LEVELLING IN ENGLISH

Our Modern English is called an analytic, or uninflected tongue. That is, present English does not rely on inflectional forms for expressing the various relations existing between nouns, adjectives, pronouns, and verbs, but either on a certain position in the sentence or on certain auxiliary words, as prepositions and auxiliary verbs. But the Indo-European family is characterized by words of the inflectional type and all members of the family partake of this characteristic.

The apparent inconsistency is explained when we know that every language belonging to the Indo-European family was in its older stages highly inflected, and only in later times is the inflectional character more or less completely lost in some members of the group, as in English, Danish, French, and others. Moreover English has not wholly lost the inflectional type, although the losses are more numerous than in some other members of the Teutonic group.

For we still retain case forms in the pronoun and one well marked case, the genitive or possessive in nouns. In the verb also we still have some inflectional forms, while others are preserved in the older language of poetry. To the question "In what way has English become an analytic tongue," it may be answered that there has been a gradual levelling of inflectional forms for centuries tinder the influence of phonetic changes affecting unstressed syllables, § 240, and of analogy, § 318. This process, too, is by no means peculiar to English. Other languages have undergone the same change, as for example the French, although present French spelling still retains numerous evidences of the older inflectional character.

In the 'Fetitonic branch, nearly all members of the Low German group have suffered similar losses, while Danish and Swedish are likewise analytic at the present time. Nor is the change in English one that has taken place in modern times, and due to causes peculiar to modern life. The change has been going on in all members of the IndoEuropean family from the earliest establishment of the inflectional system. This may be seen by comparing briefly the inflectional forms of primitive Indo-European with those of the derived languages.

The primitive Indo-European had eight cases for nouns, pronouns, and adjectives, each distinguished by a special ending. Sanskrit still retained these eight cases, the nominative, accusative, instrumental, dative, ablative, genitive, locative, and vocative, the names of which sufficiently indicate their use. But even in the classical languages the levelling process had begun, Latin having six, Greek but five cases.

This change came about by two or more cases losing their distinctive endings and so appearing in one form, although retaining the meaning and use of the original cases. Thus the genitive in Greek represents both the genitive and ablative of the primitive speech, while the dative combines the uses of the older dative, instrumental and locative. In Latin the instrumental and ablative of the primitive speech are merged in one, the ablative. The locative, on the other hand, has fallen in with the dative of the first and third declensions, and with the genitive of the second declension, while its function is performed many times by the ablative.

There were in primitive Indo-European three numbers, the singular, dual, and plural, each carried through noun, pronoun, adjective, and verb forms. These were preserved in Sanskrit and Greek but the dual does not occur in Latin.

The declensions of the primitive speech were numerous, the number being variously given by different scholars. Some idea of them may be gained, however, by observing that Whitney assigns to Sanskrit four vowels and one consonant declension, the last of which contains many varieties of stems. Greek and Latin reduced these declensions somewhat, but the consonant stems were still numerous and they may be divided into many classes.

The primitive Indo-European had a complicated and multiform verbal system. There were numerous classes of verbs, each having active, middle, and passive voices; subjunctive and optative moods; imperfect, aorist, and future tenses, with the dual number distinct in all as mentioned above. Both Sanskrit and Greek preserved this complicated system in most of its details. But latin had lost the aorist tense, and the middle voice except as it was preserved in deponent verbs. As in the case of nouns, Latin had no dual number in its verbal system.

The oldest historical form of Teutonic, the Gothic, shows some greater modifications of the Indo-European system than the classical languages. Yet Gothic possesses many forms not found in the other Teutonic languages. For example it retains the vocative singular in nouns as separate from the nominative, thus preserving the same number of cases as the Greek. Gothic also retains the dual number in pronoun and verb, although not in the noun.

In Gothic, as generally in Teutonic, the consonant stems are mainly those in *-an* (weak nouns, § 344), with a few anomalous ones, showing in this a great simplification compared with the classical tongues. In its verbal system Gothic still keeps some forms of the passive voice, but it has reduced the tenses to two, a present and a past, having lost the imperfect, aorist, and future.

For the West Germanic tongues the simplification is still greater. The extent to which these changes have gone may be best illustrated for our purpose by the oldest form of our own speech. Old English has lost the separate form of the vocative singular in nouns, a form still found in Gothic. This reduces the number of cases to four for all nouns, the dative and instrumental having separate forms only in one or two anomalous nouns, in adjectives, and in demonstrative and relative pronouns. As the nominative, vocative, and accusative are always alike in the plural and usually in the singular, the cases of most nouns are further reduced to three. Old English has no dual number except in personal pronouns, and the dual forms of these are seldom used.

Even when used they occur with plural verb forms, so that except in meaning they have no dual significance. The tendency to level the complicated inflectional system of the Indo-European is also seen in the Old English noun declensions. Nominally there are, besides the weak or consonant stems, four declensions of nouns, classified according to stems as the o, C, i, and u declensions. Practically, however, these are reduced to two, there being the merest handful of u stems, and the majority of the i stems having taken the declension of the o and C stems.

Old English has also lost all passive forms except in the case of one verb. The levelling tendency, so evident when we compare Old English with Gothic and Gothic with Indo-European, has been carried still further since Old English times. Particularly strong were the levelling tendencies during the Middle English period. Indeed this was the time when the older inflections were so thoroughly broken down that only a semblance of the original system remained.

Still other, though less numerous changes occurred in the early modern period, leaving English of to-day with slight evidences of the inflectional type originally so important a feature. From this we may see that when English is called an uninflected tongue, we only mean it has carried forward a process of inflectional levelling, common to all members of the Indo-European family, and especially characteristic of Teutonic. This process has gone so far in English that few remnants of a once complicated system are found in the modern speech. But since these changes have been going on from the earliest times, the impression that they have taken place since our English ancestors came to Britain is inaccurate and misleading.

Equally misleading is the impression, that the breaking down of inflectional forms has been directly due to the influence of foreign languages with which English has come in contact, especially Norman French, to which this levelling is often attributed. The loss of inflectional forms has occurred in other members of the Low German group where there has been slight influence from without, notably the Swedish, the Danish, and the Dutch. Moreover inflectional levelling had begun in Old English times. In late Old English it proceeded more rapidly, while in early Middle English the language was assuming its modern form, even in those localities least affected by foreign influences.

The language of Orm in the twelfth century, which shows almost no French influence in vocabulary, is nearly as inflectionless as the language of Chaucer two centuries later, which shows many French words in use. Moreover it is improbable, if not impossible, that the gradual introduction of words from the French could have influenced inflectional forms to any considerable extent. This must be conclusive from what has already been said of the relations of English and French in the Norman period.

Besides in the study of a language it is not safe to admit direct influence from without, except when it is impossible to explain the facts by natural development from within. We have already shown by a comparison of IndoEuropean and the derived languages that the levelling tendency is a natural one, common to all members of the group, and especially to Teutonic. Remembering this, we may easily discover the reason why the loss of inflections was greatly accelerated in the Middle English period. When Old English ceased to be a standard speech, that is an official and literary language, manuscripts of all kinds were written in the dialect most familiar to scribe or composer.

This absence of a standard speech removed the check upon almost indiscriminate levelling. Levelling was accelerated also by the fact that it was going on not in one locality but in many, so that part of the inflections were obliterated in one, part in another place. When a standard speech was later set up, the inflectional forms left by this many-sided levelling were few in number, and very different from those of the earlier time.

The effect of foreign tongues, especially French, was in preventing the establishment of a standard speech, rather than in directly breaking down the inflectional system of the native tongue. For it was only necessary to remove the check of standard usage to bring about all, or most of the changes taking place in the Middle English period. This will be clear from what has already been said in the chapter on Analogy.

In what has been said above the answer has virtually been given to the question, whether any of the English inflections have been borrowed from French or other foreign sources. For although borrowing of inflections has been asserted for English, the assertion his never been satisfactorily supported, and we may well fall back upon the principle already laid down that foreign influence is to be assumed only when nothing within the language will account for the fact in question.

Moreover inflections are so unobtrusive a part of speech, so closely associated with syntactical relations of the language to which they belong, that borrowing of them as distinct from words with which they are associated is in the highest degree improbable. It is true that inflections may sometimes be borrowed along with words to which they belong, as final s of the last word in the expression *knights templars.*

But in such cases it is far more natural to suppose that the expression was borrowed as a whole, rather than that the -s of the French adjective has been used as a borrowed inflection. It is far different when we assume, as in § 447, that -s of the verbal third singular has come rather from Northern English than from Midland. For in this case we must suppose that the same word, as *make*, was used for a time in the two forms maketh, makes, side by side, until finally the form with -s came to be preferred to the form with -eth. But in the case of the borrowing of an inflectional form we imply that the inflectional ending was not only borrowed along with words or expressions but that it was added to native words, becoming the predominant form.

In this sense, as said above, there has been no inflectional borrowing in English. Borrowing of inflectional endings must be separated from the adoption of formative suffixes, as French *-ess*, which have a more distinctive meaning of their own, and hence have often been attached to native words.

In considering the changes taking place in the inflections of our English speech, it must be remembered that they were brought about in the most gradual manner. As said before, there is no sharp dividing line between the language forms of different periods. Nevertheless it will be convenient to use the three divisions of our language history already mentioned and consider the inflections in relation to them.

We may thus follow Sweet in calling Old English the period of full inflections, Middle English the period of levelled inflections, and Modern English the period of lost inflections. The Middle English period is thus particularly important, and we shall consider more in detail the changes belonging in the main to this time. Still it must be borne in mind that inflectional levelling began in Old English and that it continued into the modern period.

Inflectional Chances from Old to Modern English

The inflectional levelling incident to English in the course of its history is often represented as wholly haphazard and incapable of systematic treatment. But this proceeds from a mistaken view of language and a misconception of the alterations it may undergo. In reality few changes in language are of the haphazard sort, and we may therefore expect to find, in the inflectional levelling of English, certain changes common to all forms and capable of careful and systematic statement.

These changes cannot be set down with chronological exactness, partly because there was no standard language in which alterations may be traced with ease, partly because changes were going on in some dialects more rapidly than in others. But we may still attempt to place in approximate order of time the inflectional changes which apply with regularity to more than one class of words, leaving all points of less general application to be taken up in the special chapters on nouns, adjectives, verbs, and other inflectional forms. As in other parts of the history of English we are dealing especially with the dialect from which literary English has sprung, that called Mercian in Old English and Midland in Middle English.

One of the earliest general changes in inflections was the weakening of final m to n in the dative plural of nouns, and the dative singular and plural of the strong adjective. This change was completed before the close of the Old English period, since even in late West Saxon the ending -*um* of the cases cited above had become -*un* (*on, an*). It is possible this weakening was brought about by analogy of the many inflectional forms in -*an*. Unaffected by the weakening here mentioned was the final *m*, not *um*, of pronoun forms, as for example *him, whom,* although them sometimes became *then*, as in the ME. expression *for then ones* 'for the nonce'.

One word, the archaic *whilom,* seems to have resisted the change, doubtless because as a common adverb it was no longer associated with declined forms, 336. Of more wide reaching importance was the vowel weakening that took place. By this, every unaccented *a, o,* or *u* became *e,* a change affecting the cases of nouns and adjectives, the infinitive and preterits of verbs, and other unaccented syllables with these vowels.

For example the noun endings *a, u, as, an* became *e, es, en*. At the same time the -*un* (*on, an*) OE. -*um* mentioned in the last paragraph now became -*en,* thus associating itself with other -*en* endings. Adjective endings were affected as those of nouns.

The verbal endings altered by this vowel weakening were *-an* of the infinitive, *-Að* of the present plural, and *-on, -odon, -od* of the preterit tense. In adverbs such endings as *-an* of OE. *hindan* 'behind,' *çastan* 'eastern,' and others, also became *-en*. No less widely extended were the changes of final *a* and *u* in adjectives and verbs as well as in nouns. This important vowel weakening was completed in early Middle English. Another important change concerns the Old English distinction of long and short stems. In Old English, stems containing a long vowel or a short vowel followed by two consonants were called long stems, and all others short stems. The distinction is important for Old English as it explains certain inflectional differences.

But by the lengthening and shortening of vowels that took place in Middle English times, the original distinction of long and short stems was obliterated. As a result, inflectional differences originally belonging to these two classes of words could not be kept up, and the two varieties of inflection became one. One of the principal effects of this change was in destroying the value of final *e* as an inflectional ending in the singular.

When this was accomplished, long and short stems alike often assumed an inorganic final *e*, while short steins with *e* sometimes lost that letter. Such forms as OE. *Wîf* 'wife,' *Côl* 'coal,' *Hôl* 'hole' became ME. *wife, cole, hole*. It should be said, however, that the loss of distinction between original long and short stems was not the only factor in developing inorganic final *e*, although it was a significant influence in this direction.

The addition of this inorganic final *e* not only obscured the old distinction of long and short stems both in nouns and adjectives, but it tended to obliterate the distinctive endings of the accusative and dative, so that these two case forms were more easily reduced to one. A fourth change in Middle English times was the breaking down of the Old English grammatical gender. In Old English, as in the Indo-European languages generally, gender rested upon grammatical rather than on natural grounds.

Thus OE. *wif* 'wife' was neuter, as is German *Weib*, the cognate word, at the present time. So OE. *cild* 'child' was neuter, as is German *Kind* to-day. Familiar examples also are OE. *sunne* 'sun' which was feminine, and OE. *Môna* 'moon' which was masculine. With the loss of inflectional distinctions during Middle English, and mainly owing to that loss, the grammatical gender of Old English was replaced by natural gender.

The first words to give up the older distinction were such original neuters as *wife*, which assumed natural gender very early. Later, but as early as the thirteenth century, the whole system of grammatical gender broke down, and was replaced by the modern use. Such words as *sun* and *moon* of course have gender in personification, but the gender of these two words in personification is the reverse of what it was in Old English, probably through classical or Romance influence.

A fifth general change, coming later also in Middle English times, is the loss of final *n* in the inflectional forms of nouns, adjectives, and verbs, and occasionally of uninflectional *n* endings in other words. This broke down entirely the weak declension of nouns and adjectives, and finally *n* was also lost in the infinitive and preterit plural of verbs. The change had largely taken place in nouns and adjectives before the time of Chaucer, who also sometimes omits final *n* in the infinitive while usually retaining it in the preterit plural.

Before the end of Middle English times final *n* had been entirely lost in inflectional endings except in a very few nouns where it was retained as a plural sign. An example of the latter is *oxen*, which still retains it. Under the influence of words with an inflectional final *n*, some words in which the *n* was not inflectional also suffered loss. This accounts for such forms as *ope* for open. *Misteltân*, as also for *a, my, thy* beside *an, mine, thine*. A sixth general change belonging to Middle English was the loss of final *e* in nearly all classes of words.

Not only was *e* a common ending in many inflectional forms in Old and Middle English, but it was also left at the end of many words by the change last mentioned, the loss of final *n*. Final *e* was pronounced in most words in Midland English to the close of the fourteenth century as shown by Chaucer's metre.

Even in the poetry of the latter part of the fourteenth century, however, this final vowel was regularly elided before a word beginning with a vowel or *h*, though it was usually preserved before a consonant. But by the beginning of the Modern English period final *e* had been almost wholly lost, although still preserved in the spelling of many words.

The last change to be noticed is the syncopation of *e* in certain endings, *-es* of the genitive singular, the plural of nouns, and the third singular present of verbs, *-ed* of the preterit and perfect participle, and *-en* of the perfect participle of certain strong verbs. The syncopation first took place in stems ending in a vowel or *r*, and in the second syllable from the accent. Examples of the first are *shoes, cried*; of the second *borne, sworn*; of the third *punished*.

The poetry of Spenser and Shakespeare shows *-ed* pronounced as a separate syllable in many verbs and the genitive in *-es* in some nouns. This must be regarded in so early a time as an indication of current pronunciation, rather than as poetic license. The syncopation of *e* here noticed has never extended itself to words ending in *s, z, ʃ(sh), Tʃ(ch), Dà* (*j* sound), the genitive singular and the plural making a separate syllable in such cases.

In addition to these general changes are many affecting particular classes of words. One of these, for example, is the change by which the *-es* of the nominative and accusative plural of nouns displaced the distinctive endings of the genitive and dative, so that at present all cases have the same ending in the plural. These special changes, however, belong rather to the discussion of particular classes of words, as nouns, adjectives, and verbs.

Chapter 10

The History of Non-standard Varieties of English

THE LESSER-KNOWN VARIETIES OF ENGLISH

The purpose of this section is to focus on aspects of the histories of as many as possible of those varieties of English which have often - or even always - been neglected in histories of the language. These are varieties which have been marginalised by historical linguists because they have been regarded as non-standard, and/or which have been ignored because they have been considered to be socially or geographically peripheral in some way.

We would point out, as justification for this, that there are very many more nonstandard than standard varieties of English in the world; that they are spoken by many more people than Standard English; and that to ignore them does our understanding of the history of the English language no service at all. Non-standard dialects of English have histories too, and these histories are sometimes especially helpful because, as a result of the absence of standardisation, many of the forces of linguistic change are played out in these varieties in a much more unfettered and revealing way than in the standard dialect.

We would also point out that the disregarding of varieties of English simply because the people who speak them are not White Englishmen who have for centuries been established in the southeast of England is also not only totally ethnocentric, anglocentric, 'austrocentric' and unjustifiable, but is also short-sighted in that it disregards an enormous mass of historical data from some of the most interesting and diachronically revealing varieties of the language in existence.

This is also the focus of Trudgill's paper - on lesser-known varieties of the language - which looks at the native-speaker Englishes of a surprisingly large number of small and often unknown communities in different parts of the world which are nearly always ignored by linguistics scholars and which remain untreated in most historical linguistic discussions.

The bias against non-standard varieties is tackled in the chapter by Poplack, van Herk and Harvie, which takes as its starting point the remarkable Ottawa Grammar Resource on Early Variability in English, with a particular focus on implications for the study of the history of African American Vernacular English, which in turn also does something to rectify the ethnocentrism of many histories.

Preston's paper on attitudes to varieties of English in North America also deals with the evaluation of non-standard Englishes; and, since Standard English has its origins in the south of England, the paper by Wales also inevitably confronts this issue of the importance of non-standard varieties. Finally, the chapter by Mesthrie tackles the prejudice against the Englishes spoken by non-White speakers in his fascinating examination of the history of Indian English in South Africa. This chapter also confronts the prejudice against 'new' varieties of English - 'newness' probably also being a factor in the relative lack of discussion in the textbooks of the southern hemisphere varieties generally.

Histories of the first thousand years or so of the English language obviously have to have a rather narrow geographical focus. Four hundred years ago, in 1600, English had no very important role as a foreign or second language anywhere, and was spoken as a native language in a very small area of the globe indeed: it was the native language of the indigenous population in most of England, and in the south and east of Scotland. It was, however, absent from much of Cornwall and from Welsh-speaking parts of Shropshire and Herefordshire; most of the population of Ireland was Irish-speaking; nearly all of the population of Wales was still Welsh-speaking; the inhabitants of the Highlands and Hebridean Islands of Scotland spoke Gaelic; those of Orkney and Shetland spoke Scandinavian Norn; the population of the Isle of Man was Manx-speaking; and the inhabitants of the Channel Islands were still French-speaking.

During the course of the 1600s this situation changed dramatically. English arrived as a native language - as a result of colonisation - in Ireland, in what is now the United States, and in Bermuda, Newfoundland, the Bahamas, and the Turks and Caicos Islands. It also spread during this time into many island and mainland areas of the Caribbean: Anguilla, Antigua and Barbuda, Barbados, the Cayman Islands, Jamaica, Montserrat, St Kitts and Nevis, the British Virgin Islands, the American Virgin Islands, and the mainland areas of Guyana and Belize.

And it is not widely known that areas other than these (in modern times cricket-playing Commonwealth) countries were also settled by anglophones: eastern coastal and island areas of Honduras, Nicaragua and Colombia remain English-speaking to this day. The Dutch island colonies of Saba, St Maarten and St Eustatius have also been English-speaking since the early 1600s; and the mainly Papiamentu-speaking Dutch colony of Bonaire has a sizeable number of indigenous anglophones too.

During the eighteenth century English began its expansion into Wales and north-western Scotland, and into mainland and maritime Canada. In the nineteenth century, again as a result of colonisation, English expanded to Hawaii, and into the southern hemisphere - not only to Australia, New Zealand and South Africa, as is well known, but also to the South Atlantic Islands of St Helena, Tristan da Cunha and the Falklands, and in the Pacific to Pitcairn Island and Norfolk Island.

There was also expansion from the Caribbean islands to eastern coastal areas of Costa Rica and Panama; and the repatriation of African Americans to Sierra Leone and Liberia, as well as an African-American settlement in the Dominican Republic. During this time also Caribbean Islands which had hitherto been francophone started on a slow process of becoming anglophone to different degrees: Dominica, St Lucia, Trinidad and Tobago, Grenada, and St Vincent and the Grenadines.

Other little-known anglophone colonies which still survive today were also established during the nineteenth century in southern Brazil, by American southerners fleeing the aftermath of the Civil War, and in the Bonin islands of Japan, by New England and Hawaiian whalers and seamen, and on one of the Cook Islands in the South Pacific. There are also today long-standing indigenous groups of British-origin native anglophones in Namibia, Botswana, Zimbabwe and Kenya. It is also worth noting that restructured forms of English, known as creoles, are spoken in many parts of the world: since the seventeenth century in Surinam, and since the early nineteenth century in Papua New Guinea, the Solomon Islands, Vanuatu and northern Australia.

The English-based creole Krio has also been spoken in Sierra Leone, West Africa, at least since the early 1800s, although Hancock has argued for the presence of an anglophone community there since the early 1600s. Creole varieties are, however, not discussed in this chapter. Neither are varieties of English, such as Nigerian English, which are basically second-language varieties of the language.

Of all the areas just mentioned, it is safe to say that only the English of the British Isles, mainland North America, Australasia, South Africa, and, to a lesser extent, the creoles of the Caribbean and the South Pacific, have attracted large amounts of attention from historical linguists. In this chapter I suggest that there is an alternative to this concentration on these major (in demographic terms) varieties. I examine the histories of the other - relatively ignored - native varieties of English in lesser-known areas of the anglophone world, in chronological order of their settlement. (I do not, however, deal here with the diaspora African-American English-speaking communities of Nova Scotia, Liberia, Sierra Leone, and Samana in the Dominican Republic as these are dealt with elsewhere in this volume.)

Research into the grammar and phonology of a number of these lesser-known varieties is currently in progress. Linguistic details of these varieties of English, including some rather remarkable similarities between many of them, are discussed, for example, in Trudgill et al. (forthcoming). Comments on the linguistic characteristics of these varieties in what follows are based either on my own research in the areas in question - as in the case of Bermuda, the Bahamas, Newfoundland, Cape Breton Island, Prince Edward Island, the Chatham Islands, and Guernsey - and/or on tapes that are either commercially available or have very kindly been made available to me by others.

Newfoundland

The island of Newfoundland has an area of 112,790 km^2. The population is about 550,000. About 95 per cent of these are of British and Irish origin, while fewer than 3 per cent are of French extraction.

Newfoundland was originally settled by Indians and Inuit. Viking ruins dating from about AD1000 show that Norse speakers from Iceland and Greenland were the earliest Europeans to reach the area. The official European 'discoverer' of Newfoundland was the Genoese-Venetian John Cabot, who arrived on the island in 1497 sailing under the English flag, but the Grand Banks had been known to Basque and Breton fishermen much earlier. In the 1500s English, French, Basque, and Portuguese fishermen were in competition for the fishing grounds, and by 1600 England and France were the chief rivals. Attempts made at colonisation during the 1600s were not well received by the English fishermen nor, after 1634, by the English crown. In fact, in 1699 Parliament prohibited settlement of the island except in connexion with cod fishing.

During the seventeenth and eighteenth centuries the island's population nevertheless increased, and Britain appointed a governor in 1729 and established a court system in 1792. These remained, however, only during the summer, and a settled colony was not recognised until 1824. Large groups of immigrants were brought in with the peak year of 1814-15 seeing the advent of 11,000 people, mainly Irish Catholics. Most rural areas are inhabited either by people whose ancestors came as early settlers from Dorset and Devon and/or by people with (rather later) origins in south-eastern Ireland.

The history of the settlement of Newfoundland goes a long way to explaining the current linguistic situation there. The phonology of modern Newfoundland English is characterised by considerable social variation by North American standards, and nonstandard grammatical forms, such as present-tense -s for all persons, occur very frequently and high up the social scale. It is, too, one of the few places in North America where it can be said with any degree of certainty that traditional dialects, in the sense of Wells, survive. There is also some well-documented regional variation.

A first impression for English English speakers is that speakers 'sound Irish', but closer inspection shows that this is not the case. Overall, varieties seem to be the result of a mixture of Southern Irish English and south-western English English varieties, but in different proportions in different places. In communities where immigration from Dorset and Devon played an important role, older speakers may for example still have initial-fricative voicing in *fish, thimble, seven, ship*, and a number of Irish-origin syntactic features can be found in Irish-influenced areas, such as habitual aspect expressed by *do be* as in *They do be full*.

Bermuda

Bermuda is a self-governing British colony about 900 km east of Cape Hatteras, North Carolina. Its total land area is 54 km^2, and the population is about 60,000. It is said to have been discovered by the Spanish navigator Juan Bermudez, probably between 1503 and 1511. The first anglophones to arrive were some Puritans who were shipwrecked in 1609. In 1612, sixty English settlers were sent to colonise the islands.

African slaves were transported to Bermuda beginning in 1616, and soon the Black population was larger than the White. In 1684 Bermuda became a crown colony. About 60 per cent of the population are of African origin. Whites are mostly of British origin, but descendants of Portuguese labourers from Madeira and the Azores who arrived during the 1800s are also to be found and some Portuguese is still spoken.

Bermudan English has not been extensively studied, although see Ayres (1933), Trudgill (1986), and Cutler *et al.* (forthcoming). There are noticeable differences between the speech of Blacks and that of Whites - the former being more Caribbean in character, the latter more like the English of coastal South Carolina.

The Lesser Antilles

It is well known that the majority of the populations of Belize, of Jamaica, and of the eastern Caribbean are of African origin. The English-based creoles, semi-creoles and post-creole continua spoken in many of these former, and in a few cases current, British colonies are rather well known to linguists (see Carrington forthcoming).

It is much less well known, however, that the Lesser Antilles of the eastern Caribbean contain a number of communities of White anglophones. The point about these communities is not of course that they are racially 'White' but that they are in many cases the direct cultural and linguistic descendants of immigrants from the British Isles and as such speakers of English which, while clearly

Caribbean in character, may in some respects show differences from that of Black West Indians, especially since residential and social segregation has been maintained in some places for hundreds of years.

Of the islands which have significant White populations today, direct White emigration to Barbados began in 1627, with large numbers of the migrants being unemployed or otherwise impoverished people from England, many of them coming from or via London, Bristol, and Southampton, who took positions as servants in these newly established colonies. (Immigration also began to St Kitts in 1624, but no White community survives there today.) Many of the English who arrived later in the 1650s were prisoners of the English Civil War or transported criminals. Irish immigration was also significant, particularly in the wake of Cromwell's harrying of Ireland in the 1650s, when many of the arrivals were also in fact political prisoners or prisoners of war.

The Dutch (but English-speaking) island of Saba was claimed by the Dutch in 1632 but settled by White anglophones coming, often as escapees from indentured labour, from other islands over a considerable period of time lasting until the 1830s. This isolated White community today forms about half the population of the island. Montserrat had a population of Whites until quite recently who came originally from St Kitts: there was one community of Irish-origin Catholics, and another of Scottish and English-origin Protestants. Anguilla has a community of Whites who arrived from other islands in the late 1600s, later reinforced by other arrivals from other islands who came around 1800. White immigration to St Lucia from Scotland, with some settlers arriving also from England and Ireland, dated from the 1830s, but most if not all of these have subsequently emigrated.

Some White communities descend from people who were relocated from other islands by government policy in the 1860s. This relocation was a response to the perceived poverty and unemployment of poor Whites in a number of the original communities. One community arrived in St Vincent from Barbados, and another in Bequia in the Grenadines, and a third in Grenada itself. For further details on settlement patterns and dating, see Holm.

The English of these communities has been very little studied apart from pioneering work by Williams, which looks at the very interesting question of verbal aspect in White Caribbean English and the extent to which aspectual systems derive from Irish English, British English, and/or Caribbean creoles.

The Bahamas

The Bahamas form an independent state which is a member of the British Commonwealth. They are an archipelago of about 700 islands to the southeast of Florida, with a population of about 270,000.

The Bahamas were originally inhabited by Lucayan Arawak Indians, originally from the South American continent, who had probably been driven into the Caribbean by the Caribs. In 1492 Columbus first landed in the Bahamas. Although he took formal possession of the islands in the name of Spain, the Spanish did not really make any attempt to settle them. Between 1492 and 1508, they enslaved 40,000 natives to work in the mines on Hispaniola, and by the time the English arrived the Bahamas were uninhabited.

Serious English involvement began in 1629 when King Charles I granted Sir Robert Heath, the Attorney General of England, territories in America including the Bahamas. He too made no effort to settle the Bahamas. However, in the 1640s, Bermuda was suffering from religious disputes, and in 1647 Captain William Sayle, a former governor of Bermuda, decided to look for an island where religious dissidents could worship.

The 'Company of Eleutherian Adventurers' was set up in London, and in 1648 Sayle sailed with about seventy settlers (Bermudan dissidents and others from England) for the Bahamas. It is not known where they arrived, but it is thought that they settled on the island of Eleuthera. They had planned a plantation colony. This was largely unsuccessful, however, and a number of settlers, including Sayle himself, returned to Bermuda. Other Bermudan migrants continued to arrive, however, and the island of New Providence was settled from Bermuda in 1656. In 1670 six 'proprietors' were granted the islands by Charles II, and accepted responsibility for government.

They were mostly not concerned about the islands, however. Things did not go well, and piracy became prevalent. In 1717, therefore, the King commissioned Captain Woodes Rogers as the Governor, and by 1728 he had managed to exterminate piracy. After the American Revolution, from 1782 onwards, many American loyalists fled, some of them with slaves, to the Bahamas. This had the effect of doubling the White population and trebling the Black. A minority of the population today is thus descended from English pioneer settlers and loyalist refugees. Most of the population is of African descent.

The English of White Bahamians, then, has two main sources: the Bermudan English of the original settlers, and the North American English of the Loyalists. Some of the Loyalists were from the American South, but Abaco and northern Eleuthera islands in particular were settled by Americans from New England and New York. There was also some White immigration from the Miskito coast when this area was ceded by Britain to Spain in 1786, and Andros island in particular was settled from there. It is no surprise, then, that their accents are non-rhotic (as indeed are those of Black speakers).

Black Bahamians too have different origins, some being descended from slaves who actually arrived in the Bahamas, others being originally from the American South or the Caribbean. According to Holm and Shilling Black Bahamian English is probably most like the mainland American creole Gullah. It is certainly 'closer to white English than comparable varieties in the Caribbean proper, but much further from white English than the vernacular Black English of the United

States'. The phonology differs from that of White speech in, for example, having monophthongal realisations of /ei/ and /ou/. There are also certainly a number of African American Vernacular English (AAVE) and/or Caribbean creole-like features in the syntax.

Central America

San Andrés and Providencia are Caribbean islands with a total land area of about 45 km^2 and a population of about 35,000. They lie about 180 km off the coast of Nicaragua and about 700 km northwest of mainland Colombia. They nevertheless constitute part of Colombia: Colombia controlled what is now Panama until 1903, which helps to explain this geographical anomaly. The islands were settled in 1629 by English Puritans, and subsequently also by Jamaican planters and their Black slaves. The islands were officially decreed to be Spanish in 1786, and they became part of Colombia in 1822, after Colombian independence.

The discussion by Washabaugh makes it clear that these islands, too, speak a typically Caribbean creole form of English. The Bay Islands are a group of eight small islands off northern Honduras. They have an area of 250 km2 and are situated about 55 km offshore in the Caribbean. The islands were first sighted by Columbus in 1502 and were settled in 1642 by English buccaneers. Between 1650 and 1850 Spain, Honduras, and England disputed ownership of the islands. The islands were officially annexed to Britain in 1852 but were then ceded to Honduras in 1859.

English-speaking Protestants formed the majority of the population until about 1900, when hispanic Hondurans from the mainland began settling, but indigenous anglophones still form about 85 per cent of the population, which also includes non-anglophone Black Caribs. The population is currently about 20,000: Black, White and mixed. At least at the level of acrolectal Whites, the accent is rhotic though obviously Caribbean.

The Miskito coast is the Caribbean coastal area of Nicaragua and Honduras consisting of a strip of lowland about 70 km wide and 350 km long. Columbus visited it in 1502, but there was not much European presence there until the arrival of buccaneers in the 1650s. England established a protectorate over the local Miskito Indians, who the region is named after, and the area was a British dependency from 1740 to 1786.

In Nicaragua, the British founded the principal Miskito coast city of Bluefields. Spain, Nicaragua, and the United States at different times disputed the legitimacy of this dependency. The issue was settled as far as Nicaragua was concerned by the occupation of what is now the Nicaraguan part of the coast by Spain in 1786, and later by a British-American treaty of 1850.

There are about 30,000 native speakers of English in this area of Nicaragua who look to Bluefields as their centre. Most of them are of African origin. Several hundred, however, are Rama Indians, and another several hundred are so-called Black Caribs, who were transported from their native island of St Vincent to this area by the British in the late 1700s. The Miskito Indians number about 70,000. Some of them, too, are native speakers of English and are included in this figure, but, of those who have retained their own language, a large number also speak the local variety of English as a second language.

According to Holm and O'Neil (1993) it is a typically Caribbean form of English with many creole features. English is also spoken in many different locations on the Caribbean coast of mainland Honduras where, however, language shift to Spanish seems to be taking place. As far as I know, these varieties have not yet been investigated by linguists.

The anglophone Corn Islands of Nicaragua, Great and Little Corn Island, lie in the Caribbean about 80 km offshore from Bluefields. The population is about 2,500. The islands were leased by treaty to the United States by Nicaragua from 1916 to 1971. The English of these islands is also typically Caribbean. For a general overview of this area, see Lastra (forthcoming). For further details on settlement patterns and dating, see Holm.

Saint Helena

This island is a British colony in the South Atlantic Ocean, 1,950 km west of Africa. It is about 120 km^2, and the population is about 6,000. It was discovered in 1502 by the Portuguese but the English learnt of it in 1588. It then became a port for ships travelling between Europe and the East, and in 1659 the East India Company took possession. By 1673 nearly half the inhabitants were imported slaves. Napoleon was confined on the island from 1815 until his death in 1821. The island's population is largely of mixed British, Asian, and African descent.

The English of St Helena is perhaps best described as a creoloid. It has, for example, a number of creole features such as copula deletion, but is nevertheless obviously English.

The Cayman Islands

These are a British colony of three major islands in the Caribbean, about 290 km northwest of Jamaica. The population is about 25,000. About a quarter of the Caymanians are European, mostly of British origin; about one-quarter are descendants of African slaves; and the remainder are of mixed ancestry. The Islands were first sighted by Columbus in 1503. They appear to have been uninhabited, but known to Carib and/or Arawak Indians.

They were subsequently visited by Spanish, English, and French ships but were not claimed by any nation until they were ceded to England in 1670. Most of the settlers were British mariners, buccaneers, shipwrecked passengers, plus land-grant holders from Jamaica and African slaves. The Cayman Islands were a dependency of Jamaica until 1959, when they became a separate dependency.

Turks and Caicos Islands

The Turks and Caicos are a British crown colony consisting of two small groups of islands at the south-eastern end of the Bahamas about 145 km north of the Dominican Republic. The Turks group consists of Grand Turk and Salt Cay. The population is about 14,000.

A pre-Columbian Indian - possibly Arawak as on the Bahamas - culture may have existed on the islands, but they seem to have been uninhabited at the time of their 'discovery' by the Spanish explorer Juan Ponce de León in 1512. They were not settled by Europeans until 1678, when Bermudans arrived and set up a salt industry. The Caicos Islands were also settled by loyalist refugees from the USA after the War of Independence.

As in the Bahamas, they established cotton plantations employing slaves. In 1799 the islands were annexed by the Bahamas, but in 1848 they were granted a separate charter. After the abolition of slavery in 1843 the plantation owners left the islands, leaving their former slaves in control. The colony was placed under the control of Jamaica from 1874 until 1959, and became a separate crown colony in 1962 when Jamaica became independent. Over 90 per cent of the inhabitants are Blacks.

The speech of the islands is often described as being very close to Bahamian English. It is clearly true that there are many phonological and grammatical similarities, but Cutler (see Cutler *et al.* forthcoming) reports that a number of Bahamian lexical items are not known on Grand Turk. Holm also suggests that the English may be somewhat different from that of the southern Bahamas. He reports (personal communication) that certain students at the College of the Bahamas in Nassau where he taught in 1978-80 were said by other students to have 'Turks accents'.

Turks Islanders claim that people in the Caicos Islands speak differently. This is possible but awaits investigation. Grand Turk was settled mainly by Black and White Bahamians, while the Caicos Islanders descend from American slaves brought there by American loyalist planters in the 1780s. They have traditionally been more isolated and had less access to education.

India

English first arrived in India as a significant feature as a result of British colonisation and administration especially from about 1750 onwards, although the English had had commercial interests in India much earlier than that. It is well known that a distinctive second-language form of Indian English is today widely used as a lingua franca among educated elites in India, and that English plays an important role in government, education, and the media, although only a very small minority (nevertheless constituting many millions of people) have a good command of the language.

The linguistic characteristics of Indian English are also well known. However, it is less well known that a form of Indian English is the native language of the Eurasian or Anglo-Indian community in India, which includes about 100,000 people who are of mixed British and Indian origin. The phonology of this variety is outlined in Wells.

The Canadian Maritimes

In the seventeenth and eighteenth centuries Nova Scotia was the site of a struggle for power between England and France. Halifax was founded by the British in 1749 to counteract French influence with a population of about 4,000 British settlers. In the 1750s the French Acadian settlers, who had refused to swear allegiance to the British crown, were expelled, and new immigrants arrived from the British Isles and New England.

Gaelic-speaking Scottish Highlanders settled in a number of areas of Cape Breton Island, where some Gaelic is still spoken to this day. Protestant Germans founded the town of Lunenburg in 1750, and Ulster Scots set up farms in the Truro and Onslow districts. After the American War of Independence about 35,000 American loyalists arrived and by 1800 New Englanders formed about half of the population. Later, Irish people arrived via Newfoundland or directly from Ireland and settled in and near Halifax.

Prince Edward Island was claimed by France early on but was not colonised until 1720, when 300 settlers from France arrived. Fishermen and trappers from the francophone Acadian mainland colony in New Brunswick established several other small communities on the island. The British occupied the island in 1758, expelling most of the French-speaking settlers, though some francophone families still remain in some areas.

The island was formally ceded to Britain in 1763. More than three-quarters of the population are descendants of early settlers from the British Isles: Highland Scots, Ulster Scots, English, and southern Irish, but as in Nova Scotia there are also descendants of American Loyalists who arrived after the American War of Independence. In the 1800s religious tensions between people of Irish Protestant and Catholic origin was not unknown.

The British took over New Brunswick in 1713 and expelled most of the French-speaking Acadian settlers in 1755. Many of them went to Louisiana, and some later returned. The first English-speaking settlers came north from New England and moved into the St John River valley in 1762. There was then a big influx of 14,000 loyalist Americans after the War of Independence, who came mostly from the New York area. The English-speaking majority today - about two-thirds of the population - thus consists largely of descendants of American loyalists, together with the descendants of Scottish, Irish, and English settlers who arrived in the 1700s and 1800s.

Canadian English as it is spoken from Vancouver to Ontario has been very well described. The English of the Maritime Provinces is, however, not so well known to linguists, and while the English of younger educated speakers in urban areas such as Halifax is not radically different from that of the rest of Canada, rural Maritime English is distinctively different, having a number of similarities with the English of Newfoundland, and phonological features which appear to owe much to Irish and/or Scottish and/or American influence.

Quebec: the Magdalen Islands

The Canadian Iles de la Madeleine are in the Gulf of St Lawrence between Prince Edward Island and Newfoundland,

240 km southeast of the Gaspé Peninsula. There are nine main islands with a total land area of 230 km^2.

The largest islands are Havre-Aubert (Amherst), Cap aux Meules, Loup (Wolf), and Havre aux Maisons (Alright). The islands were 'discovered' by Jacques Cartier in 1534, although Basque and Breton fishermen had known about them long before that. They acquired a settled population in 1755, when many of the Acadian French colonists of Nova Scotia who were expelled by the British escaped there.

The islands were ceded to Britain in 1763 and annexed to Newfoundland, but were made a part of Quebec in 1774. At the end of the 1700s the population was reinforced by further Acadians who had earlier taken refuge on the French-owned islands of St Pierre and Miquelon, but who now preferred the British Monarchy to the French Republicans. The population today is about 14,000. About 90 per cent of these, as this history would lead one to suspect, are French-speaking. However, there is a long-standing community of about 1,500 anglophones who are mainly of Scottish and Irish origin and who today live for the most part on Ile d'Entrée and La Grosse Ile.

Pitcairn Island

This isolated British colony is about 2,200 km southeast of Tahiti in the south Pacific. The main and only inhabited island has an area of about 5 km2, and the population in 1992 was fifty-two. It was 'discovered' in 1767 by British navigators, but, though uninhabited, showed signs of previous Polynesian habitation or at least visitation. The modern population, as is well known, is descended from the mutineers of the British ship HMS Bounty and their Tahitian companions. After a lengthy stay on Tahiti, the crew, led by the first mate, Fletcher Christian, mutinied when their voyage to the West Indies had got only as far as western Polynesia, and set their captain William Bligh and a number of loyal sailors adrift. They headed back to Tahiti, where they collected a number of local women and a few men, and, fearing discovery by the Royal Navy, set off again.

They reached Pitcairn in 1790, where, in the interests of secrecy, they burnt their ship. The island community survived undiscovered until found by American whalers in 1808. In 1856, because of overpopulation, some of the islanders were removed to Norfolk Island. The population is currently declining owing to emigration to New Zealand.

A range of varieties of English appear to be open to islanders. The most basilectal of these resembles an English-based creole and has many features of Polynesian origin. There has been some considerable controversy about its exact status, but I have suggested the term 'dual source creoloid' for this variety.

Tristan da Cunha

This South Atlantic British dependent territory consists of six small islands which are about half-way between southern Africa and South America. The only populated island, Tristan da Cunha, has an area of about 100 km^2 and a population of about 290. It is said to be the most remote permanently inhabited settlement in the world, the nearest habitation being St Helena, which is about 2,000 km distant. The islands were discovered in 1506 by a Portuguese sailor, Tristao da Cunha. A British garrison was stationed on Tristan da Cunha in 1816, as a result of fears that it might be used as a base for an attempt to rescue Napoleon from St Helena and the islands were formally annexed to Britain.

When the garrison left in 1817, three soldiers asked to stay, and during the 1800s they were joined by shipwrecked sailors, a few European settlers, and six women from St Helena. By 1886 the population was ninety-seven. In 1961 a volcanic eruption threatened the settlement, and the inhabitants were evacuated to England. Most of them returned to Tristan in 1963. The English is remarkable. It is mainly of English dialect origin but shows some signs of pidginisation, though probably not enough to be considered a creoloid. It has a number of grammatical features found nowhere else in the anglophone world.

Bonin Islands

Almost certainly the least-known anglophone community in the world, these Japanese-owned islands, known in Japanese as Ogasawara-gunto, are in the central Pacific Ocean, about 800 km southeast of Japan proper. There are three main island groups: the Beechey Group; the Parry Group; and the Bailey Group. The population is about 2,000. The islands were discovered by the Spanish navigator Ruy Lopez de Villalobos in 1543.

They were then claimed by the USA in 1823 and by Britain in 1825. The islands were formally annexed by Japan in 1876, but, after World War II, they were a placed under US military control. They were returned to Japan in 1968. The English appears to be mainly American in origin and has many similarities to New England varieties. It also has similarities to a number of other island Englishes which are not necessarily very easy to explain.

Palmerston

Palmerston English is a variety spoken on Palmerston Island, Polynesian Avarau, a coral atoll in the Cook Islands about 430 km northwest of Rarotonga, by descendants of Cook Island Maori and English speakers. What we know about the settlement is that William Marsters, a ship's carpenter and cooper from Gloucestershire, England, came to uninhabited Palmerston Atoll in 1862. He had three wives, all from Penrhyn/Tongareva in the Northern Cook Islands. He forced his wives, seventeen children and numerous grandchildren to use English all the time.

Virtually the entire population of the island today descends from the patriarch. Ehrhart-Kneher considers Palmerston English a dialectal variety of English rather than a contact language. She writes that it appears to be a classic case of mixing and vernacularisation of a type which has 'produced languages which, while new languages, are varieties of English rather than new languages without genetic affiliation in the usual sense'.

The Falkland Islands

This British colony in the South Atlantic Ocean lies about 500 km east of the South American mainland. There are two main islands, East Falkland and West Falkland, with a total land area of about 12,200 km2 and a population, of British descent, of about 2,100. In 1690 the English captain John Strong made the first recorded landing on the islands. The islands' first settlement was established in 1764 by the French under de Bougainville, closely followed by a British settlement in 1765 on West Falkland.

The Spanish purchased the French settlement in 1767, and succeeded in temporarily expelling the British from West Falkland between 1770 and 1771. The British withdrew from West Falkland in 1774 for financial reasons but without renouncing their claim to sovereignty. The Spanish settlement on East Falkland was in turn withdrawn in 1811. In 1820 the Argentinean government, which had declared its independence from Spain in 1816, proclaimed its sovereignty over the Falklands, but in 1831 an American warship attacked an Argentinean settlement on East Falkland and in 1833 a British force expelled the few remaining Argentinean officials.

In 1841 a British governor was appointed for the Falklands, and by 1885 a British community of about 1,800 people had been established on the two islands. The Falklands became a British colony in 1892. A new focused dialect of English has developed in the capital and only town, Port Stanley, but in rural West Falkland each village apparently shows connections with the particular part of England from which it was settled.

The Chatham Islands

This island group is about 800 km east of New Zealand. The largest island, Chatham Island, is 900 km2 in area. Pitt Island is about 21 km to the southeast. The indigenous population was the Polynesian Moriori, who were conquered and exterminated by the New Zealand Maori from 1835 onwards. The islands were annexed by New Zealand in 1842.

The current population of about 750 is mainly White with some people of Maori or mixed Maori and Moriori origin. The English is indistinguishable from that of New Zealand, but 'broad' New Zealand accents are found much higher up the social scale than in New Zealand itself.

The Channel Islands

The islands of Jersey, Guernsey, Herm, Sark, and Alderney were until the 1800s Norman French-speaking in spite of the fact that they had been under the English and British crown since 1066, as they still are today, though they are not actually part of the United Kingdom as such but rather autonomous dependencies.

The local French patois is now very much in retreat, but the English which has now mostly replaced it has a number of distinctive characteristics which have been little described; but see Ramisch and Barbe (1995), who discuss features of the local syntax and morphology, which appear to owe something to the influence of French as well as to the dialects of the southwest of England. Ramisch indicates, and I can confirm, that the pronunciation of English at least on Guernsey is basically of a rhotic southwest of England type, though with some second-language features such as *th*-stopping.

Norfolk Island

This is an Australian dependent territory in the south-western Pacific, about 1,600 km northeast of Sydney. The island, with an area of 35 km^2, has a population of about 2,750. Captain Cook discovered the uninhabited island in 1774. It was claimed by New South Wales in 1788 and settled by a small group which included fifteen convicts. This was abandoned in 1814, but a new penal colony was established there from 1825 to 1855, when it was relocated in Tasmania. In 1856 the Pitcairn Islanders, descendants of the mutineers on the Bounty, were resettled on Norfolk Island.

Not all of the islanders were happy, however, and eventually two separate groups returned to Pitcairn. Norfolk

Island's current population includes about one-third who can claim to be the descendants of mutineers, the remainder being descendants of later settlers, mostly from Australia and New Zealand. A strong Polynesian influence, stemming from the Tahitian input into Pitcairn, is still apparent in the culture and customs of the island. The local English of Norfolk Island, which is spoken by only about 25 per cent of the current population, is still rather like that of Pitcairn, but less basilectal, and it has been argued that it is really a 'cant' or 'antilanguage'.

Brazil

At the end of the American Civil War in 1865, thousands of Americans from the defeated South left the United States for ever. Some went to Mexico and the West Indies, and some even made it as far as Japan and Egypt, but the largest number of those that left went to Brazil, perhaps as many as 40,000 of them, where they founded a number of settlements. The best known of these is called Americana, which is situated about 150 km northwest of Sao Paulo, and which has today about 200,000 inhabitants.

The conservative southern English of this community, as described by Montgomery and Melo, as well as by Bailey and Smith, is of considerable interest for reconstructing the history of English in the southern United States. The language of the community was for many decades a Southern variety of American English, and there are many hundreds of older people today who still speak a conservative form of English which has its roots in, particularly, Georgia and Alabama. Gradually the community has become bilingual in English and Portuguese, and most younger people are as comfortable in Portuguese as in English, if not more so.

Southern and Eastern Africa

English is the official language of Zimbabwe, and much teaching in schools is also carried out in English, except in the case of the youngest Shona- and Ndebele-speaking children. Zimbabwe has had a White, mainly British-origin population since settlers arrived from Botswana in 1890. However, only about a quarter of the White population at independence in 1980 were born in Zimbabwe.

About 50 per cent had immigrated from Europe, mainly Britain, and about 25 per cent from South Africa. There are also Zimbabweans of mixed race, called 'coloureds', who are mainly anglophone. The Zimbabwean English of the native anglophone population resembles very closely that of South Africa, but according to Wells it has never been systematically studied. Native English-speakers make up less than 1 per cent of the total population of 11 million.

Botswana was a British protectorate from 1885 and an independent Commonwealth nation since 1966. White settlement in Botswana, consisting of some Afrikaners and fewer English-speakers, dated from the 1860s and has always been confined to farms in areas bordering South Africa. At its greatest, the White population never totalled more than 3,000. The English of the local population is South African in type.

British interest in Kenya began in the 1880s, and in 1890 Kenya became a British protectorate. Large-scale settlement by Whites began in 1901, many anglophones coming from South Africa as well as from Britain. Modern European Kenyans, mostly British in origin, are the remnant of that farming population. At the time of independence in 1963, most Europeans emigrated to southern Africa, Europe, and elsewhere. Most of those remaining today are to be found in the large urban centres of Nairobi and Mombasa.

They now constitute much less than 1 per cent of the 30 million population. The English of the settlers has not been systematically investigated, as far as I know, but it clearly resembles that of South Africa to a perhaps surprising extent.

Namibia, as Southwest Africa, was a German colony from the 1880s. In 1915 it came under South African control, and it achieved independence as a member of the Commonwealth in 1990. About 6 per cent of Namibians are of European ancestry: Afrikaners constitute about 3.5 per cent and Germans about 1.5 per cent of the population.

Anglophones of British origin thus constitute only about 0.5 per cent of the total population although English is the national language and is said to be the home language of about 3 per cent of the population. About 10,000 people of European origin have left Namibia since independence. Native Namibian English is, unsurprisingly, of a South African type.

Studies of the history of the English language up to 1600 obviously have to be confined to the British Isles, though it has to be said that the standard histories most often have relatively little to say about Scotland, or about the anglophone enclaves in Ireland. After 1700 there is, however, no real excuse for histories of the language which confine themselves to England, or even to England and the United States.

It is true that, increasingly, historical linguists have been looking at the development of English in the other major anglophone nations: Canada, South Africa, Australia, and New Zealand. But, with the honourable exception of Holm, the minor anglophone locations have been widely ignored. In the above I have dealt mostly with the external history of the lesser-known varieties of English.

I have referred, however, at a number of points, to other works, including forthcoming works, dealing with the internal, linguistic histories of these varieties. It seems that some of the most important sociolinguistic and linguistic developments involving English have taken place in these other, 'alternative' parts of the world where English is spoken natively, and that much work remains to be done on their internal, linguistic history also.

Index